146 ''

THE ORIGINAL VERMONTERS
Native Inhabitants, Past and Present

THE ORIGINAL VERMONTERS
Native Inhabitants, Past and Present

WILLIAM A. HAVILAND

MARJORY W. POWER

PUBLISHED FOR UNIVERSITY OF VERMONT

BY UNIVERSITY PRESS OF NEW ENGLAND

Hanover and London, 1981

UNIVERSITY PRESS OF NEW ENGLAND

Sponsoring Institutions

BRANDEIS UNIVERSITY

BROWN UNIVERSITY

CLARK UNIVERSITY

DARTMOUTH COLLEGE

UNIVERSITY OF NEW HAMPSHIRE

UNIVERSITY OF RHODE ISLAND

TUFTS UNIVERSITY

UNIVERSITY OF VERMONT

Library of Congress Catalog Card Number 80-55465
International Standard Book Number 0-87451-196-8
Printed in the United States of America
Library of Congress Cataloging in Publication data
will be found on the last printed page of this book.

*Publication of this volume has been aided by a grant from
the* NATIONAL ENDOWMENT FOR THE HUMANITIES.

CONTENTS

ILLUSTRATIONS

TABLES

PREFACE

THIS BOOK is an attempt to make available to the general reader what anthropologists have learned (and are still learning) about Vermont's original inhabitants, past and present. In it, we have striven for synthesis, rather than presentation of detail, so that the book might have the broadest possible appeal. Our presentation is kept as uncomplicated as possible, with the concepts employed emerging, or made clear, in the course of it. What we have to offer, then, is a general statement about how people lived in Vermont before the arrival of Europeans, why they lived the way they did, and what has been their fate in the wake of foreign intrusion and domination.

A statement of this kind is needed to counter the extraordinary amount of misinformation which exists on the subject of Vermont Indians. Most books on Vermont simply repeat one or another version of the old myth that Indians never lived in the state, or else they repeat information that is at least thirty years out of date and quite inaccurate. Whenever one of the world's cultural heritages is lost, we are all the poorer for it. That of Vermont's native peoples has not yet been lost, but through distortion or outright neglect it has come perilously close to it. It deserves to be better known, and not just to Vermonters.

Although we have not written this book for an audience of professional anthropologists, it does have something to offer them, as well as more general readers. For one thing, a lot of research is currently being done, particularly in archaeology, which is of major importance for improving our understanding of the origin and development of aboriginal culture in Vermont. Much of this has not yet been published, but our colleagues need to know about it. We have been able to draw on this unpublished research, which will alert other anthropologists to its existence and importance. But beyond this, there comes a time in any field of research when we must get away from the minutiae and look at the broad pic-

ture. What do all those minutiae mean, when they are put together? From such broad synthesis, we can examine anew old as-
sumptions, redefine the issues, and recognize new avenues of
research to which we would otherwise be blinded.

The beginnings of this book go back to 1965, when I first came
to the University of Vermont. In the fall of that year my colleague
Clark Johnson asked me where there was an archaeological site
he could show his students. Since I had written an honors paper
in 1956 and a master's thesis in 1958 on the archaeology of
Maine, I had a general overall knowledge of northeastern archaeology and I knew that there were prehistoric archaeological sites
in Vermont. A number of them were shown on a map of Lake
Champlain published in 1922 by Warren K. Moorehead. Moorehead, who was field director of the R. S. Peabody Foundation's Archaeological Survey of New England, spent part of the summer
of 1917 traveling around the shores of the lake, together with
George Perkins of the University of Vermont, looking for prehistoric sites. The largest which they found was at Colchester
Point, where according to Moorehead the ground was literally
covered with artifacts, stone-chipping debris, and burned stones.
It sounded like a good site to look at, so Clark and I went out one
Saturday to do this. What we found was not the remains of an ancient Indian village, but a relatively new housing development.
The site had been bulldozed into oblivion, to be replaced by
neatly cropped suburban lawns.

This lack of success led me to believe that the best way to track
down existing sites would be to ask around. This I did, and it was
then that people began to tell me that "Indians never lived in Vermont." The first few such assertions I dismissed without a second
thought. But as I heard this repeated over and over again, and as I
began reading books about Vermont and its history, I was aghast
to learn just how pervasive this myth was. In his book, *The Invasion of America*, the historian Francis Jennings has accused his
colleagues of being willfully and consistently misleading about
Native Americans and their role in North American history. For
reasons which are, I think, unwitting rather than willfull, writers
of books on Vermont have been no less misleading.

Eventually, I did find some people who were aware that Indians
once lived in Vermont, and who knew where archaeological sites

were to be found. These were collectors of prehistoric artifacts who generally were as taken aback as I at the conventional wisdom that "Indians never lived in Vermont." They were genuinely interested in learning about Vermont's aboriginal occupations, but were hampered by their limited knowledge of both modern archaeology and the prehistory of northeastern North America. In this they were victims of the literature. With few exceptions, the sources most readily available to them consisted of works such as Huden's *Archaeology in Vermont* or Willoughby's *Antiquities of the New England Indians* which were hopelessly out of date. More recent material was usually buried in specialist journals which either were not known to them, hard to find, or written in such a way as to be difficult to comprehend without a substantial background in anthropology.

Obviously, something needed to be done about all this, but in the 1960s I was heavily involved in a ten-year program of research at the ancient Maya site of Tikal, in Guatemala. My field involvement in the Tikal Project did not end until 1967, at which point I had four file drawers of data which I was obligated to write up before I could commit myself to any other major undertaking. But there were some things of a stop-gap nature which I could do. In 1968, with student assistance and a small institutional grant from the University of Vermont, I began collecting information on known site locations. This work was directly responsible for the founding, in 1968, of the Vermont Archaeological Society. And I was able to bring to the university other archaeologists who, unencumbered with research responsibilities in other areas, were able to work directly in Vermont archaeology. The first of these was Louise Basa, who was followed by Marjory Power, and most recently, Peter A. Thomas. Working with the other university archaeologists and the archaeological society, I was privileged to be able to assist in the writing and enactment of Vermont's Historic Preservation Act of 1975, and in the recruitment of the first State Archaeologist, Giovanna Neudorfer.

In addition to these promotional activities, I was able to publish short summaries of Vermont's prehistory in *Vermont Life* and the series of *Lake Champlain Basin Studies*, and to assist some of our anthropology students in the production of a film, *Prehistoric Life in the Champlain Valley*. With Gordon Day's excellent 1965 article in *Vermont History*, these made a start at combating the prevailing misinformation about Vermont Indians. And when Huden's *Archaeology in Vermont* was republished in 1971, I was able to persuade the publisher to include an introduction which, however gently, tried to warn the reader that much of the material in the book was out-dated. To aid in the further dissemination of reliable information on Vermont natives, Marjory Power and I prepared under the auspices of the Vermont Historical Society an annotated bibliography and list of resources for the study of Vermont archaeology for teachers. At about the same time, we instituted at the university a regular course offering on Vermont Indians.

Whatever value these efforts may have had, they still were no substitute for a thorough book on Vermont's native peoples. Up to now, my various other commitments have not allowed me the time to write such a book. And even now, I couldn't do it without the able assistance of Marjory Power. I hope that our joint effort is effective in presenting the story of Vermont's original inhabitants, stripped bare of all the misinformation and inaccuracies which have so distorted that story.

My interest in the native peoples of northeastern North America goes back to my boyhood on the coast of Maine. In the 1930s and '40s, I was privileged to know the late Theodore Mitchell, one-time Governor of the Penobscots. I can't claim to have known him well, but he was a born raconteur, and I never tired of listening to him when he came to visit each summer. This experience supplemented my awareness of a past native presence all around me in the form of the numerous shell middens which dot the islands of Penobscot Bay. The two influences together led me, as an anthropology student at the University of Pennsylvania, to seek out the works of Frank Speck on the Penobscot. These enabled me to make some sense, in human terms, of what was then known of the archaeology of Maine. Had it not been for this background, I would not now be collaborating on a book about Vermont natives.

Nor would I be collaborating on such a book were it not for support granted by the University of Vermont, the National Endowment for the Humanities, and the Cecil Howard Charitable

Trust. The university, by granting me a full year sabbatical, provided me with the time necessary to fulfill the responsibilities of a senior author. The National Endowment, by granting me a fellowship for independent study, provided me with sufficient funds so that I could afford to take a full year's sabbatical. The Cecil Howard Charitable Trust, for its part, provided funds to help defray costs of manuscript preparation. By their actions, all three institutions provided valued endorsements of the concept of a book on Vermont's original inhabitants; I am grateful for this as well as for their more direct support.

I am also grateful to all those whose archaeological, ethnographic, linguistic, and historical research has made it possible for us to write this book. Their names are too numerous to list here, but will be found throughout the text as appropriate, and in the bibliographical notes at the end. I wish to thank, too, those who read critically parts or all of our manuscript as it was written: Michael Green of Dartmouth College's Native American Studies program and the publisher's anonymous readers, who read the entire manuscript; Peter A. Thomas of the University of Vermont's Anthropology Department, who read all but the last chapter; Gordon M. Day of Canada's National Museum of Man, who read Chapters 1, 3, 5, and 6; Giovanna Neudorfer, Vermont's State Archaeologist, who read Chapters 1, 2, and 3; Howard Russell, who read Chapters 5 and 6; John Moody, who read Chapters 6 and 7; Ian Worley and Philip Wagner of the University of Vermont's botany and geology departments, who read Chapter 2; graduate students James B. Petersen and Lauren Kelley, who read Chapter 4; and Miles Jensen and Jean Sbardellati, who read Chapter 7. Their reactions and comments were of immense value to us, but of course they should not be held responsible for the use we have made of them.

For technical assistance, we are indebted to Kevin Crisman, who expertly drafted the various charts, maps, and drawings which were prepared specifically for this book. John Smith and his staff at the University Photo Service were invaluable in copying drawings and producing quality prints. Dick Adams of Vergennes made it possible to photograph material from the Reagen site and Donovan site. The monumental task of typing the manuscript was handled almost entirely by Kathy Greer. I am sure her patience was sorely tried at times, but she kept her good humor through it all.

We owe a major debt to Vermont's Abenakis, whose decision to "go public" in the 1970s forced researchers to carefully reexamine the conventional picture of what happened to Vermont's native population following the French loss of their North American possessions. We have found Vermont's Abenakis to be a friendly and cooperative people with those who are willing to listen to what they have to say. Moreover, their steadfast refusal to renounce their cultural heritage in the face of tremendous pressures to do so should prompt us all to stop and think about our own traditions, and our attitudes toward those whose traditions may differ from our own.

Yet another debt is owed to the students who have enrolled in our course on Vermont Indians. It was in that course that we began to gather the materials and try out the ideas which have become this book.

To conclude on a more personal note, I wish to thank my wife and children for having put up with my preoccupation with this book. It could not have been easy for my wife, when trying to study for a psychology exam, to have me ask for her reaction to a phrase or an idea which eventually found its way into this book.

Burlington, Vt.   W.A.H.

September, 1980

THE ORIGINAL VERMONTERS
Native Inhabitants, Past and Present

I. INTRODUCTION

Prior to the coming of the Whiteman, the present state of Vermont was largely an uninhabited no-man's-land. The entire area was a disputed hunting ground claimed by the Algonquin tribes of Indians, who resided in what now is Canada, and the powerful Iroquois federation, whose principal villages were in what is now New York State.

SO SAYS the *Vermont Atlas and Gazetteer,* a handsome volume published in 1978. Such a statement might be dismissed as misinformed, were it not that similar statements are to be found in almost every book which touches in one way or another on Vermont history. The tenacity of this myth (for that's what it is) that "Indians didn't live in Vermont" is amazing. The early European explorers and colonists, French and British alike, were perfectly aware that native people lived in the region. The British traded with them and then fought them as enemies. The French traded with them, fought with them as allies against the British and Iroquois, were assisted by them in their explorations into the heart of North America, and even established a mission at one of their villages, near the mouth of the Missisquoi River. In the 1760s, when English settlers really began to pour into Vermont, hundreds of acres in the Champlain and Connecticut valleys were found already cleared of trees, where people had grown their crops; Champlain spoke about "fertile fields of maize" in this region in 1609.

Today, an awareness that Vermont was once inhabited by Indians is largely confined to their descendants, anthropologists, and collectors of prehistoric artifacts. Most authors of books about Vermont and its history, on the other hand, are content to repeat in their own words the last inaccurate statement about Vermont's supposed emptiness prior to settlement by Europeans. How this myth came into being will be made clear later in this book. What is really surprising is its continued widespread acceptance; most authors who write about Vermont are readers of the journal, *Vermont History,* which has carried a number of articles on aborigi-

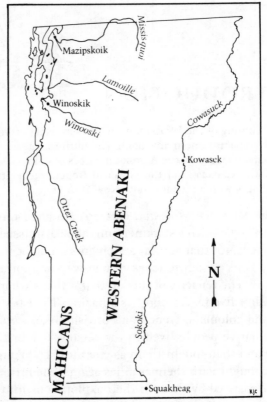

FIGURE I–I. Abenaki bands in Vermont, ca. A.D. 1600.

nal occupations, among them one by Stephen Laurent, himself a descendant of earlier Vermont natives, and another by the anthropologist-ethnohistorian Gordon M. Day of Canada's National Museum of Man, who has devoted over two decades to the study of evidence from archival and informant sources on Vermont's native peoples. The Vermont Historical Society, for its part, began a survey of prehistoric sites in the 1940s, and sponsored archaeological investigation of a prehistoric settlement near Vergennes in the 1950s. Why so many writers continue to ignore all this and other relevant research is a mystery.

Native Peoples of Vermont
The people who lived in Vermont in the seventeenth century when Europeans first appeared on the scene consisted of various bands of Abenaki peoples (Figure 1–1). The only exception to this

was in that part of Vermont which lies west of the Green Mountains and south of the Otter Creek watershed, a part of the upper Hudson watershed which was the home of the Mahicans. This is attested by linguistic data, oral traditions which have survived among some Abenaki peoples down to the present day, and a scattering of early colonial documents. The only discordant note is Champlain's brief but oft-quoted statement that the east shore of the lake belonged to the Iroquois. Unfortunately, Champlain is quite unreliable on this, according to Gordon M. Day. Champlain traveled down the west side of the lake near the New York shore and saw Vermont only from a distance. He could not see for himself who was living there, and had to rely on what his Canadian Indians told him. Either they didn't know themselves who lived there or, perhaps more likely, Champlain simply misunderstood what he was told.

Linguistic Affiliations

The Abenaki and Mahicans spoke languages which were parts of a chain of related languages stretching from the Maritime Provinces of Canada down the eastern seaboard as far as the Carolinas. Where such chains occur, it is possible to travel easily from one group of people to the next with little trouble understanding what is said; however, the differences between languages at the two ends of the chain are of such magnitude that they are not mutually intelligible. This chain of languages is known as Eastern Algonquian and is classified within a larger family of languages known as Algonquian (which is not to be confused with Algonquin, the name of a group of people in Canada who spoke an Algonquian language). Algonquian is the most widespread of all native North American language families. Besides Eastern Algonquian, it includes within it the chain of Central Algonquian languages, which stretch north of the St. Lawrence from the Atlantic coast through the Great Lakes, as well as the languages of such Plains people as the Blackfeet, Cheyenne, and Arapaho. While the languages of the Algonquian family are not mutually intelligible, the similarities between them are of the same order as those between, say, the Romance languages or the Germanic languages.

Just as the Romance and Germanic languages are classified together with a number of others spoken by peoples native to Europe and Asia in a larger category known as Indo-European, so the Algonquian languages are placed in a comparable category known as Algonquian-Ritwan, which includes the languages spoken by the Yurok and Wiyot of California. Algonquian-Ritwan, in turn, may belong with the Muskogean languages of southeastern North America in a Macro-Algonquian phylum, much as the Indo-European languages are thought to belong with ancient Hittite in a phylum known as Indo-Hittite.

Linguistic classifications such as those just summarized are constructed in such a way as to reflect historical relationships between languages. Simply put, the classification of the Algonquian and Ritwan languages together means that they diverged a long time ago from an ancient ancestral language, which we may call Proto-Algonquian-Ritwan. Proto-Algonquian-Ritwan and Proto-Muskogean, in turn, may have diverged from an even more ancient ancestral language known as Proto-Macro-Algonquian. The geographical distribution of Algonquian and Muskogean languages suggests that there was once an uninterrupted belt of Proto-Macro-Algonquian dialects in eastern North America. Following a separation, divergence took place between the northern and southern dialects, leading to the development of two daughter languages, Proto-Algonquian in the North and Proto-Muskogean in the South. Linguists estimate this separation to have occurred sometime between 4000 and 3000 B.C. The Algonquian languages spoken at the time of European contact are the result of further linguistic divergence from Proto-Algonquian. The breakup of Proto-Algonquian into separate speech communities is estimated to have taken place over the last 4000 years (since 2000 B.C.).

Speakers of Central and Eastern Algonquian were all hunters and gatherers until about 1500 to 1000 years ago, and many of them continued living this way until recent times. It is typical of hunters and gatherers, when they are not impeded too much by natural obstacles in their terrain, to maintain a relatively uniform language for a long period of time over a large area, despite low concentrations of population and slow means of travel. When the regional differentiation of a language into dialects does occur, as it always does with time, it takes on the typical chain formation. Thus, it is likely that Central and Eastern Algonquian peoples were living where Europeans found them for a very long time;

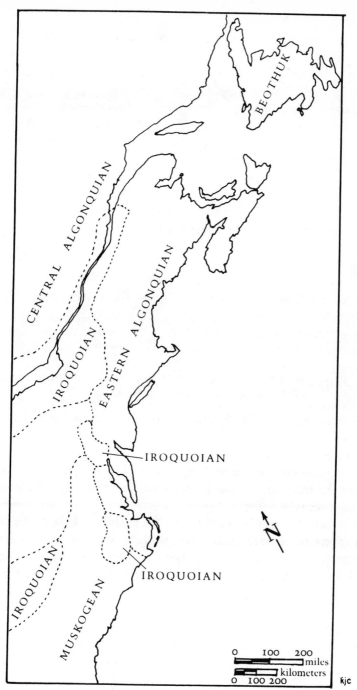

FIGURE 1-2. Major language groups of northeastern North America.

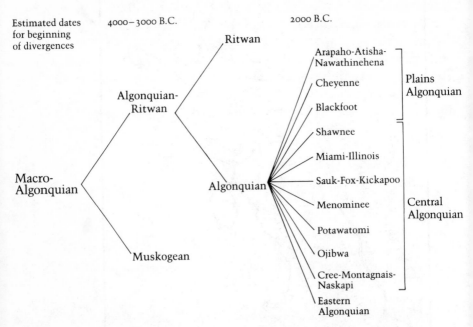

FIGURE I–3. This diagram shows the relationships of the Algonquian languages to one another, as well as to the Ritwan and Muskogean languages.

possibly, since the divergence of Proto-Algonquian from Proto-Muskogean. Furthermore, there is nothing in any of the Eastern Algonquian languages to suggest that the region was ever inhabited by speakers of any non-Algonquian language, from whom Algonquian intruders would be expected to have borrowed some words.

Appearing to form a wedge between Central and Eastern Algonquian–speaking peoples are the speakers of the Iroquoian languages (see Figure I–2). This family of languages includes those spoken by the Susquehannocks of Pennsylvania, the Five Nations Iroquois of New York, the Huron of Canada, the St. Lawrence Iroquois (who were encountered in 1535 by Cartier, but who had disappeared by Champlain's time), and the Tuscarora and Cherokee of the Carolinas and adjacent portions of Tennessee and Georgia. The Iroquoian languages are part of the Macro-Siouan phylum, along with Siouan and some other languages of the Plains and the Southeast. This classification reflects the fact that Iroquoian and Algonquian resemble each other about as much as English resembles Chinese. Differences of such magnitude are the result of many thousands of years of separate development.

The geographical distribution of the Iroquoian languages vis-a-vis the unrelated Central and Eastern Algonquian languages suggests that at some time in the past there had been an intrusion of Iroquoian speakers into the Northeast from a homeland elsewhere. The connection between the northern Iroquoian languages, Cherokee, and Tuscarora suggests that this homeland could have been located in the Appalachian uplands. (Just when this intrusion might have taken place is a question we shall take up in Chapter 3.)

The Environmental Setting

Human survival depends upon the ability of a people to adapt themselves to the environment in which they live; this requires that they develop patterns of behavior that will help them to utilize the environment to their advantage. Such patterns, or more precisely, the appropriate standards of behavior which underlie them, are what anthropologists call *culture.* A basic principle of anthropology is that to understand any human culture, one must view it within its environmental setting.

The environment to which Vermont's original inhabitants had to adapt is part of a lake-forest belt which extends from west of the Great Lakes eastward across southern Canada and the northern United States. This region has a relatively cold and humid climate, with a marked seasonal variation between warm summers and cold winters, at which time snow can build up to depths of 120 inches and more in the mountains. By and large, this is the way things have been for the last 4300 years or so. Before that the environment to which people had to adapt was rather different; these differences are discussed later in appropriate chapters of this book.

The Green Mountains form the backbone of Vermont, with lowlands lying to the east and west. This topographic variety is important, for certain resources are available at higher elevations which are not to be found in the lowlands, and vice versa. By moving back and forth between uplands and lowlands, people had available far more in the way of resources than they would have had by limiting their activities exclusively to one or the other zone.

The most extensive of the lowland regions is the Champlain

Valley, to the west of the Green Mountains. These lowlands are one segment of a longer lowland corridor which opens to the north into the St. Lawrence Valley, and runs south through the Lake George trough and the Hudson Valley. Though far from flat, the gently rolling hills do not impede travel, which is easy both by land and by water from the St. Lawrence to the Hudson. In these low hills are to be found numerous outcrops of stone such as chert, jasper, and quartzite, useful for making a variety of tools; large chert quarries are known at Mount Independence and St. Albans, and a quartzite quarry at Monkton Ridge.

The soils of the Champlain Valley consist of water-deposited sands, silts, and clays, with glacial drift at higher elevations. These are some of the richest farmlands in the state and are easy to cultivate with simple hand tools. These soils, a growing season of 130 or more frost-free days, and an annual precipitation of 33 inches made the valley suitable for native horticulture—the cultivation of domestic plants by means of simple hand tools. Where not cleared by natural forces such as fires, floods, and high winds, or by humans for farming, the land was covered by a forest in which northern hardwoods, especially sugar maple, beech, and yellow birch were dominant. In the bottomlands, ash, red maple, and elm were to be found; elsewhere there was some basswood, butternut, chestnut, oak, white birch, hemlock, cedar, red spruce, and white pine. The trees of this forest were huge by modern standards, reaching heights of 100 feet or more, with diameters of several feet. A relatively open canopy permitted the growth of various shrubs and herbs beneath these trees. This kind of forest supports a rich fauna, including such edible species as deer, bear, and turkey.

The dominant feature of the Champlain Valley is Lake Champlain itself. It receives its water from eleven major rivers including, on the Vermont side, the Poultney, Otter Creek, Winooski, Lamoille, and Missisquoi. In these waters are to be found sturgeon, salmon, perch, pickerel, catfish, bass, turtle, and otter. Along the edges of the lake and its rivers are extensive wetlands which attract over thirty species of waterfowl in season, and provide a habitat for muskrat and beaver. Much of the wetland vegetation is useful to humans, both as food and as raw material for mats and baskets. Besides providing an abundance of food, the lake and its rivers permit canoe travel throughout the Champlain lowlands; in addition, the major rivers provide easy access to the uplands to the east.

On the east side of Vermont, the Connecticut Valley occupies a position analogous to the Champlain Valley on the west side; though less broad, it contains the same sorts of rich soils, adequate rainfall, and sufficient frost-free days for native horticulture. Its forests are similar to those of the Champlain Valley, and in the seventeenth century the Connecticut Valley with its tributaries was one of the highest fur-yielding territories in all of New England. As part of the Atlantic Flyway, along with Lake Champlain, migratory waterfowl are abundant in their season. Several species of fish and turtles, including annual runs of Atlantic salmon and shad were to be found in the river. In colonial times, one of the best salmon and shad fishing areas on the whole river was at Vernon. Travel is easy on or along the Connecticut all the way from Canada to the Long Island Sound, and its major tributaries—the West, Saxtons, Williams, Black, Ottauquecee, White, Ompompanoosuc, Waits, Wells, and Passumpsic—give access to the uplands to the west.

Vermont's least extensive lowland region is the Vermont Valley. Ranging in width from a few hundred yards to as much as eight miles, it extends southward from Brandon and forms another link between the Hudson and Champlain Valleys. Its floor rises gently to a point north of Bennington which marks the divide between the Otter Creek watershed and that of the Batten Kill (which, with the Wallomsac and Hoosic around Bennington and Pownal, ultimately flows into the Hudson). It is an easy matter to pass from one watershed to the other. The soils of the Vermont Valley, like those of the other lowlands, are suitable for native horticulture: there are 130 frost-free days, and adequate precipitation (37 inches). Its forests are like those of the Champlain Valley, and there are extensive wetlands along Otter Creek.

The coldest, wettest, and most prominent of Vermont's upland regions are the Green Mountains, which rise rather sharply east of the Champlain and Vermont valleys. From twenty to thirty-six miles in width, they extend the length of the state into Quebec on the north and Massachusetts on the south. Formed largely of ancient quartzites and marbles, glacial deposits are common be-

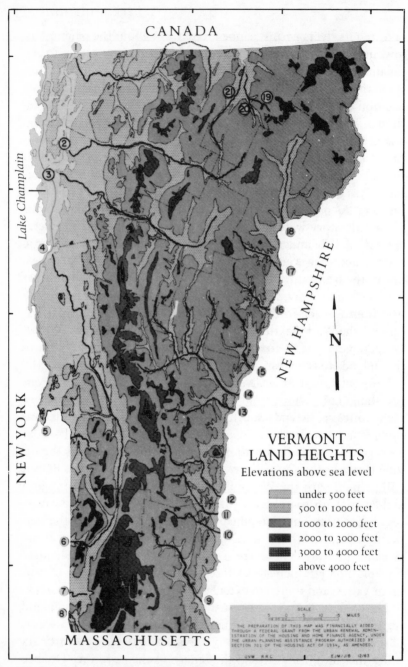

FIGURE 1–4. Land heights and rivers of Vermont: 1, Missisquoi; 2, Lamoille; 3, Winooski; 4, Otter Creek; 5, Poultney; 6, Batten Kill; 7, Wallomsac; 8, Hoosic; 9, West; 10, Saxtons; 11, Williams; 12, Black; 13, Ottauquechee; 14, White; 15, Ompompanoosuc; 16, Waits; 17, Wells; 18, Passumpsic; 19, Willoughby; 20, Barton; 21, Black. From *Vermont in Maps*, by Edward J. Miles (University of Vermont, 1963), by permission of author; rivers added by us.

low 3100 feet, with lake sediments and gravels frequent below 2000 feet. Generally, the soils are all rough, stony, and acidic. Such poor soils, coupled with a short growing season—90 days at 3000 feet—effectively ruled out native horticulture.

The Green Mountains average 2000 feet in height, with several peaks rising above this up to the maximum 4393 feet of Mount Mansfield. Forests of northern hardwoods cloak the lower slopes of the mountains below 2400 feet. By 2400 feet yellow and white birch become more prominent along with hemlock, red spruce, and balsam fir. At 3000 feet the mixed forest gives way to a boreal forest dominated by red spruce and balsam fir, with some white birch still present. The higher peaks are clad with alpine-tundra, a mixture of lichens, heaths, sedges, and stunted, twisted firs. The higher forests, above 1500 feet, provide habitat for such animals as moose, marten, and lynx.

The Green Mountains would constitute a formidable barrier to east-west travel in Vermont, were they not breached at various points. On the west, the Winooski and Lamoille rivers both cut well through the mountains, so that it is relatively easy to move from the headwaters of the Winooski and its tributaries to the White, Waits, and Wells rivers, which feed the Connecticut, or from the Lamoille to the northern Black River which flows into Lake Memphramagog. One can also reach Lake Memphramagog from the upper Missisquoi. Further south, we know that Abenakis were accustomed to crossing the mountains from Otter Creek to the southern Black River, which flows to the Connecticut. One can also portage from Roaring Brook, a tributary of Otter Creek, to the headwaters of the West River.

Between the Green Mountains and the Connecticut and Passumpsic valleys is an extensive upland region known as the Vermont Piedmont. This is made up of low rolling hills with a few prominent monadonocks such as Mount Ascutney (3144 feet) and Burke Mountain (3267 feet). The hills slope gently from north to south, and from the Green Mountains to the Connecticut. Among them are numerous small streams, lakes, and ponds which contain such cold water species of fish as rainbow, lake, and brook trout, and which provide habitat for such fur-bearing animals as beaver and otter. The largest body of water is Lake Memphramagog, which gives access to Canada. From its feeder streams, the Black, Barton, and Willoughby rivers, one can travel easily to the Connecticut River via the Passumpsic, or to Lake Champlain via the Lamoille or Missisquoi.

The growing season in the Vermont Piedmont is generally less than 130 days, and the stony soils are generally poorly suited for horticulture. Although fertile sand, silt, and clay may be found along rivers, glacial tills lie thick in the valleys. The forest consists mostly of white pine, hemlock, and northern hardwoods, with conifers more prominent at higher elevations.

East of the Passumpsic, the uplands continue as the Northeast Highlands, a heavily folded granite and schist extension of the White Mountains. This is rugged country with swampy plateaus, much of which is above 2000 feet in elevation. The soils are generally either swampy and mucky or stony and acidic, and the growing season ranges from 90 to 110 days—not sufficient for native horticulture. The region's forest is heavy in white pine, hemlock, spruce, and fir, with some northern hardwoods.

Vermont's one other upland region consists of a northward extension of the Taconic Mountains on the west side of the Vermont Valley. These are a mass of rugged mountains and hills which contain important sources of slate and quartzite for the making of stone tools. Their soils consist largely of stony glacial tills and gravels along with some lake bottom sediments. These are not very good for farming, and the growing season is less than 130 days. The forest is heavy in hemlock and white pine to the west, with spruce, fir, and hardwoods on the east.

Chronological Periods

In the rest of this book, we will be looking in detail at the ways of life of the native people who lived in the land just described. Our presentation will be chronological, beginning with the first people who lived in Vermont and ending with a section on Native Americans in Vermont today.

Our chronological presentation is organized in terms of a few broad time periods: Paleoindian, Archaic, Woodland, Ethnographic Present, and Historic. The first three are in common use among archaeologists; their precise dating will be discussed in Chapters 2, 3, and 4. Unfortunately, they are commonly used in other ways as well: as the names of cultural traditions, and as labels for broad developmental stages through which native North American cultures have evolved. This is not so much of a problem with the term Paleoindian, for the time period is virtually synonymous with the Paleoindian, Big Game Hunting way of life, out of which Archaic culture did develop. The terms Archaic and Woodland though, are another matter. Woodland culture really is exemplified by the Adena and Hopewell culture of the "mound builders" which developed in the Midwest. While Vermont natives in the Woodland period shared certain features with Adena and Hopewell, such as use of the bow and arrow, pottery, and native horticulture, there were very significant cultural differences between them. Vermont natives in the last millennium b.c. began to adopt elements of Woodland culture, but these only modified, without any fundamental change, what remained an Archaic way of life right down to the time of European contact. In other words, although the Archaic period ended in Vermont in the last millennium b.c., the Archaic as a cultural tradition did not end in Vermont until native culture had been seriously disrupted by the impact of European intrusion and domination. Woodland culture in Vermont, then, is a modified version of Archaic culture, and not the same as Woodland culture in the Midwest.

In the rest of this book, we will try to be as clear as possible about what we mean by the terms Archaic and Woodland, whenever we use them. Fortunately, no such complications surround use of the terms for our other two periods. The Ethnographic Present, a standard concept in anthropology, marks the transition from prehistory to history. It is that time following first contact with Europeans, but prior to substantial modification of native culture. In Vermont, it may be said to begin with Champlain's visit of 1609 to the lake which now bears his name. We have rather arbitrarily set the date for its end at 1650.

Radiocarbon Dating

Our dating of events in these last two periods is based on written records. For the earlier periods, we are dependent on radiocarbon, or carbon 14, dating. This method works because all living things absorb a heavy radioactive isotope of carbon of mass number 14 (carbon 14) from the atmosphere and reach equilibrium with that

FIGURE 1–5. The "ethnographic present" in Vermont begins with Champlain's visit of 1609 to the lake which now bears his name. Here he is shown, with his Algonqui friends, fighting a force of Iroquoians on the New York side of the lake. Photo courtesy of *Vermont Life*.

in the atmosphere. This absorption ceases with death, and the carbon 14 begins to decay at a fixed rate into nitrogen 14, emitting beta particles in the process. This rate at death is about 15 beta radiations per minute per gram of material. The rate of decay of a radioactive substance is measured in terms of its *half-life*, the time it takes for half of its atoms to disintegrate. The half life of carbon 14 as of 1963 is 5730 years; therefore it takes 5730 years for half of the original carbon 14 to break down into nitrogen 14. After 5730 years, beta radiation will be about 7.5 counts per minute per gram. In another 5730 years, one-half of the remaining carbon 14 will also have decayed: after 11,460 years, one-fourth of the original amount of carbon 14 is left. Thus, when a piece of organic material such as wood, charcoal, shell, or bone is found in a hearth, burial, storage pit, or the like, its age can be determined by counting the beta rays emitted by the remaining carbon 14. Actually, for a variety of technical reasons, its age can be determined only as probably lying within a certain range of time, even though a more specific date is stated. For example, the date for a piece of bone from an early Vermont site discussed in Chapter 3 is 5120 ± 210 years before present ("present" is defined as A.D. 1950). What this really means is that there are two out of three chances that the correct date lies somewhere in the 420 years between 4910 and 5330 years ago. The chances are even better, nineteen out of twenty, that it lies in the 840 years between 4700 and 5540 years ago. One must always remember that carbon 14 dates are not as precisely accurate as they may seem.

Until 1970, it was thought that radiocarbon years were equivalent to calendar years. Then, it was demonstrated that they are not. With the exception of a brief period around A.D. 1500, the difference is insignificant back to 1500 B.C., but by then radiocarbon and calendar years begin to diverge significantly. For periods older then 1500 B.C., carbon 14 dates become progressively younger, or too recent, relative to calendar years. This means that most published 14 dates for Paleoindian, Archaic, and very late Woodland materials are too young and will need to be corrected. It also means, in the case of carbon 14 dates used in recent publications, that one must know whether the author is using "raw" or corrected dates.

Carbon 14 laboratories have not yet reached final agreement as to how radiocarbon dates should be corrected, and until they do, they have recommended that we not try to correct them. Nevertheless, various correction formulas are in use. None of them, however, go back beyond about 5400 B.C.; so dates for Paleoindian and early Archaic materials cannot be corrected, whether one wishes to do so or not. In this book, then, we use uncorrected dates throughout, although for dates in late Archaic and late Woodland times we include the calendar equivalents, as determined by one widely-used formula. For uncorrected dates, "b.c." and "a.d." are used; actual calendar years are indicated by "B.C." and "A.D."

Archaeological Method

People have been living in Vermont for 11,000 years or so, yet eyewitness accounts of their way of life and remembered traditions take us back only a few centuries. Unless we turn our backs on the greater part of aboriginal history in Vermont, we must turn to archaeology for our knowledge of native culture over the millennia preceding the seventeenth century A.D.

Therefore, the next three chapters of this book are archaeological in nature. They deal with the formation and subsequent development of native culture in Vermont. The primary data of archaeology are artifacts—objects made by people—and the ground they were left in. These objects, and the precise way they were left in the ground, reflect certain aspects of human behavior. The archaeologist uses these data to reconstruct and explain past ways of life by means of analogy, resting on the premise that similar forms imply similar functions. For example, if an ancient people are identified as hunters and gatherers, it is because their tools, their trash, and their settlements are more like those of historically known hunters and gatherers than they are like those of historically known pastoralists or horticulturalists. Furthermore, it is probable that their social and political organization, as well as their religious beliefs and practices, had more in common with those of known hunters and gatherers than with those of known pastoralists or horticulturalists.

Probability always plays a prominent role in archaeological reconstruction and explanation. Usually, we cannot be 100 percent certain that a particular reconstruction or explanation is correct, and so we must see which alternative the weight of the evidence favors as most probable. This lack of absolute certainty may bother some people, but it is the way of science. Truth, in science, is not considered to be absolute, but rather a matter of varying degrees of probability; what is considered to be true is what is most probable. This is true of archaeology, just as it is true of biology or physics. As our knowledge expands, the odds in favor of some explanations over others are generally increased, but sometimes old "truths" must be discarded when alternative explanations are shown to be more probable.

Because the raw data of archaeology are things and the associations between things, a good deal of the writings of archaeologists are of necessity devoted to the description and analysis of things such as projectile points and pot sherds, as opposed to descriptions and explanations of how the people who used them lived. All too often this makes it difficult for someone else to see the forest for the trees. Here we shall try to summarize details and synthesize particular observations into a broader outlook, rather than describe archaeological materials in detail. We will spend less time with particular things such as types of projectile points (so dear to the hearts of northeastern archaeologists) and more time analyzing what these things can tell us about human behavior in general. Those who want more descriptive details can consult the primary sources which we list at the back of the book unless, of course, the details have not been published. In such cases, we have tried to present those details necessary to make a more general point, but in such a way as to not disrupt the flow of the narrative.

Ethnohistoric Method

The last three chapters of this book are largely ethnohistoric in nature. Ethnohistory is a kind of historic ethnography which studies cultures of the recent past through accounts left by explorers, missionaries, and traders; through systematic interviews with individuals still living who remember events and traditions of the past; and through analysis of such records as land titles, birth and death records, and other archival materials. Unfortunately, there are problems with all of these sources of data. For example, the early explorers and other observers were not trained ethnographers and frequently misunderstood what they observed or were told. Furthermore, they had their own self-interests to look out for, and these are reflected in what they wrote. The same applies to living individuals and what they remember; moreover, memories may become blurred as the events remembered fade further—especially several generations—into the past. Nor are other archival materials entirely reliable. For example, early land speculators often got people to sign deeds who really had neither the right nor authority to do so, in order to protect themselves from the possibility of challenges to their titles or in order to challenge someone else's title. Thus, the ethnohistorian can neither ignore nor take at face value any one source of information. Only by sifting through all available sources of information, carefully cross-checking them for accuracy, can a substantial body of reliable data be amassed.

The last chapter brings us to matters which were the subject of a good deal of controversy in the late 1970s. For awhile, emotions ran high on all sides, to the point where arguments by assertion, rather than fact, were the rule. Not wishing to become embroiled in emotional debate, we have tried to stay as close as we can to the facts currently available. This is a cautious approach, and one which we feel will make the best contribution toward the ultimate resolution of the controversy.

2. PALEOINDIANS:

The First Vermonters

IN 1492, Columbus discovered America—or so most of us were taught in school. Of course, he was not the first European to do so; the Norsemen beat him by about 500 years. But even they must be ranked as relative newcomers, for it is a known fact that they were preceded tens of thousands of years earlier by a now nameless people from northeast Asia. These Asians made their way across a land bridge where the Bering Straits now lie, probably between 33,000 and 40,000 years ago. It is unlikely that they had any idea that they were discovering a "new world," but that's all right, Columbus didn't know he was either.

Late Glacial Environments

When Columbus came to America, the world's climates were much as they are today, but they were far different when the earlier northeast Asians arrived. Then, the world was locked in the grip of the last of the great ice age glaciations, which had its beginnings 60,000 or 70,000 years ago. With so much of the world's water supply taken up by great continental ice masses, there was a world wide lowering of sea levels, causing an emergence of land joining Siberia to Alaska. But because the cold was less intense at some times than others during the Wisconsin glaciation, as it is called in North America, there were occasional minor recessions of the ice. One of these took place about 33,000 years ago, releasing enough water to drown the Bering land bridge. It also opened an ice-free corridor along the McKenzie River Valley. With these events, human populations in Alaska and the northern Yukon were cut off from their fellow Asians and became, in effect, the first Americans. Gradually, these first Americans worked their way south through the McKenzie corridor before it was closed by the next period of intense cold, about 23,000 years ago.

The same expansion of the Wisconsin ice which closed the McKenzie corridor also placed much of the Northeast, including Vermont, off limits to expanding human populations. All of New England and the Maritime Provinces including the now sub-merged continental shelf were buried deep beneath the Lauren-tide ice, one of the major Wisconsin glaciers. The Laurentide ice grew from a nucleus in central Canada and terminated south of New England at Long Island, New York. In places this ice reached thicknesses of up to 20,000 feet, and its weight was such as to de-press the land as much as 3300 feet below present sea level. In short, the Northeast was an ice desert, all but devoid of life and totally unsuited to human occupation.

Conditions in the Northeast remained this way until climates began to warm up a bit, starting about 16,000 b.c. This began the melting of the Laurentide ice, which continued, with minor set-backs, until the ice was totally dissipated around 6000 b.c. By 11,000 b.c., southern and northern coastal New England were ice-free, and deglaciation was under way in Vermont. As this pro-ceeded, the ice acted as a huge dam, impounding meltwater in the Champlain Valley until it reached such depth as to be able to drain southward into the Hudson Valley. This Lake Vermont, as it is called, had a water level 400 to 700 feet higher than the present Lake Champlain. Another large body of glacial meltwater, Lake Hitchcock, filled the Connecticut Valley from Middletown, Con-necticut to East Thetford, Vermont. This filled an irregular basin, its northern part anywhere from one to twelve miles in width. In the uplands between lakes Vermont and Hitchcock, smaller gla-cial lakes formed. No matter what their size, all these lakes had three things in common: youth, exceedingly cold waters, and changing configurations. Such a combination severely limits bi-otic productivity, so these lake waters contained little in the way of edible resources. Coupled with rivers like the Hudson, swollen far above their present levels by glacial meltwater, the larger lakes must have been impediments to the eastward movement of peoples. To be sure, these rivers and lakes could have been crossed on the winter ice, but the general north-south trend of major river and lake valleys in eastern New York and western New England would have made northward, rather than eastward, movement easiest. Most, if not all, of New England seems to have remained uninhabited by human populations at this time.

By 10,500 b.c., although some glaciers may have survived in the Green Mountains, the front of the principal ice sheet had retreated slightly north and west of the St. Lawrence River, releasing the waters of Lake Vermont northward. Although forests were beginning to recolonize deglaciated areas to the south, they had not yet reached New England, where tundra conditions prevailed. Nor had human populations, although there is evidence that people were beginning to expand northward along the west side of the Hudson River. Their archaeological remains have been found at Dutchess Quarry Cave in southeastern New York and radiocarbon dated at 10,580 ± 370 b.c.

The release of such vast amounts of formerly frozen water by glacial recession, not just in North America but throughout the world, raised the world's sea levels dramatically, particularly in those areas where the land had been depressed by the weight of the glacial ice. This had a significant effect on Vermont; following the release of Lake Vermont's waters, marine waters flooded the St. Lawrence and Champlain lowlands. At its maximum extent, in 10,000 b.c., the Champlain Sea covered an area of 20,500 square miles or more. Wider in the north than south, it reached as far east as Enosburg Falls, as far west as Lake Ontario, and as far south as Whitehall. Soon, though, the Champlain Sea was affected by another consequence of glacial recession: the removal of the tremendous weight of the ice which had depressed the land. Northern land masses began to rebound, much as a piece of foam rubber will rebound when a heavy object is removed from it. There is a slight lag between removal and rebound; subsequent rebound will be greatest where the weight had been greatest, causing the most depression. Since the weight of the Laurentide ice was greatest at its center, decreasing towards its margins, postglacial rebound has been greater in Canada and northern New England than it has to the south.

As the land rebounded in Vermont, the level of the Champlain Sea dropped relative to the elevation of the land, especially at its northern end. Probably by 8200 b.c., and certainly by 7400 b.c., the land north of the present Lake Champlain had risen above sea level, preventing the entry of tidal waters and so ending the Champlain Sea. Over in the Connecticut Valley, erosion breached the dam of Lake Hitchcock, but there is continuing debate over when this occurred. Lake Hitchcock may have disappeared by about 8700 b.c., but a successor lake, known as Lake Upton, survived in the Connecticut Valley between Springfield, Vermont and St. Johnsbury. It was sometime prior to the demise of the Champlain Sea that the first human populations entered Vermont.

The Reagen Site

The people usually referred to as Paleoindians, whose archaeological remains have been found over much of North America, were the first people to inhabit the area now known as Vermont. In Vermont, Paleoindians are known primarily from finds in the Champlain Valley, although a few finds are known from elsewhere in the state. The best known Paleoindian remains are those from the Reagen site, in East Highgate. The site was discovered in the 1920s by two amateur archaeologists, William Ross and Benjamin Fisher; it was the first recognized Paleoindian site in New England. Standing on a high, sandy bluff, eight miles from Missisquoi Bay, one looks south and west over the broad valley of the Missisquoi River. The river itself is three quarters of a mile distant, and some 300 feet lower in elevation. North and east of the site the land rises steeply another 200 feet.

Our understanding of the Reagen site is distinctly limited, for it was never professionally excavated, and adequate records of how artifacts and other materials were distributed over the site were not kept. Nor has the complete series of artifacts been adequately studied, although William A. Ritchie, former New York State Archaeologist, carried out a partial study in the 1950s. For our account here, we have supplemented Ritchie's study with our own preliminary observations on the artifacts which were not a part of his study.

The Reagen site seems to have been about two acres in size and was covered by a thin layer of yellowish sand. Beneath this were bits of charcoal and fire-cracked rocks, presumably the remains of hearths. With these were at least 230 stone artifacts, as well as numerous chips and flakes of chert (a flint-like stone), and a few chips and flakes of rhyolite and jasper (more colorful stones that

FIGURE 2–1. This picture shows some of the scraping and cutting tools from the Reagen site made by retouching flakes of chert (top two rows), and three gravers (bottom row). The graver on the left is of rhyolite, the others are of chert. None of the artifacts in this picture have ever been illustrated before.

FIGURE 2–2. This picture shows a plano-style projectile point (top left) and two specially shaped "knives" (top center and right) from the Reagen site. The knife in the center was broken anciently, and then reworked along one edge (the left, as shown here) of the larger surviving fragment. The large implement below the knives and projectile, never before illustrated, apparently served as a combination chopping and scraping tool. The bifacially worked rounded edge is suitable for chopping and the steep, unifacially worked "straight" edge fits comfortably against the palm of the hand. This same steep edge makes an effective hide scraper and the tool is also comfortable to hold as a scraper.

may be worked in the same way as chert). Of all the artifacts, roughly 70 percent are flakes of various sizes which have been retouched on one or both sides to serve as scraping or cutting tools (although a few were used as is, without any retouching). Most of these flakes are irregular in shape, but a few are long and blade-like, with parallel edges.

Some of these flake scraping and cutting tools are illustrated in Figure 2–1. Generally, the thicker flakes were made into scraping tools by retouching the edges and/or the ends, usually on one side only, to produce steeply beveled faces. The thinner flakes were generally made into cutting tools by retouching the edges, usually on both sides, to produce a sharp cutting edge. Not infrequently such flake knives, once dulled, seem to have been reworked for use as scrapers. Thus, the distinction between flake knives and scrapers is not always a clear one. A few flakes with sharp points were apparently used as gravers, and a few with concave working edges were "spokeshaves," used for smoothing down spear shafts and the like.

Other utilitarian artifacts from the Reagen site consist of about a dozen specially shaped knives, a large semilunar implement useful for both chopping and scraping, and about fifty-five projectile points (Figure 2–2). Some of these projectiles are fluted—that is, large channel flakes were removed from both surfaces at the base (Figure 2–6). Taken with the flake cutting and scraping tools just discussed, these are the sorts of tools useful to hunters. They suggest the killing and butchering of animals, and probably the working of hide and bone. The charcoal and burned stones indicate the cooking and eating of food. The chips and larger unused flakes of chert, and some apparently unfinished projectiles, indicate that stone tool making took place at the Reagen site.

Included among the Reagen artifacts are fifteen objects, three of soapstone and the rest of talc, which are unlike anything ever found at any other Paleoindian site in North America. Four of these are shown in Figure 2–3. Most have holes drilled in them, apparently so that they could be worn as pendants. They contrast markedly with the utilitarian nature of all the other artifacts.

The stone used to make the Reagen artifacts includes several different kinds of chert, rhyolite, basalt, quartzite, jasper, soapstone, and talc. The materials seem to have been carefully se-

FIGURE 2–3. Objects of soapstone (top, bottom, and middle left) and talc (middle right) from the Reagen site, never before illustrated. The object at the top could have been worn suspended as an ornament, and another object like that on the middle right is perforated near the tip for suspension. The significance of the other two grooved objects is unknown.

lected for their flaking properties; they come from a wide range of sources, many of them outside of Vermont. For example, some of the chert seems to have come from New York state, while the rhyolite probably came from Mount Jasper in Berlin, New Hampshire.

Apparently the Reagen site was occupied by a hunting people. Its large size suggests that it may have been recurrently occupied over a number of years, perhaps by a small band of people who returned for a particular season of food gathering activities. Other such Paleoindian sites are known in the Northeast, one of the better known being the Debert site in Nova Scotia. This site is securely dated at 8635 ± 47 b.c. Here, eleven living floors were found, eight in a nuclear area of three acres. Over 3000 artifacts

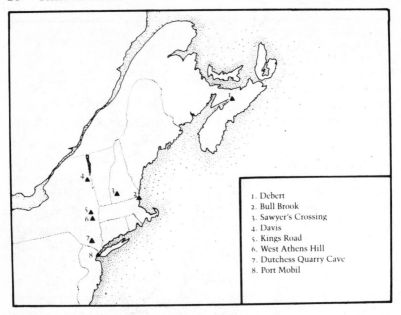

1. Debert
2. Bull Brook
3. Sawyer's Crossing
4. Davis
5. Kings Road
6. West Athens Hill
7. Dutchess Quarry Cave
8. Port Mobil

FIGURE 2–4. Other Paleoindian sites in the Northeast.

were recovered, including fluted projectiles and some scrapers and knives like some of those from the Reagen site. The scrapers and knives clearly had been used for working hides and cutting meat. Debert was located between what was then open tundra and forest, where caribou almost surely migrated back and forth from their sheltered winter feeding grounds in the forest and their summer feeding grounds on the tundra. It is likely that Debert was recurrently occupied by hunters in order to take advantage of the annual caribou migrations.

Another large Paleoindian site in the Northeast is Bull Brook at Ipswich, Massachusetts. Like Reagen, it is on a high terrace, overlooking low country to the north and east. Forty-five concentrations of chipping waste, artifacts (4000 of them, including fluted projectile points), fire-cracked stones, and charcoal were found here. A large number of the artifacts were made of stone from sources in the Mohawk and Hudson River valleys and the Catskills. Each of the forty-five "hot spots," some of which were as much as forty-one feet in diameter and four feet deep, may indicate a single occupation by a small group of people, who returned here year after year. Radiocarbon dates suggest that this occurred around 7300 b.c., but these dates are not regarded as reliable.

The dating of the Reagen site remains a problem. The site was excavated long before the advent of radiocarbon dating, and material suitable for radiocarbon dating is no longer available. Close resemblance of the artifacts to those from a dated Paleoindian site would suggest a comparable date for Reagen. The trouble with this is that the Reagen collection remains unique; no other collection from the Northeast is quite like it. There are, however, some helpful clues. First, the diversity of projectile points are reminiscent of late Paleoindian sites in southeastern North America. Second, triangular points, scrapers, knives, and flakes from Labrador which date back to 6900 b.c. appear to be derived from artifacts much like those found at the Reagen site. In addition, the sand on which the Reagen people camped was deposited by the Champlain Sea at its maximum. Thus, the site must postdate 10,000 b.c., or the camp would have been a wet place indeed. Throughout the Northeast, Paleoindians are known to have preferred high, well-drained spots for their camps, which were not only dry, but commanded a view of surrounding terrain where one would expect game animals to be plentiful. These conditions were not met at Reagen until after the waters of the Champlain Sea had withdrawn from the Missisquoi Valley.

Another clue to the age of Reagen is afforded by the nonfluted projectile points. Many of these resemble what in the Midwest are called Plano points: long, nonfluted, lance-like points which show fine, parallel flake scars. Plano points are characteristic of a late Paleoindian stage west of the Mississippi, where they first appear around 8000 b.c. This would place the Reagen site in a period of time about which little is known, archaeologically, in the Northeast. This would account for the so far unique nature of the Reagen collection. Further support for this position is provided by recent work in New Hampshire, where a radiocarbon date of 7665 ± 210 b.c. applies to Plano-like material near Lake Winnipesaukee.

Other Paleoindian Sites in Vermont

Although the Reagen site is Vermont's best-known Paleoindian site, Paleoindian material has been found at other localities in the

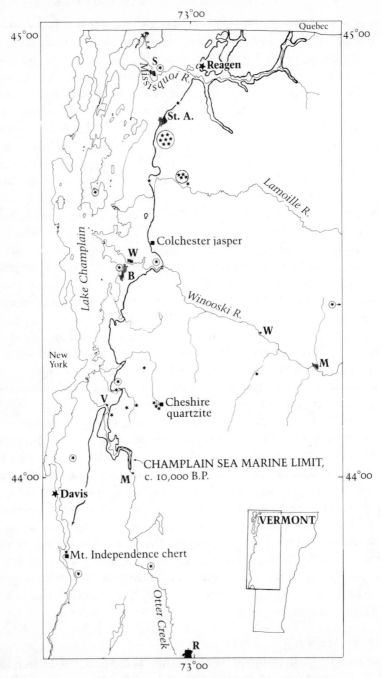

FIGURE 2–5. Shoreline of the Champlain Sea ca. 10,000 b.c. relative to Paleoindian sites (large stars) and fluted point "find spots" (small stars). Where only the approximate location of a find is known, the star is enclosed by a circle. Map courtesy of Stephen Loring and *Man in the Northeast*.

TABLE I. *Fluted Point Finds from Vermont*

Town	No. of Points	Material
Swanton	1	Fine black chert; from Mt. Independence?
St. Albans	1	Dark grey chert
Milton	1	Colchester jasper
Fairfax	5	4 Rhyolite, 1 crystal
Grand Isle	1	Crystal
Milton/Fairfax/Georgia (exact location unknown)	7	3 Fine black chert; from Mt. Independence? 1 Colchester jasper 1 Cheshire quartzite 1 Blue-green chert 1 Maroon red to banded black jasper (exotic; from Penna?)
Burlington	1	Colchester jasper
Essex Jct.	1	Colchester jasper
Danville	1	?
Ferrisburg	4	1 Colchester jasper 1 Cheshire quartzite 1 Dark brown chert; from Hudson Valley? 1 Mottled brown chert; from Hudson Valley?
Monkton	1	Dark brown chert; from Hudson Valley?
Moretown	1	Black flint
Bristol	3	2 Cheshire quartzite 1 Red-brown jasper; from Colchester?
Waltham	1	Cheshire quartzite
Addison	1	Crystal
Orwell	2	1 Normanskill flint; from New York 1 Brown chert
Brandon	1	Crystal

state. In most cases, little is known save the approximate location of the finds. Nevertheless, these stray finds are useful in any attempt to discover when Paleoindians arrived, and where they hunted.

Table I lists those fluted points which have been found in the Champlain Valley, as well as elsewhere in Vermont. To these might be added a Plano-like point of chert from Colchester, and a shouldered point from Addison, found a short distance from a fluted point noted in Table I. This shouldered point resembles some of the nonfluted points from Reagen, and Paleoindian San-dia points from the North American southwest. Outside Vermont, but still in the Champlain Valley, is the Davis site, near Fort Ticonderoga. This small site, only one-third of an acre, produced ten artifacts, including fluted points. Most were of local stone, but one was of exotic (nonlocal) flint, and two were of exotic jasper. The Davis site was probably a one-time encampment.

Of the Paleoindian finds from the Champlain Valley, the localities at Colchester, Grand Isle, Swanton, and the Davis site were surely under water at the time of the Champlain Sea maximum. The Grand Isle point is a problem, for it is reputed to have been found where fill had recently been trucked in from elsewhere. However, it is safe to conclude that the Davis site, as well as the Swanton and Colchester points, postdate the Champlain Sea maximum.

Fairfax, Monkton, Bristol, and two of the Ferrisburg finds were made well east of the maximum extent of the Champlain Sea. Theoretically, then, these could be as old as 10,000 b.c. The Milton/Fairfax/Georgia, Essex Junction, Waltham, Orwell, and one of the Ferrisburg finds are a bit problematical. The Orwell localities surely were not underwater at the time of the Champlain Sea maximum, but could have been some distance east. Information on the others is not sufficiently precise to indicate where they were relative to the maximum extent of the sea.

The St. Albans, Milton, and one of the Ferrisburg finds seem, like Reagen, to have been directly on beaches associated with the Champlain Sea maximum. The two Addison finds come from just above and below what seems to be the same shore line; they could have been lost then, but it is perhaps more likely that they were lost after sea levels had receded. And as the Reagen case demonstrates, location on a shore of the Champlain Sea maximum is no guarantee that site and shore are contemporary. But after 9300 b.c. this old shore level at Addison and St. Albans would have provided a favorite kind of Paleoindian stopping place: a high, well-drained spot overlooking low country frequented by game animals. This is probably true for the Milton and Ferrisburg sites as well.

As noted, some of these Paleoindian finds could be as old as the Champlain Sea maximum, but there is no proof for this; they could be more recent, as is the Reagen site. On the other hand, some of the finds are surely no older than about 9300 b.c., before which the locality would have been under water. Since there is no Paleoindian material elsewhere in New England or the Maritime Provinces which can be dated as early as the tenth millennium b.c., it is unlikely that any of the Vermont Paleoindian finds predate 9300 b.c. at the earliest.

Outside the Champlain Valley, fluted points have been found in Brandon, on a knoll along the Otter Creek; Danville; and Moretown, on a ridge near a small brook. No fluted points are known from the Vermont side of the Connecticut Valley, but Mary Lou Curran of the University of Massachusetts in Amherst is currently investigating a Paleoindian site in southwestern New Hampshire, which is on a tributary of the Connecticut River. The site, Sawyer's Crossing No. 1, has produced fluted points and other artifacts. A preliminary report describes one locality of fourteen square feet which produced 1500 flakes of chert and quartzite, including scrapers and other used flakes, pieces of two fluted points and an endscraper. The site is said to date around 9000 b.c. It documents the presence of Paleoindians in the upper Connecticut Valley, in spite of the lack of reported finds in Vermont.

Paleoindians and the Late Glacial Environment

The data reviewed thus far seem to indicate that Paleoindians were moving into Vermont by 9300 b.c. This is consistent with their appearance in the southern Hudson Valley around 10,500 b.c., and in Nova Scotia by 8600 b.c. When they came, park-tundra conditions prevailed in the state. Scattered growths of spruce, fir, larch, and birch were separated by open country covered by grasses, herbs, sedges, willow, and alder. This is ideal country for human hunters, for it provides long vision as well as many opportunities for trapping prey. It is also the kind of habitat that will support large numbers of grazing animals, including large herds of caribou. There is direct evidence from sites in Michigan and southeastern New York, as well as indirect evidence from Debert, Nova Scotia, that Paleoindians hunted caribou. Almost certainly, caribou were hunted by Paleoindians in Vermont.

In addition to the caribou and whatever other animals were

available to them on the land, Paleoindians may also have made use of the resources of the Champlain Sea. The world's arctic and subarctic marine waters are generally rich in edible resources, and the Champlain Sea was no exception. Moreover, the reduction in size of the sea with time would cause a concentration of these resources, making them more accessible to the people exploiting them. The several narrow tidal arms and estuaries of the sea provided many good hunting, fishing, and beaching sites.

The marine resources of the Champlain Sea included mollusks, crustaceans, and fish, and we know from archaeological remains in Pennsylvania that Paleoindians had no aversion to eating fish. The sea also contained a rich assortment of sea mammals: beluga, finback, and bowhead whales; ringed, harp, bearded, and hooded seals; harbor porpoises; and possibly walrus. Many of these would have been available only in summer, but some species—ringed and harp seals—could have been hunted from the ice. While we have no direct evidence that Paleoindians hunted any of these species, it is hard to imagine that a hunting people capable of killing mammoths, as Paleoindians did in western North America, would overlook such a readily available source of red meat. This might be one reason why their sites seem to be more common near the Champlain Sea than elsewhere in Vermont, although in view of the unsystematic nature of present evidence, it is best to be cautious about such a conclusion.

The marine resources of the Champlain Sea remained available to Paleoindians until 8200 b.c., and possibly as late as 7400 b.c. On the land, the park-tundra gave way to forests dominated by spruce and fir, which lasted until about 7500 b.c. More open than modern northern evergreen forests, these provided good habitat for browsing animals, such as the mastodon, known from fossils in Vermont and available in the Northeast until 7200 b.c., at least. Other animals in this forest included the now-extinct moose-elk, woodland caribou, and musk ox, as well as modern species of elk, deer, moose, beaver, and wolf. Although we as yet lack direct evidence that any of these species were hunted by Paleoindians in Vermont, we do know from remains in western North America that Paleoindians were capable of hunting any and all of these, including mastodons.

Though our knowledge of Vermont Paleoindians may be limited, they clearly represent a variant of what Gordon Willey, dean of American archaeologists, has called the North American Big Game Hunting Tradition. This tradition is known best in the West from archaeological remains including distinctive, lance-like projectile points and a variety of other tools which reflect a way of life in which an emphasis was placed on the killing of large game animals. Their kill sites are known from the edges of ancient swamps and rivers, and their campsites are known from high ground overlooking from strategic distances the places to which large animals came for water.

The earliest manifestation of the Big Game Tradition is known as Clovis, after the site in New Mexico where their archaeological remains were first identified. The hallmark of the Clovis hunters is the distinctive Clovis fluted point (Figure 2–6). Clovis points have been found all over the United States from the Rocky Mountains east to the Atlantic seaboard, and from central Canada south as far as the Panama Canal. West of the Mississippi, they are frequently associated with mammoth kills. In the East, mammoths were available, but apparently not common. None have been found which were killed by Clovis hunters; apparently the easterners relied on other game.

Clovis hunters were widespread in eastern North America from Dutchess Quarry Cave in New York, south to the Gulf of Mexico, by 10,500 b.c. Their greatest concentration was along the lower Mississippi, Ohio, Cumberland, and Tennessee rivers. The frequent occurrence of exotic lithic material on eastern sites suggests that the Clovis hunters moved about rather widely. This is to be expected, for the large herd animals which the hunters preferred were themselves high mobile. Caribou, for example, may cover 800 miles in a single direction and seem to have been the game animals preferred by those Clovis hunters in the East who lived just south of the Laurentide ice. We should not assume aimless wandering on the part of these people, for such wandering is not characteristic of any historically known hunting and gathering people. Rather, hunters and gatherers usually move about within a clearly recognized home area, reoccupying old campsites as appropriate to the subsistence cycle. And Paleoindian sites in the Northeast, such as Debert, in Nova Scotia, appear to have been regularly reoccupied. In the case of contemporary caribou

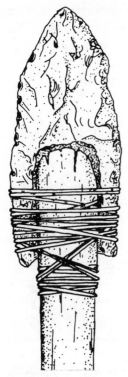

FIGURE 2−6. The photo on the right is of a Clovis-style fluted point, and the drawing on the left shows how such points may have been hafted as spear points. The point shown here, at approximately actual size, was found on Grand Isle and is unusual for having been made of quartz crystal. Photo by John F. Smith.

hunters, home areas are apt to be quite large; for example, the Inuit in the interior of Alaska who depend on the caribou for subsistence range over areas of close to 8300 square kilometers.

Although some upland remains are known, most Paleoindian remains in the Northeast, including Vermont, have been found in river valleys. This suggests that river valleys served as corridors for travel, as they did later on in the region. This is not to imply that Paleoindians had water craft; there is no evidence one way or the other. But these people, like any people, needed some means to orient themselves, and in the absence of roads and compasses, rivers are a convenient device. Moreover, the terrain along rivers is apt to be less hilly than elsewhere, making for easier travel. An added attraction for the Paleoindians is that game trails are far more well-defined in river valleys than they are in low to moderate hill country. Thus, hunting would generally have been easier for them along rivers than elsewhere.

How Paleoindians Came to Vermont

When Paleoindians first moved into the Northeast in the wake of glacial recession, they probably did so along the major river valleys. Generally, outwash rivers, and rivers from glacially dammed lakes, provide excellent open arteries for travel. Along such rivers today in places like Alaska, northern Canada, and New Zealand, one can easily cover up to thirty-five miles in a day on foot.

Of particular significance to Vermont is the Hudson River Valley. Swollen beyond present levels as the glacial ice melted, it would have constituted a major impediment to east-west movement, although crossings in the winter over the ice were probably possible. The Hudson Valley constitutes the south segment of lowlands which extend northward into the Champlain Valley, and movement up this lowland corridor, eventually into western Vermont, would have been relatively easy for Paleoindian peoples. It may be significant that no Paleoindian site has been reported to date on the east side of the Hudson River. The one stray fluted point which has been found on the east side compares with about 100 such finds from the west side. Further north, Paleoindian finds seem to be far more common in and near the Champlain Valley than in other parts of Vermont. This suggests the priority of the Champlain Valley over other parts of the state for Paleoindian settlement. But again, given the lack of systematic search for Paleoindian sites in Vermont, as well as on the east side of the Hudson River, it is best to be cautious about this. Especially needed now is research throughout the Connecticut Valley, which we might expect to have been an important corridor for movement of Paleoindians into eastern Vermont.

It is highly unlikely that the movement of Paleoindians into Vermont and other parts of the Northeast took place as actual migrations. To appreciate why this is so, one must have an understanding of the nature of hunting and gathering as a way of life. Studies of historically known hunters and gatherers indicate the critical importance of an intimate knowledge of the wild food resources on which their survival depends. They must know where and when they will be able to find the necessary plant foods, and they must know in detail the habits of game in their region in order to know exactly where to find it when meat is needed. To leave a known area for one which is unknown is to place one's very survival in jeopardy, for the knowledge necessary for success is not there. Historically known hunting and gathering peoples, therefore, do not leave their home territories, unless forced to do so. This has happened, for example, in various parts of the world where peoples who rely for their subsistence on the raising of their own food have frequently displaced earlier hunting and gathering populations. Such farmers and pastoralists may migrate with impunity, for they can carry their means of subsistence— seeds or herds of domestic animals—with them. But in North America there were no farmers or pastoralists until several millennia after Paleoindian times.

Even though hunters and gatherers tend to remain within the home areas with which they are familiar, it is nonetheless a fact that they may come to live in regions far from those in which their ancestors lived. The mechanism, however, is one of gradual movement, rather than migration. The key to this is the usual hunter-gatherer idea of "home." Hunters and gatherers typically identify with a region, rather than a specific place, within which they shift their habitation sites as necessary. This is true, even though they may define their home in terms of a specific place. For example, the aborigines of central Australia may speak of a specific place within a territory as "home," but they do not actually live there; it is where their ancestral spirits dwell, and where they keep their ceremonial paraphernalia. Their living sites shift from place to place, as required by subsistence activities.

While hunters and gatherers may define their home areas in various ways, they do not normally do so in terms of fixed boundaries. This is important, for it allows the areas in which they move about to fluctuate in size, thereby adjusting to differences in size of the home and neighboring groups, as well as supplies of basic resources. Because boundaries are not precisely defined, this can be done without anyone seeming to lose ground, or gain it at someone else's expense. To hunters and gatherers, then, "home" is a large area without precisely defined boundaries, within which they are usually fairly mobile. As we have already seen, Paleoindian home areas are apt to have been quite large.

In this kind of situation the growth of human populations follows a pattern which in its general outline is characteristic of most mammals. What happens is that a growing population will gradually extend its food-getting activities outwards, and this ultimately leads to gradual movement into previously empty areas, providing such areas are available. This "spill over" into empty areas need not amount to very much in a single generation. All that happens is that people extend their activities just a little bit further in a particular direction than they used to, while the bulk of their home area remains as it was. Because precisely defined boundaries are not crossed, each generation sees itself as operating within its traditional home area. But if this process continues steadily over many generations, the end result is a major penetration into what once was uninhabited country.

In humans as in other mammals, this kind of population growth will result from any kind of adaptation that makes life significantly easier than it had been. In the language of biology, selective pressures are reduced, reproduction becomes easier, more offspring survive than before, and so populations grow. The difference between humans and animals is that the former achieve new adaptations through culture, and animals do not. By inventing better tools, more efficient means of organization and the like, humans may make life significantly easier for themselves. This is precisely what Paleoindians did when they invented Big Game Hunting as a subsistence strategy.

That this new strategy was successful is indicated by three things. The first is the great rapidity with which people adopted it over so vast an area. Within 500 years certainly, it spread to all inhabited portions of North America east of the Rockies. Generally, people will stick with known techniques, unless a new one stands out as clearly superior. The more obviously superior new techniques are seen to be, the more rapidly they are adopted. The success of the Big Game Hunting strategy is further indicated by its adaptability. Big Game Hunting could be pursued successfully in the tundra-like regions south of the ice, as well as in the forested regions along the gulf coast; it was not limited in any significant way by environmental conditions. Finally, success is indicated by the long time Big Game Hunting lasted—as much as 6000 years on the Great Plains. Such stability indicates that it effectively met peoples' needs better than any alternatives that may have been available to them.

Given the success of Big Game Hunting, it is no surprise to find that the archaeological evidence indicates that North American populations were substantially larger after the invention of Big Game Hunting than before. Population growth was probably slow but steady. This is not to say that populations ever became especially dense. For example, studies of recent northern hunters, such as the Naskapi of northeastern Canada, suggest that population densities remain below ten people per 100 square kilometers. Among the caribou hunting Inuit of interior Alaska they are far lower: about six people per 100 square kilometers. In the case of Paleoindians living just south of the glaciers, we would expect that as population growth increased population densities, dispersal into available uninhabited regions began to take place. This would have been promoted by the gradual northward movement of the southern ice margin and the associated movement of forests into what had been park-tundra. The northern forest fringe and the southern ice margin were probably both significant landmarks in the home regions of northern Paleoindians. In northern regions today, such landmarks are often more sharply defined than other features of the landscape. Thus, their gradual northward movement would likely bring with it a gradual northward shift in Paleoindian home areas. Twelve hundred years, more or less, is ample time for all this to have brought people from the southern Hudson Valley well up into the Champlain Valley, without anyone ever consciously having "left home." It would involve a rate of movement on the order of .34 km per year. Even if the movement was accomplished in half the time allowed here, the rate of movement would still be less than 1 km per year.

Summary

To sum up what we know, or what we think we know, about the first Vermonters, Paleoindians probably did not arrive in the state until about 9300 b.c. They probably moved into the region up the Champlain and Connecticut valleys, perhaps a bit earlier in the former than the latter. The movement seems to have been gradual, brought about by a combination of population growth in previously inhabited regions to the south and west, and the northward movement of the ice margin and forest fringe which were probably important landmarks for the definition of home areas.

These first Vermonters were hunters of large herd animals, such as the caribou, and possibly some of the marine mammals so abundant in the Champlain Sea. The chief weapon of the hunt was a spear tipped with fluted, Clovis-like points or (later) unfluted Plano-like points. Although their stone tools indicate an emphasis on hunting, Paleoindians elsewhere in the Northeast are known to have fished and gathered wild plant foods as well; however, the latter were probably of minor importance. Among historically known hunting and gathering peoples inhabiting cold parts of the world, as Vermont was 11,000 years ago, meat accounts for the bulk of the diet. Such plant collection as did take place was the work of the women, while the men did the hunting, for this sexual division of labor is universal among hunting and gathering people.

The first Vermonters were highly mobile, probably ranging over large home areas which included upland, as well as lowland, regions. Movement back and forth between uplands and lowlands may have occurred along major watercourses, for Paleoindian finds seem to be most frequent along them. Along the Missisquoi are the Reagen site and the Swanton fluted point; along the Lamoille are the Milton and Fairfax fluted points; along the Winooski are the Burlington, Colchester and Essex Junction points, and the Moretown point comes from a tributary of the Winooski; the Brandon point was found near the Otter Creek. This is suggestive of a pattern which we will see for all later native peoples of the region.

Paleoindian populations in Vermont seem not to have been large, and densities were probably less than ten people per 100 square kilometers. Perhaps densities were greater near the Champlain Sea, with its rich marine resources, than elsewhere. Based on our knowledge of recent hunting peoples—especially those of the far north—these populations were probably broken up into small family groups, either single families or bands of a few related families. Among the caribou-hunting Inuit of interior Alaska, bands are made up of four or more related families, averaging

FIGURE 2−7. This drawing gives an idea of what life in a Paleoindian camp might have been like.

about fifty people. Probably, married couples had the option of associating with either the wife's or the husband's relatives, for this is the usual practice among hunting and gathering people. It provides a means of equalizing the numbers of people between bands, which is important in maintaining a balance with resources. For example, if the resources at the disposal of the husband's relatives are overtaxed, but those of his wife's are not, the couple can go and join her relatives. It also means that, for children, maternal as well as paternal relatives are of potential importance, and so ties are maintained with both sets for life. The result is that each individual has relatives living in several different bands who can be appealed to for aid in times of extreme need.

Though we have no direct evidence, our knowledge of recent northern hunters leads us to expect that the first Vermonters entertained some kind of animistic religious beliefs—that is to say, they believed in the existence of various animal and other spirit beings capable of interacting with humans. Wherever such beliefs are found, there is always one member of each group who is especially skilled at contacting and manipulating supernatural beings and forces. This individual is known as the shaman, and shamanism is highly developed among all northern hunting people of whom we have record. Moreover, we have evidence that this sort of system goes back at least 40,000 years in the northern parts of Europe and Asia.

The evidence presently available suggests that Paleoindians in Vermont were able to go about their business until sometime in the eighth millennium b.c. The question is, what happened then? The answer currently seems to be that Vermont was largely, if not completely, depopulated. The explanation for this is thought to lie in the environmental changes which continued to take place as a result of glacial recession. On the land, pollen samples from bogs indicate that, sometime around 7500 b.c. in the Burlington area (7300 b.c. in north central Vermont) Vermont's forests began to change in important ways. They still included spruce, fir, larch, birch, and alder, but there was much less spruce and fir, while pine and oak increased substantially. This changing forest seems to have been one of low diversity and low productivity. While it supported animals such as the red fox, marten, wolverine, and lynx, it appears to have been poor for such species useful to human hunters as caribou, deer, bear, elk, and turkey. In addition, the large ice age animals, such as the moose-elk and mastodon, had recently become, or were soon to be, extinct. The last dated mastodon remains in the Northeast date to 7200 b.c. In short, it looks as if there was no longer an ample and reliable supply of red meat, nor were plant resources sufficient to compensate adequately for this.

To compound the problem, the Champlain Sea, with its abundant marine resources, ceased to exist, possibly as early as 8200 b.c., certainly by 7400 b.c. Once cut off from the sea as a consequence of continued rebound of the land, the salt water was probably completely flushed out of the Champlain basin within ten years. This is much too fast for most marine organisms to have adapted to fresh water conditions, although a few species, such as smelts and salmon, did survive the change. A further problem, though, is that the extensive wetlands of today's Lake Champlain, which are critically important in sustaining life in the lake, did not exist until some time after 6000 b.c. The result seems to have been a freshwater lake of low productivity to match the apparent low productivity of the forests on land.

Earlier in this chapter, the suggestion was made that the marine resources of the Champlain Sea were important to the Paleoindians living along its edge. In view of the abundance of these resources, we might suppose that they became increasingly important with time, although this remains to be demonstrated. To people relying on them, the demise of the Champlain Sea would have been a severe blow. However, marine resources were still available to them; all they had to do was travel up to the St. Lawrence Valley to get them. To Paleoindians, traveling such a distance would not have been an unusual undertaking. Eventually, as the postglacial rebound which had drained the Champlain Sea continued, there would have been continued recession of marine waters. The logical response on the part of Paleoindian hunters of marine mammals would have been a gradual movement northeastwards toward the coast.

The idea of such a Paleoindian withdrawal from the Champlain Sea to the Gulf of the St. Lawrence is presently being actively explored by Stephen Loring, a graduate student in anthropology at the University of Massachusetts at Amherst. Meanwhile, we do know that archaeological materials from southern Labrador, dating to about 6900 b.c., show an obvious, though not precise, similarity to materials from the Reagen site in Vermont. This is exactly what we would expect if the withdrawal hypothesis is correct. Although the work needed to prove it remains to be done, it may be that our late Vermont Paleoindians had a hand in the development of the Maritime Archaic, a new way of life we shall learn about in Chapter 3.

3. THE ARCHAIC:
A New Way of Life Comes to the Northeast

THE END of the glacial period in North America, as elsewhere in the world, brought with it momentous changes. Overall climates became warmer, and in some places, drier. This trend reached its climax in the Hypsithermal period, between roughly 6000 and 1500 b.c. At that time—especially around 3000 b.c.—temperatures were on the average a few degrees warmer than today. With the reduction in amount of glacial meltwater, the erosion of dams of glacial debris, and changes in the elevation of land relative to sea levels, substantial changes in drainage systems also took place. Simultaneously, the distribution and composition of forests continued to change until around 2300 b.c., when the eastern half of the continent was covered by forests more or less like those of today. As its vegetation changed, so too did the animal life of North America. By 7000 b.c., over 100 species of large mammals, such as the mammoth, mastodon, and moose-elk, became extinct. Others, like the caribou and musk ox, moved north with the tundra.

Given such profound changes, it is scarcely surprising that human lifestyles changed in important ways. Many of the animals on which Paleoindians had depended for food, clothing, and shelter, were no longer available to them. In the forests, such animals as remained were for the most part smaller and perhaps not so easy to hunt as once was the case; however, plant foods were more abundant than they had been, and there were new and abundant sources of fish and other food around lake shores, bays, and rivers. Hence, people developed new and ingenious ways to catch and kill deer, bear, and a variety of smaller animals, while they devoted more energy to fishing and the collection of wild plant foods. This new way of life, based on the hunting and gathering of a wide variety of plant and animal resources, is known as the Archaic. The term is unfortunate, for it has a con-notation of staleness and obsolescence. Actually, as we shall see here and in Chapter 5, the Archaic way of life was extremely effective, and apparently fulfilling to those who followed it.

The Origin of Archaic Culture

Archaic culture was developing in the Midwest—what is now Missouri and Illinois—by 8000 B.C., out of Paleoindian begin-nings. It used to be thought that the Archaic spread from this cen-ter to other parts of eastern North America; since the mid 1960s, however, evidence of development from Paleoindian into Archaic has emerged throughout eastern North America, well up into New York State as well as Connecticut, Rhode Island, and Mas-sachusetts. North of Massachusetts, developmental sequences from Paleoindian into Archaic are known for Lake Winnepesau-kee in New Hampshire and southern Labrador. Unfortunately, much land that might have been occupied by late Paleoindian and early Archaic peoples in the coastal region of Maine and the Mar-itimes has been submerged by rising sea levels—about one foot per 100 years. Nonetheless, some early Archaic materials have been found, especially along rivers that lead from the coast into the interior. It is now clear that human populations from Lab-rador to the Gulf of Mexico were all engaged in working out new solutions to the problems of human existence in the postglacial era. Although their solutions differed somewhat from region to region, regular interaction between populations facilitated the spread of useful ideas and innovations from one region to another.

To date, similar developments have not been documented for Vermont or northern New York, although the situation appears to be changing in the Champlain Valley. Otherwise, the Archaic in this interior lake-forest region is represented for the most part by archaeological materials which postdate 5000 b.c. This has gener-ally been taken to indicate a lack of human habitation for some 2000 to 3000 years, although there is now considerable debate about this. Critics have argued that we have just learned what earlier Archaic materials look like, and they have not been sys-tematically sought out in the region. Moreover, they suggest that many earlier Archaic sites may have been located in places such as old flood plains which have long since eroded away. In short,

Vermont and adjacent parts of the Northeast may not have been vacant at all between late Paleoindian and later Archaic times.

The issue of an early Archaic hiatus in the northern interior lake-forest region is by no means settled, and deserves careful investigation. At least for the Champlain Valley, the critics seem to have a point. With the demise of the Champlain Sea, the level of the lake which remained was very much lower than that of today's Lake Champlain; as much as sixty feet lower toward its south end. Later, there was extensive back-flooding which may have drowned many an early Archaic site. On the other hand, it is hard to see why earlier Archaic sites in other parts of Vermont and northern New York would have been any more vulnerable to destruction than Paleoindian sites. It is true that early Archaic materials have not been sought out in Vermont, but New York State Archaeologist Robert Funk has been searching the northern part of his state since 1961 for material which would bridge the gap between Paleoindian and late Archaic times. His efforts have met with the most limited success. At the moment the weight of the evidence still favors a hiatus or at least a reduced population in earlier Archaic times, compared to later Archaic populations. Possibly such a population was confined to a very few restricted geographical regions, of which the Champlain Valley may have been one. In other words, if abandonment was not complete, it may have been at least partial. We shall return to this problem after a discussion of the late Archaic in Vermont.

Ketcham's Island and the Vergennes Archaic

The best known Archaic materials from Vermont pertain to what has come to be known as the Vergennes Archaic. This was first defined on the basis of excavations conducted in 1937 by John Bailey at the Donovan site near Vergennes, at the junction of the Dead and Otter creeks. Bailey's material, unfortunately, was thoroughly mixed with later artifacts. In 1955, however, an amateur archaeologist, Game Warden Tom Daniels, discovered a site further up the Otter Creek where Vergennes Archaic materials were unmixed with later remains. The site is not far from Rutland, on a small island in an extensive swamp along Otter Creek. Ketcham's Island, as it is called, is a rocky wooded island of about three

FIGURE 3–1. Typical Vergennes Archaic artifacts from Vermont. At the top is a ground slate ulu and at the bottom center a ground stone plummet, shaped to resemble a turtle. The other artifacts are, *from left to right*, a chipped stone Otter Creek point, two ground slate points, a ground stone atlatl weight, and a ground stone gouge. All were found in the northern part of the Champlain Valley. The plummet is from the collection of K. E. Varney, the others are from the Fleming Museum. Photo by John F. Smith.

acres, which rises no more than about twenty feet above the surrounding swamp.

Although a proper site report has never been published, we still know a good deal about Ketcham's Island, or KI, as the site is usually called in the literature. Daniels, assisted by Mrs. Kathleen Rowlands of Poultney, excavated sporadically there until his death in 1962. William A. Ritchie, then New York State Archaeologist, participated briefly in 1959 and 1960, and in 1966 he returned with his assistant Robert Funk for a week of intensive excavation.

The KI site is about an acre in size, occupying most of the high ground on the island. The site was covered by about 9 cms of humus, beneath which was up to 2.5 cms of gray podzol—a type

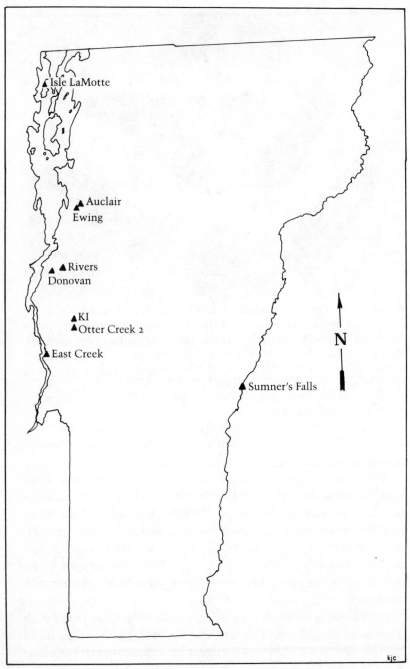

FIGURE 3-2. Archaeological sites in Vermont mentioned in Chapter 3.

of leached soil which typically forms under cool, humid forest conditions in northern regions. The podzol overlayed a finely textured sandy clay mixture full of water-worn pebbles and an occasional cobble. The top of this sandy clay was yellow to reddish in color and anywhere from 5 cms to 20.5 cms deep. Below this, the clay content was higher and the color a darker tan to brown. Its thickness over the uneven, glacially marked marble bedrock beneath varied from 2.5 cms to 30.5 cms. These two parts of clay graded into each other with no sharp boundary between them.

Artifacts, chipping debris from the manufacture of stone tools, burned rock, scattered charcoal, and burned bone were found in all strata at the site, but were four times as common in the upper part of the sandy clay as in any of the others. Apparently this represents the actual occupation layer. The deeper sandy clay must represent soil into which the occupants of KI trampled some of their litter, although later rodent burrowing and root penetration may also have worked occupation debris down into it. The podzol and humus pretty clearly postdate occupation, but rodent activity, upheaval by roots and tree falls, and frost action would have worked some of the occupation debris up into higher strata.

A complete inventory of artifacts from KI is presented in Table 2. The bulk of them are of the sorts useful for the procurement and processing of animal carcasses for meat and skins. We do not know the full range of animals hunted, but a bear claw and deer toe bone could be identified among the burned bone scraps. The weapon of the hunt seems to have been the spear, for the bulk of the projectiles (including the slate points) are too large and heavy to have served as arrow points. The most common spear point was the chipped stone "Otter Creek" type (Figure 3–1), but there were a few triangular, eared, and smaller side-notched points, in addition to the ten made of slate. The spears were used in conjunction with the atlatl, or spear thrower, based on the presence of the seven atlatl weights (atlatl is the Aztec word for spear thrower). Spear throwers are wooden devices which may or may not be weighted. One end is held in the hunter's hand, and the other end has a hole or a hook in or against which the end of the spear is placed. It is held so as to increase the length of the hunter's arm, thereby increasing the velocity of the spear when

TABLE 2. *Inventory of Artifacts from Ketcham's Island Site*

Category	Artifact	No.	Percent of Total
Chipped Stone	Projectiles	76	34.7
	Bifacially worked blades	41	18.7
	Scrapers	7	3.2
	Preforms	2	.9
	Drills	2	.9
	Chopper	1	.5
Ground Stone	Slate points	20	9.1
	Stone rods	20	9.1
	Atlatl weights	7	3.2
	Celts	7	3.2
	Ulus	4	1.8
	Abraders	3	1.4
	Gouges	3	1.4
	Pestles	2	.9
	Plummets	2	.9
	Perforated stone	1	.5
Pounded Stone	Hammer stones	15	6.8
	Anvil stones	3	1.4
	Hammer-anvil-mano	2	.9
Copper	Gorge	1	.5

SOURCE: Wright 1972

thrown. The spear and spear thrower when used together make for more efficient hunting than does the use of the spear alone.

For reasons known only to themselves, the occupants of KI, in common with late Archaic peoples throughout eastern North America, used atlatl weights far fancier than required for the job at hand. Before their true use was known, archaeologists frequently referred to them as *bannerstones*, a term still used by some collectors. It was thought that such finely made objects, drilled as they were for the insertion of a round piece of wood, must have served a function analogous to the sceptre of an Old World monarch. It was not until bannerstones were found in place as atlatl weights in some midwestern burials that their true function was learned.

Not only were late Archaic atlatl weights such as those at KI more finely made than one would expect for their utilitarian purpose, they were also heavier than one would expect. Unless the spear thrower were made of a particularly tough but flexible wood, it would soon snap from the stress of the throw. Such a wood is iron wood, and it is probably no accident that the distribution of iron wood is virtually the same as that of stone atlatl weights in eastern North America.

The blades, chopper, and ulus are the implements most likely to have been used for skinning and cutting up animal carcasses at KI, though perhaps some of the projectiles and slate points were used as knives. The ulus are thin, semilunar implements of slate identical to the Inuit ulu, from which the name comes. Until recently, Inuit ulus were made of ground slate, and were used exclusively by women for processing meat and fish. That the KI people fished, too, is indicated by the gorge, which would have been used on the end of a handline, and possibly the plummets. The latter could have served as sinkers on nets and lines, although they would have served equally well as bolas stones. Bolas stones are tied on the ends of lines for throwing at birds such as ducks, which certainly frequented the wetlands along Otter Creek. When the line hits the bird, the stones carry the ends of the lines around the legs, for example, tangling the bird long enough for the hunter to retrieve it.

The KI people had scrapers for working animal hides, and stone drills for making holes so that skins could be sewn. The pestles, and possibly the stone rods, were used for processing plant foods. The celts (used as axes), adzes, chisels, scrapers, and gouges were certainly employed in woodworking. Among other things, they would have served well in the making of dugout canoes. Considering the location of KI on an island, the suitability of the Otter

GURE 3−3. This series of pictures shows how a spear is cast with an atlatl. he hunter begins his throw on the right and completes it on the left.

Creek for dugout canoe travel, its status as one of the best streams in Vermont for hunting from a canoe, and the evidence for fishing, the KI people surely must have made use of dugout canoes.

In addition to woodworking, the occupants of KI were also engaged in the making of chipped stone tools. This is certainly indicated by the abundance of chipping waste, along with the pre-forms—chipped stone objects which had not yet been worked into finished tools. The implements used for this were probably the hammer stones, anvil stones, and perhaps the hammer-anvil-manos (but these could have been used for cracking open nuts as well). To make their implements the KI people made use of materials available locally, or at least not too far distant: quartzite (which constituted the bulk of the chipping waste), slate, phyllite, chert, sandstone, and siltstone. The source of the copper is unknown; it could be from as far away as the Great Lakes.

In addition to the artifacts, four hearths and the remains of some sort of dwelling were unearthed at KI. The hearths were shallow, basin-shaped features filled with burned earth, stones and a few pieces of charcoal. The dwelling was represented by a circular pattern of three-inch post holes, about fifteen feet in diameter, the whole covered by a low earthen mound. A dome-shaped hut built on a frame of bent wooden poles covered by

FIGURE 3–4. In this picture, the hunter has just thrown his bolas at the bird.

FIGURE 3–5. Making a dugout canoe. Probably, fire was used to char the wood which was to be removed or dug out with gouges of ground stone.

skins or bark, with earth placed on top, would leave exactly this sort of ruin. In the floor, covered by quartzite cobbles, was a human skeleton with red ochre (an iron oxide pigment) sprinkled lightly over it. It looks as if someone who lived in the hut, or the relative of someone who did, was buried beneath its floor. Although the artifacts from KI were for the most part randomly distributed, some were reportedly clustered in such a way as to suggest the presence of other huts. How many of these there were, how they were spaced, and precisely how the artifacts were clustered has not, unfortunately, been reported.

The KI site was clearly home to a people who hunted, fished, and gathered wild plant foods for subsistence; who traveled about in dugout canoes presumably of their own making; and who made their stone tools of locally available materials. How many people lived there is not known, but the small size of the site suggests habitation by a small group of people, perhaps some sort of family band. How long they lived there also is not known. The earth-covered hut suggests more than a transitory occupation, but the wild food resources of the northeastern lake-forest region are best exploited on a seasonal basis, as was done by late Archaic peoples in other parts of the Northeast. The occupation of KI was probably seasonal, but which season is not known. By way of speculation, fishing would be difficult, if not impossible, and canoe travel would be impossible during the cold of winter; nor would the plant resources of the swamp, useful for making mats and containers as well as a source of food, be accessible. The earth covering of the hut seems more appropriate to the cool weather of spring or fall as opposed to the heat of summer. In these two seasons, waterfowl would be most abundant in the swamps, and Ketcham's Island is well situated for bird hunting. At the same time, fish and swamp vegetation were available, and canoe travel was possible. Therefore, a spring and/or fall occupation of KI seems likely.

Other Vergennes Archaic Sites

While KI remains the best known Vergennes Archaic site in Vermont, others exist at least in the Champlain Valley. The Donovan site, at the junction of Dead and Otter Creeks, has already been mentioned. Here, mixed with later materials in a thin black soil stratum, John Bailey found typical Vergennes Archaic Otter Creek projectiles, scrapers, lance-like and ovate biface blades like those from KI, drills, ground slate points, including a fragment of a bayonet-like form, ulus, gouges, celts, abraders, atlatl weights, and anvil stones. Across Dead Creek, on a point of land between it and Otter Creek, lies the Rivers Site. Again, mixed with later materials, Bailey and others have found Otter Creek points, a fragment of an atlatl weight, a gorge just like that from KI but of bone, rather than copper, and some other possible Vergennes Archaic chipped stone artifacts.

Elsewhere on the Otter Creek, Ritchie in 1970 located and tested no less than five Vergennes Archaic sites. One of these, Otter Creek No. 2, was excavated from 1971 until 1977 by Mr. and Mrs. Richard Passino, amateur archaeologists from New York, with periodic assistance from Ritchie. Although small—the Vergennes deposit covered a maximum area of 15 m. by 9 m.—Otter Creek No. 2 yielded a rich assortment of Vergennes Archaic artifacts (Table 3), along with quantities of spalls, flakes, cores, and preforms from the manufacture of stone tools. These were scattered mostly at random in a dark, midden-like soil which also included a number of animal bones. These bones indicate something of the diet of the Vergennes Archaic occupants of Otter Creek No. 2: deer predominated, but bear, beaver, muskrat, possibly dog, turkey, possibly great blue heron, smaller unidentifiable birds, and turtle were also eaten. The gorges indicate that fish, too, were eaten, but their bones have long since decomposed. The

TABLE 3. *Inventory of Vergennes Archaic Materials from the Otter Creek No. 2 Site*

Material	No.	Object
Chipped stone	69	Projectiles (includes 34 whole and 14 fragmentary Otter Creeks)
	35	Knives (includes 1 ulu-like knife of slate)
	14	Scrapers (5 varieties represented)
	1	Drill
	3	Large choppers
Ground slate	9	Points
	6	Ulus
	2	Rod-like objects
Other ground stone	4	Gouges
	2	Celts
	1	Adze
	1	Atlatl
	1	Plummet
	6	Abrading stones
	30	Hammer stones
	1	Muller-hammer stone
Copper	5, possibly 6	Gorges
Bone and antler	4	Barbed bone points
	1	Spearpoint
	5	Awls
	3	Used antler tines
Other	1	Graphite paintstone (produces grey pigment)

combination muller-hammer stone testifies to some use of plant foods.

Six fragmentary burials—an infant, three children, and two adults—were found on or close to bedrock at Otter Creek No. 2. They seem to represent individuals who died elsewhere, and whose remains were saved for ultimate burial here. They contained no evident grave goods with the exception of a dog that was buried with one of the adults. The site has also provided one reliable radiocarbon date for the Vergennes Archaic (Figure 3–6).

South of Otter Creek, where East Creek enters Lake Champlain, a party from the Museum of the American Indian Heye Foundation began excavations in 1933 at a site of such importance that it was placed on the National Register of Historic Places in the 1970s. Unfortunately neither a site report nor proper field records exist for this work; but Stephen Loring, whose work on Paleoindians in Vermont was mentioned in Chapter 2, has spent considerable time in Vermont and at the Museum of the American Indian in New York City tracking down every scrap of information available on the East Creek site. While the bulk of the materials clearly relates to the Woodland and Historic periods, a few objects attest to a late Archaic occupation. These include one Otter Creek projectile, two fragments of atlatl weights, a ground stone gouge, and a celt which was manufactured from a broken gouge.

Further north in the Champlain Valley, the Auclair and Ewing sites on Shelburne Pond (see p. 65) have produced characteristic Vergennes Archaic artifacts, including Otter Creek projectiles, an ovate blade, slate points, ulu fragments, and pieces of adze and/or gouge. Private collections and collections at the Fleming Museum at the University of Vermont include a number of slate points, ulus, gouges, adzes, and Otter Creek points which were collected up and down the Champlain Valley from the Missisquoi River south to the Poultney River.

Outside Vermont, but still in the Champlain Valley, an important Vergennes Archaic site was discovered in 1967 on the Little Ausable River not far from its mouth. This discovery was the result of sand removal operations, which shortly destroyed the site. Although the Bridge site, as it is known, is larger than KI, its environmental setting is the same. From here to its mouth, the Little Ausable is slow moving, with extensive marsh. The artifact inventory virtually duplicates that from KI, though it is far richer in ground slate (15+ ulus, 30+ slate points) and plummets (12).

Further afield, the Vergennes Archaic, or something very much like it, is known at the Hirundo site on a tributary of the Penobscot River in central Maine. This site seems to have been strategically located for salmon fishing. What looks like Vergennes Archaic material has also been found in northern Maine, New Brunswick, and Nova Scotia. The Vergennes Archaic is also known at various small sites around Lake George. As one goes south from Lake George in the Hudson Valley, such typical Vergennes Archaic artifacts as Otter Creek points, ground slate points, gouges, and plummets become far less common, and it is clear that the Vergennes Archaic, as an identifiable entity, is not present in the lower Hudson Valley. A comparable situation may be seen in New England south of Vermont, where late Archaic materials have much in common with those of the Hudson Valley. Here, the southernmost sites which have produced assemblages of Vergennes Archaic materials, as opposed to occasional isolated elements such as Otter Creek points, are the Neville site in Manchester, New Hampshire, and a site in the Connecticut Valley just south of Vermont. In both cases, the material appears to us to be similar to what we think is late Vergennes Archaic material in the Champlain Valley (see below).

North and west of Vermont the furthest extension of the Vergennes Archaic seems to be a site on Allumette Island in the Ottawa River. Here, along with a typical assortment of Vergennes Archaic artifacts, is a rich assortment of copper spears, fishhooks, gorges, awls, and knives. Objects of copper are normally exceedingly rare at Vergennes Archaic sites; here, their presence can probably be explained as a result of trade. The Ottawa River forms a natural east-west route for trade between the upper Great Lakes and the coast, and the center of native copperwork was in the Great Lakes region. But a short distance upstream from Allumette Island is Morrison's Island; here, the late Archaic is represented not by Vergennes, but by Brewerton materials such as are characteristic of northern New York from the Adirondacks westward. It looks as if a rather sharp cultural boundary ran between the two islands.

The Age of the Vergennes Archaic

The dating of the Vergennes Archaic has been, and remains, somewhat of a problem. The first attempt at radiocarbon dating utilized charcoal from hearths at KI. Unfortunately these were contaminated from more recent forest fires, and so the dates (Figure 3–6) are wholly unacceptable. The radiocarbon date for Otter Creek No. 2 seems to be reliable; it agrees with one of three dates from Allumette Island. Unfortunately the other two dates are inconsistent. Since they fall within a few hundred years of the unreliable KI dates, they too must be regarded as unreliable. Two dates that are reported to pertain to the Vergennes-like material at the Hirundo site in Maine fall within a thousand years of the early date from Allumette Island, and the date for Otter Creek

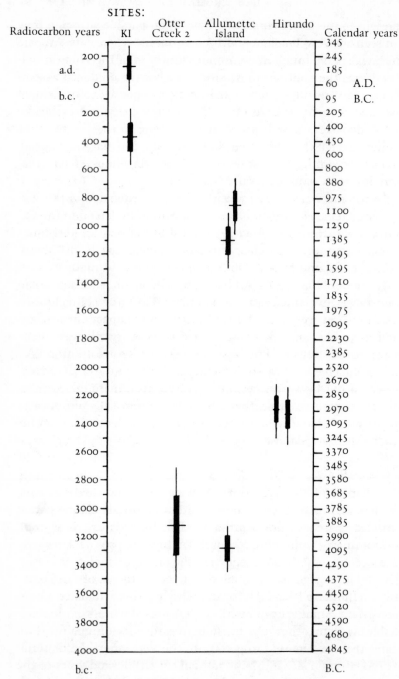

FIGURE 3–6. Radiocarbon dates for the Vergennes Archaic.

No. 2. At this point, it is safe to conclude that the Vergennes Archaic began by 3500 b.c., and perhaps a few centuries earlier.

How late the Vergennes Archaic lasted is an open question. Traditionally it has been regarded as the earliest phase of something called the "Laurentian Archaic," the later phases of which are known as the Vosburg Archaic and the Brewerton Archaic. Since Vosburg and Brewerton dates run as early as 2800 b.c., this would suggest that the Vergennes Archaic did not last beyond about 3000 b.c. In fact, a date of 3500 b.c. for Vosburg in the Delaware Valley—and Brewerton could be just as old—would suggest that the Vergennes Archaic ended as soon as it began. That it did not is indicated by the two dates from the Hirundo site. If these are reliable, and there is no reason to assume that they are not, then the Vergennes Archaic could not have ended before about 2500 b.c., at the very earliest.

In our opinion, the time has come to abandon the Laurentian concept. While Vergennes has been found stratigraphically beneath Vosburg in the upper Hudson–Lake George region, nothing transitional between them has ever been found. Otherwise, Vosburg and Brewerton both, save for some projectiles to be discussed shortly, have never been found in the Vergennes Archaic area, nor the Vergennes in theirs. Rather, the three seem to be roughly contemporary regional manifestations of the late Archaic: Vosburg south of Vergennes and Brewerton to the west. The Lake George–upper Hudson situation is easily explained as a southward extension of the Vergennes Archaic, which soon was displaced by a northward movement of Vosburg. To the north in the Champlain Valley, there is nothing to indicate that Vergennes did not continue to flourish. Since Vosburg lasted until about 2200 b.c. and Brewerton until about 2000 b.c., perhaps Vergennes did too. In fact, the Hirundo dates are compatible with its survival until sometime between 2200 and 2100 b.c., and Otter Creek points have occasionally been found in Brewerton sites dating around 2000 b.c. In Wisconsin, points comparable to Otter Creeks are known until 1800 b.c. Looking to the east, ground slate and other ground stone implements comparable to those of the Vergennes remained in use well into the second millennium b.c. All things considered, we doubt that the Vergennes Archaic ended before 2000 b.c., and we wouldn't be surprised if it didn't last into the second millennium. In order to be certain about this, though, we need a good series of radiocarbon dates for Vergennes sites in Vermont and elsewhere in the Northeast.

The Origin and Significance of Ground Stone Tools

When Vergennes Archaic artifacts first came to light in the Northeast, collectors were struck by the resemblance of the ground slate implements with historically known Inuit implements. This led some to believe that a people similar to the Inuit once lived in the region; others suggested a diffusion of ground slate technology from the Inuit to the other people of the Northeast. All such notions have long since been abandoned, for we now know that ground slate tools were made by people in northeastern North America long before the Inuit began making them. With the demise of these theories, the idea developed that late Archaic peoples moved into the Northeast from regions south and west. This, of course, made sense so long as it appeared that there was no one living in the Northeast between Paleoindian and late Archaic times. And the chipped stone tools of the Vergennes Archaic gave support to the idea, for they clearly derive from earlier prototypes south and west of Vermont. For example, Otter Creek-like projectiles occur widely in the East and appear in southern New York, at Sylvan Lake, in levels dated as early as 4000 to 4600 b.c. Along with Otter Creek points, the simple and notched end scrapers, bifacial blades, and drills of the Vergennes Archaic all have earlier prototypes in regions to the south and west.

With the discovery of earlier Archaic materials in much of the Northeast, and a better understanding of the significance of the ground slate and heavy woodworking tools of the Vergennes Archaic, the time has come to take a whole new look at the origins of this late Archaic culture. We may best begin by discussing the ground slate and woodworking tools, returning then to the question of earlier Archaic remains in Vermont.

The center of ground slate technology in northeastern North America is now known to have been the coastal area stretching from southern Labrador down into Maine. Ground slate points made their appearance by 5500 b.c. in southern Labrador; thereafter they achieved a prominence and diversity unmatched any-

TABLE 4. *Species of Marine Animals Known to Have Been Hunted by Maritime Archaic Peoples*

Birds	Black guillemot
	Canada goose
	Common loon
	Common murre
	Cormorant
	Curlew
	Dovekie
	Eider duck
	Gannet
	Goldeneye duck
	Great auk
	Gull
	Harlequin duck
	Merganser
	Puffin
	Red-throated loon
	Shearwater
	Swan (trumpeter swan?)
	Tern
	Thick-billed murre
Fish	Cod (otoliths only)
	Shark (mackerel shark?)
	Skate (barn door skate?)
	Swordfish
Mammals	Blackfish (pilot whale)
	Polar bear
	Porpoise
	Seal (harp seal and others?)
	Walrus
	Whale (killer whale?)
	Whale (large baleen whale)
Shellfish	Blue mussel
	Sea urchin

SOURCE: Tuck (1975a: 258)

where else in the northeast. Ground slate ulus, too, appeared in the same region between 4900 and 4200 b.c. North, south, and west from this coastal area, ground slate implements are much less common; they are virtually unknown west of the Vergennes Archaic region save for an occasional piece that was probably traded west (as objects of copper were occasionally traded east).

The people responsible for this invention and elaboration of ground slate technology are known as the Maritime Archaic people. The Maritime Archaic was a way of life based on the intensive utilization of marine resources (Table 4). To procure some of these, they had to take their dugout canoes considerable distances offshore. On the land, to supplement the produce from the sea, they hunted the bear, beaver, caribou, fox, otter, marten, and moose. They also developed the first elaborate burial cult in the Northeast, the famous "red paint" burials of Maine and the Atlantic Provinces. The roots of the Maritime Archaic lie in the area of its florescence, as earlier Archaic people became more and more efficient in their utilization of the resources of the sea.

The Maritime Archaic peoples are not the only people in the world to have developed a ground slate technology. Such technologies were also developed completely independently by people in the North Pacific, Northern Europe, and Scandinavia. In each case, the development was associated with an intensification of marine hunting, and a general de-emphasis on chipped stone tools. The same phenomena can be seen among other people, such as the Inuit, who have adopted a ground slate technology from some other source of innovation. Conversely, ground slate tools are rarely adopted by interior peoples, even when they live just inland from users of slate tools. It is now possible to state as a general principle that northern maritime cultures tend to develop ground slate tools while interior cultures do not.

The reason for this is that ground slate is particularly well-suited for the processing of marine mammals and fish. The mammals are a main source of hides for clothing, tents, and thongs; but they are more difficult to clean than the hides of land mammals, on account of the adherence of blubber. Similarly, the splitting for drying of large fish requires long hours and sharp knives. For both tasks, ground slate is superior to chipped stone. For one thing, knives must be frequently resharpened. In the case of a chipped stone knife, this is done by reflaking, which "uses up" the tool quite rapidly. A slate knife, by contrast, can be quickly resharpened, but will not be used up as fast. Also, the smooth edge of a slate knife is better for cutting soft flesh, like that of fish, than the nicked edge of a chipped stone knife. Finally, a smooth edge is essential for scraping hides where the application of maximum pressure over a large surface is required, without damaging them. This is particularly true in the processing of gut for waterproof clothing.

By contrast, interior peoples do not have to deal with marine mammals, with all their blubber, and large fish are not likely to play quite such a large role in their subsistence; thus, skin preparation is a good deal easier. Overall, chipped stone tools and flakes are perfectly adequate for them.

In form, the Vergennes Archaic slate tools are quite like those of the Maritime Archaic. Sometimes the similarities are very precise: the slate bayonet from Donovan and one of the points from Otter Creek No. 2 virtually duplicate points from Newfoundland. This, along with the relative dating and distributional evidence, makes it quite clear that the ground slate implements of the Vergennes Archaic derive from the Maritime Archaic. The same may be true for the Vergennes bone technology; James Tuck, the foremost authority on the Maritime Archaic, has remarked that at least one barbed bone point from Otter Creek No. 2 probably derived from the Maritime Archaic. Other indications of some kind of significant connection between the Vergennes and Maritime Archaic also come from Otter Creek No. 2: the rod-like objects and one of the chipped stone projectiles duplicate items which have been found in Maritime Archaic graves in Maine.

It is also apparent that many, although not necessarily all, of the heavy woodworking tools of the Vergennes Archaic have their origins in the Maritime Archaic. Among maritime peoples in general, cutting, scraping, stabbing, and piercing tools of slate are almost always accompanied by heavy woodworking tools, including gouges and adzes of ground stone. In fact, ground stone gouges similar to those of the Vergennes Archaic appeared in southern Labrador by 5500 b.c., where they were important for the making of dugout canoes. This suggests that the Vergennes people derived their canoes, as well as the tools used for making them, from the Maritime Archaic. And the celts, plummets, and even atlatl weights of the Vergennes Archaic all have their counterparts in the Maritime Archaic.

Heavy woodworking tools also were made and used by Archaic peoples in southern New England, where the full grooved axe is close to 7000 years old, and where gouges may be equally old. Although full grooved axes have been found in Vermont, they are conspicuously absent from known Vergennes Archaic materials, again suggesting an eastern, rather than southern, origin for the heavy woodworking tools of the Vergennes.

Early Archaic Culture in Vermont

There can be no doubt that the Vergennes Archaic was strongly influenced not just from the south and west, as their chipped stone tools show, but from the east as well. Before coming to grips with the meaning of these influences, though, we must consider how the Vergennes Archaic may have been influenced by earlier Vermonters. This, of course, brings us back to the question of an early Archaic hiatus in Vermont.

Between 6000 and 7000 b.c. there were small, scattered populations of early Archaic peoples living in southern New England. Their distinctive projectile points, which have bifurcate bases (Figure 3–7), are thinly scattered in Connecticut, Rhode Island, Massachusetts, and parts of New Hampshire. Not much is known about them, but a lack of identifiable tools specifically intended for the processing of plant foods indicates that the emphasis in subsistence was on hunting.

Some bifurcate-base points have been found in Vermont, but not very many. So far, none have been found outside of the Champlain and Vermont valleys, where they appear to be about as common (or uncommon) as they are in southern New England. Most are surface finds, but three were found in the course of excavations by the Burlington Chapter of the Vermont Archaeological Society at the Auclair site on Shelburne Pond in the Champlain Valley. However, they were found along with other materials which postdate 6000 b.c. in southern New England; the fact of the matter is that we don't know for sure that bifurcate-base projectiles ceased to be used after early Archaic times, even in southern New England. In southern New York and at the head of Lake George, bifurcate-base points have been found in contexts dating to the sixth millennium b.c., and there is even one from the late Archaic Brewerton site. In Vermont, there is one report of a bifurcate-base point from what surely was an early Woodland cemetery at Swanton; unfortunately, the report dates from the nineteenth century, and we cannot be sure that the association was not accidental. At Otter Creek No. 2, a fragment of a bifurcate-base point was found stratigraphically overlying the Vergennes Archaic materials.

In short, we have no firm evidence that anyone lived in Ver-

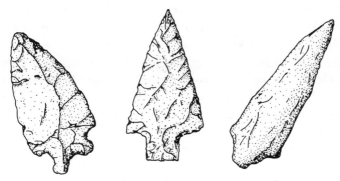

FIGURE 3–7. *Left to right*: bifurcate-base, Neville, and Stark projectile points.

mont between late Paleoindian times and the start of the sixth millennium b.c. If they did, there probably were not many of them, and they seem to have been restricted to the lowlands of western Vermont. And even if the makers of bifurcate-base points did occupy the Champlain Valley prior to 6000 b.c., there is nothing to rule out the possibility that they had moved gradually into the region through the lowland corridor leading from the Hudson Valley to the Champlain Valley even as much as 1000 years after late Paleoindians are thought to have withdrawn down the St. Lawrence River.

Evidence for pre-Vergennes habitation of Vermont sometime after 6000 b.c. is somewhat, but not a whole lot, more substantial. The best evidence we have so far comes from two sites on either side of Muddy Brook where it flows out of Shelburne Pond. These are the Auclair site, on the east side of the brook, and the Ewing site, west of the brook. The Auclair site we have already mentioned; the Ewing site was excavated between 1962 and 1967 by Ken Varney, one of the founders of the Vermont Archaeological Society. His work was continued by the Burlington chapter of the society until 1977.

Excavations at the Auclair site produced some 200 artifacts, ranging all the way from bifurcate-base projectiles, through Otter Creek and ground slate points and ulu fragments, to middle and late Woodland pottery and artifacts. Along with the bifurcate-base and Otter Creek projectiles were a variety of stemmed and side-notched chipped stone projectiles, including some very much like what are called Neville points in southern New England. Neville points are broadly triangular with tapered stems which have been thinned at the base by removal of a single flake (Figure 3–7). This, and an occasional example with a bifurcate base, bespeaks a bifurcate-base ancestry. On the Merrimack River in New Hampshire, Neville points date to the millennium between 6000 and 5000 b.c., although a few could be as recent as 4000 b.c. Unfortunately, at Auclair these points are mixed together in the plow zone with all but just a few of the Vergennes artifacts.

The Ewing site is made up of three loci, the largest of which is on a low, gently sloping wooded area just above the present-day marsh. The other two are thirty and twenty-five feet higher on two terraces of a limestone ridge just behind the low area. The three loci together take up no more than about half an acre. The top of the site consists of a layer of humus 30 cms deep, in which most of the artifacts have been found. Below this is about 20 cms of sandy gravel which is full of cobbles and broken limestone. Few artifacts are contained in this stratum, and none are in the underlying clay.

Like the Auclair site, Ewing contains materials from Archaic through middle and late Woodland, and they are not stratigraphically separated. Included among them are other Neville-like points, small gouges, and grooved plummets such as appear in the middle Archaic of southern New England. Unfortunately, in southern New England, such gouges and plummets continued to be used into late Archaic times, and late Archaic materials are present at Ewing: Otter Creek points, ovate blades, and ground stone adze or gouge fragments. All we can say, then, is that pre-Vergennes material may be present at Ewing, as it seems to be at Auclair.

In addition to those from Ewing and Auclair, Neville-like points have been collected elsewhere in the Champlain Valley, from Shelburne Pond south as far as the Poultney River. Generally, they are a bit broader of blade than those from elsewhere in New England, and they are usually made of locally available chert or quartzite. Other occasional finds (less than ten are known) up and down the Champlain Valley are more pointed, stemmed projectiles very similar to what are known as Stark points in southern New England (Figure 3–7). Stark points made their appearance there as early as 5000 b.c.

Although Archaic materials which predate the fourth millennium b.c. are not as rare in Vermont as once was thought, they appear to be nowhere near as abundant as are late Archaic materials. This correlates rather well with environmental changes. As discussed in Chapter 2, the Champlain Sea, with its rich marine life, was gone by the latter half of the eighth millennium b.c., replaced by a freshwater lake poor in food resources. Between 7500 and 7300 b.c. the forest was changing to one of relatively low productivity in terms of available plant and animal foods. Things stayed this way until the Hypsithermal period, when the wetlands, which are so essential to the maintenance of life in Lake Champlain, began to develop. At the same time, extensive back-flooding of the lake, caused by continued uplift of land in the north, created broad swampy areas along the lower reaches of many rivers, thereby increasing the areas in which the new wetlands could flourish. On the land, the forests began to develop more diversity, as hemlock and hardwoods became more abundant. Mast (nut) producers such as oak, beech, and chestnut became more common, as did animals such as deer, elk, bear, and turkey.

These changes would have made Vermont far more attractive for human habitation than it was for the approximately 1500 years prior to 6000 b.c. Of course, it did not become so overnight. Conditions in the Champlain Valley may have begun to improve somewhat earlier, but in southern Vermont they were just starting to improve around 6000 b.c. It probably wasn't until around 4500 b.c. that hardwood-hemlock forests were really well established in most of the region. Thus, we might well expect a slow build-up of human populations in Vermont, beginning a bit before 6000 b.c. in places, but no really large population until sometime after 4500 b.c. So far as it goes, the archaeological evidence is consistent with this interpretation, but we obviously need further investigation.

Roots of Vergennes Archaic

To return, now, to the question of the roots of the Vergennes Archaic: we can regard it as a way of life made up of elements derived from the Maritime Archaic and other Archaic cultures to the south and west, probably combined with elements carrying over from a local pre-Vergennes Archaic culture. That the Vergennes should be such a cultural hybrid is not at all surprising, for all human cultures are made up of borrowed elements, as well as those which they invent for themselves. Although the relative mix may vary greatly, as much as 90 percent of a given culture may derive from outside sources. What keeps cultures from being mere grab bags of traits is that they are always selective about their borrowing, and borrowed traits are always integrated with other elements to produce new and distinctive patterns. Consistent with this, foreign elements are prominent in the Vergennes Archaic, while indigenous elements are not; yet the Vergennes as a whole is a unique and distinctive entity when compared with the other late Archaic cultures of the Northeast.

Influences from the south and west which went into the making of the Vergennes Archaic are reflected in the chipped stone tools used by these people. Because such tools account for the bulk of the artifacts at Vergennes sites, we might suppose that influences from the south and west were far more important than those from the east. There are, though, reasons to question such a supposition. Most Vergennes Archaic chipped stone artifacts seem to have been used to procure and process the carcasses of land mammals for meat and hides. While hunting was undoubtedly important to the Vergennes folk, we do not know precisely how important; it is very easy to overestimate its role in the economy of a hunting and gathering people. It takes more in the way of equipment to kill and butcher game than to gather and process plant foods, grubs, snakes, caterpillars, and similar delicacies. All that is required for the latter is a good stout stick for digging, a bag or basket to carry collected food back to camp, and rocks of a size to be held in the hand to grind or pound tough substances, such as nuts and seeds. Thus, equipment associated with the hunt is likely to be over-represented and that associated with gathering under-represented at archaeological sites, even where the bulk of the food eaten came from the gathering activities of women, rather than the hunting activities of men. And among documented hunting and gathering peoples, only in the far north does the bulk of the food come from the hunting activities of men.

James Tuck has observed that close to 20 percent of all tools at the KI site ultimately have their origins in the tools of the Maritime Archaic. Considering that we know nothing about the bone tools used at KI, this may be too low a figure. The evidence from Otter Creek No. 2 suggests that Vergennes bone tools may clearly have their origins in the Maritime Archaic, too. And we have already speculated that the dugout canoes of the Vergennes Archaic may have their origins in the Maritime Archaic. Even in the absence of things made of wood or bone, Maritime Archaic derived tools seem to have accounted for more than 20 percent of those from the Bridge site.

As we have already seen, interior peoples almost never adopt a ground slate technology from neighboring coastal people. On the other hand, chipped stone technology seems to diffuse from one people to another quite easily. This means that a straight comparison of the frequency of chipped stone versus Maritime Archaic derived tools in the Vergennes Archaic is likely to lead one to seriously underestimate the importance of the Maritime Archaic in the development of the Vergennes Archaic. Considering this, along with the improbability of the diffusion of ground slate technology in particular, the only satisfactory way to account for such strong influences from the Maritime Archaic is through an actual influx of Maritime peoples.

Considering everything we have covered in this chapter so far, we are now in a position to offer a tentative reconstruction of the emergence of Archaic culture in Vermont. As discussed in Chapter 2, Vermont was abandoned totally or almost totally by its Paleoindian population. A few people may have lingered on in the Champlain Valley, or it may have been deserted for 500 to 1000 years before small numbers of people began to drift northward, very gradually, through the lowlands that lead from the Hudson Valley into the region. Around 6000 B.C., as the forests of southeastern Vermont became more like those in which people already lived to the south, a similar northward drift of peoples probably began in the Connecticut Valley. The process was probably very much like that which we discussed for the earlier Paleoindians: population growth in inhabited areas causing a very slow but steady dispersal into previously unoccupied territory.

As Archaic peoples were gradually drifting northward in Ver-

mont, important developments were taking place around the
Gulf of St. Lawrence. Here, the development in the sixth millennium b.c. of an effective technology for the intensive utilization
of abundant marine resources was the same kind of revolutionary
development as was the earlier Paleoindian invention of Big
Game Hunting as a subsistence strategy. As we would expect, the
result seems to have been the same: a population explosion of
sorts. This led to a dispersal of Maritime Archaic peoples to the
westward, probably along river valleys for the most part. The
largest river valley in the region is the St. Lawrence, the lower
part of which isn't so much a river as it is a 1500 mile estuary
reaching westward just beyond the mouth of the Ottawa River,
near present-day Montreal. Maritime Archaic peoples lived on
both shores of the Gulf of St. Lawrence as far west as the locality
of the present-day city of Quebec, and the St. Lawrence estuary
was a logical passage for population expansion. There were few, if
any, people already there to block such an expansion, and many,
though not all, of the marine resources to which they were accustomed remained available to them. Presumably, as they expanded up the estuary, they continued to exploit such large fish
and marine mammals as were still available to them. Had they
not done so, we would expect their ground slate technology to
have fallen away, and it obviously did not. In fact, ground slate
tools—which are almost without exception found near water—
are known up and down the St. Lawrence estuary, and they survived in the Vergennes Archaic. At the same time, more land
hunting would have been necessary to make up for those marine
resources which were no longer available.

The descendants of these Maritime people, for that is who we
think the Vergennes people were, eventually got as far west as Allumette Island, which is about 150 miles beyond the western end
of the St. Lawrence estuary, but still on the navigable portion of
the Ottawa River. Others came down the Richelieu River to Lake
Champlain. That they got no further west may be attributed to
two factors: their culture, though modified as it had become by
then, was not well adapted to conditions beyond the estuary;
their way may have been blocked by populations which were
drifting eastward down the St. Lawrence. That they were able to
penetrate the Champlain Valley suggests that human populations

there were not so large as to block expansion, and that the culture of the newcomers from the north was reasonably well adapted to the region. From this standpoint, the lake may be thought of as a kind of inland sea, containing resources long exploited by Maritime Archaic peoples with the aid of their ground slate tools: seals, which have been seen in the lake up into the nineteenth century, and salmon (Tuck thinks that Atlantic salmon was important in the summer diet of Maritime Archaic people).

Upon their entry into the Champlain Valley, if not before, the newcomers probably encountered a sparse population of the people who had been drifting up from the South. The mixing of these people would have contributed further to the modification of what was on the way to becoming the Vergennes Archaic. While we think that ground slate and other Maritime elements were introduced into Vermont by an actual influx of peoples, we don't think this was the case with the chipped stone technology which was introduced from regions to the south and west. For one thing, chipped stone technology seems to diffuse from one people to another quite easily. For another, although people prefer to stick with techniques and equipment to which they are accustomed, they are quick to borrow, through diffusion, new techniques and equipment which appear to be clearly superior to what they already have. Generally speaking, the more obvious the superiority, the more quickly diffusion will take place. In the development of the Vergennes Archaic, we seem to begin with a people whose technology was well-suited to the intensive utilization of marine resources, supplemented by land hunting. The most important land mammal hunted was the woodland caribou, and Tuck thinks that the weapon normally used to hunt them was the ground slate bayonet. As these people moved further inland from the coast, they were forced to rely more and more heavily on land hunting to make up for marine resources no longer available to them. But the move inland presented a problem: the herds of woodland caribou on which they depended in the maritime forests of the Northeast were not to be found, at least in any great numbers, in the forests of Vermont and adjacent regions. Instead, the available large game animals were moose and deer, which are more solitary in their habits. So not only were the newcomers from the east forced to do more land hunting, they had to change their whole way of hunting so as to be even more successful at getting deer and moose than they had been at getting caribou. Fortunately for them, their expansion into the interior would have brought them increasingly into contact with people who were already accomplished hunters of deer and moose. These were peoples who were expanding in a generally northeasterly direction. With a long tradition of hunting in interior forests behind them, their hunting technology is likely to have been perceived by the newcomers from the east as clearly superior to their own, and so it was adopted rapidly by them.

It is evident that this expansion of Maritime peoples and development of the Vergennes Archaic was not limited to the St. Lawrence, Richelieu and Champlain valleys. The distribution of Vergennes-like material in central and northern Maine, New Brunswick, and Nova Scotia has already been mentioned (see p. 56). Probably all rivers flowing to the coast of Maine and the Maritimes, as well as those which, like the Richelieu, flow northward into the St. Lawrence estuary, were involved. We have seen, too, that the Vergennes Archaic spread beyond the Champlain Valley to Lake George and the upper Hudson Valley. But there its rather abrupt replacement by the Vosburg Archaic indicates, we think, a failure of Vergennes. It is a fact that many of the fish thought to have been important to Vergennes people in the Champlain Valley and elsewhere, such as salmon, could not ascend the falls to Lake George, the outlet of which is 70 meters above the level of Lake Champlain. Hence, the Vergennes was not as well adapted to that region as was the Vosburg.

Linguistic Frontiers

The apparent geographic distribution of the Maritime and Vergennes Archaic is shown in Figure 3–8. If one compares this with Figure 5–1, which shows the distribution of Wabanaki peoples (Abenaki, Passamaquoddy-Maliseet, Micmac) in the ethnographic present, one is struck by a marked resemblance between the two. The situation is similar to a number of others in which native cultures have persisted over several millennia in North America. Typically, the boundaries of the areas occupied by these cultures fluctuate over time, in response to environmental and cultural factors, but their cores remain stable. This brings us to

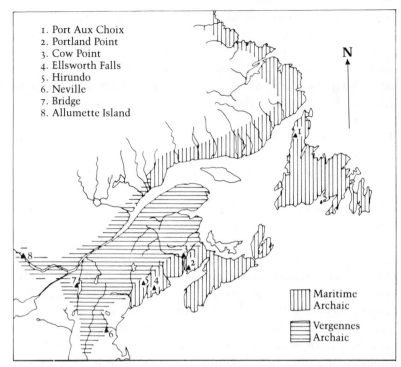

1. Port Aux Choix
2. Portland Point
3. Cow Point
4. Ellsworth Falls
5. Hirundo
6. Neville
7. Bridge
8. Allumette Island

N

Maritime
Archaic

Vergennes
Archaic

FIGURE 3–8. Areas occupied by Maritime Archaic peoples, and probably occupied by Vergennes Archaic peoples. West of the Vergennes were the Brewerton peoples, while the region north of the Vergennes and west of the Maritime Archaic was occupied by Shield Archaic peoples. The latter had spread eastward through the boreal forests and were ancestral to the Central Algonquian–speaking Cree-Montagnais-Naskapi, who held the lands north of the St. Lawrence in early Historic times. Map modified from Tuck (1978).

some linguistic considerations which are consistent with the reconstruction of Vergennes origins which has just been presented. A word of caution is in order at the outset, though, for there are plenty of cases where language and culture do not coincide. In some parts of the world, people who speak different languages share the same culture; in other places, there are people who speak the same language but possess different cultures. Still, there are enough cases of correspondence between language and culture in the Americas to make the study of linguistic distributions and relationships worthwhile for the prehistorian.

As we saw in Chapter 1, linguistic distributions in the Northeast are such as to suggest that the Algonquian-speaking peoples have been a very long time in place, although at some time in the past there has been an intrusion of Iroquoian-speaking peoples from a homeland in the Appalachian uplands. Archaeologists James Tuck and Dean Snow have argued persuasively that Maritime Archaic peoples spoke an early Algonquian language ancestral to dialects spoken in Maine and the Maritimes in the ethnographic present. This would mean that the Vergennes folk spoke the same language, or at least a closely similar dialect. The people with whom the Vergennes folk came in contact on the west seem to have been drifting eastward from somewhere south of the Great Lakes, and so would have spoken a different language than the Vergennes folk. Thus it appears that a frontier between Algonquian peoples closely related to those of Maine and the Maritimes and peoples speaking some other language was established in late Archaic times just west of Lake Champlain, close to where the frontier between Abenaki- and Iroquoian-speaking peoples was located in the seventeenth century A.D.

As originally established, this frontier probably did not separate early Iroquoian from early Algonquian speakers. Although it is generally accepted that Iroquoian peoples have been living in New York State and southern Ontario for at least the past 2000 years, it has not yet been established when they first arrived in the region from their Appalachian homeland. Since the western neighbors of the Vergennes folk seem to have come from the Great Lakes region, rather than the Appalachian uplands, they probably did not speak an early Iroquoian language. The earliest archaeological candidates for the status of early Iroquoian immigrants are the Lamoka folk, who established themselves in southwestern New York by 2500 b.c. Their small-stemmed projectiles and other tools are quite different from those of the Brewerton and Vosburg neighbors of the Vergennes folk, and the origins of these tools seem to lie further south in the Appalachian uplands. Furthermore, skeletal remains indicate that the Lamoka folk closely resembled other Archaic peoples living in Kentucky, rather than peoples indigenous to the Northeast.

If the western neighbors of the Vergennes folk did not speak an early Iroquoian language, they probably spoke a dialect of Proto-Algonquian. Prior to their eastward movement, and the westward

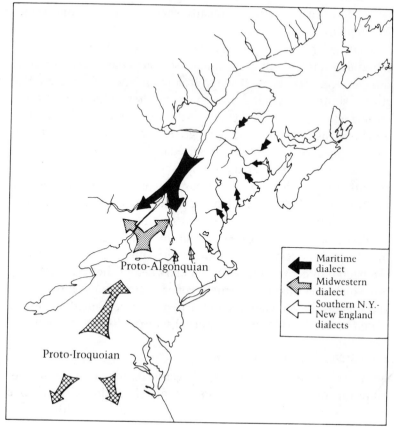

FIGURE 3–9. Late Archaic expansion of Algonquian- and Iroquoian-speaking peoples in the Northeast.

movement of the maritime ancestors of the Vergennes folk, speakers of Proto-Algonquian dialects probably lived in a belt stretching from the Great Lakes across southern New York and New England, and up along the coast of northern New England and the Atlantic Provinces of Canada to southern Labrador. These dialects would have taken on the typical chain formation discussed in Chapter 1. This being so, when descendants of Proto-Algonquian speakers from the Great Lakes region made contact with descendants of Proto-Algonquian speakers from the Gulf of St. Lawrence, they may not have been able to understand one another's language. In short, the languages of the Vergennes folk and their western neighbors probably were not mutually intelligible even though, technically speaking, both spoke Proto-Algonquian.

What began as a frontier between speakers of mutually unintelligible Proto-Algonquian dialects seems to have become a frontier between speakers of early Iroquoian and Algonquian languages sometime around 2000 b.c., as it remained down to the ethnographic present. Linguists estimate that Proto-Algonquian was breaking up into separate languages around that time; this is also when the Brewerton Archaic came to an end. The most likely cause of a final separation between Central and Eastern Algonquian would have been further expansion of Iroquoians into the Northeast. This would have severed whatever links remained in the old Proto-Algonquian chain of dialects, and would have displaced or absorbed the Brewerton folk of northern New York. In fact, there is evidence of conflict between Lamoka and Brewerton people in central New York shortly before the end of Brewerton. Following this final intrusion of early Iroquoians, any eastern and western Proto-Algonquian speakers who remained in contact would probably have spoken mutually unintelligible dialects.

Evolution of the Vergennes Archaic

As far as we can tell now, the Vergennes Archaic lasted in Vermont for some 1500 years, if not longer. The stability which this implies, though, should not be taken to indicate that things were static. Occasional Otter Creek projectiles in places like southern New England and central New York; an occasional, though rare, slate point found west and southeast of the Vergennes region; and the copper gorges at KI and Otter Creek No. 2 suggest that the Vergennes folk maintained contacts with other peoples. Where such contacts are maintained, it is inevitable that ideas will be exchanged. Such exchange, we think, explains the presence of typical Brewerton and Vosburg projectiles in Vermont.

In a study of projectile points from the Champlain Valley, Mariella Squire has recognized the presence of chipped stone points which are typical of the Vosburg Archaic. They have been found up and down the length of the Champlain Valley, but are far more common in the south than in the north. This supports the idea of their introduction from the Vosburg heartland, which is south of Lake Champlain. At the Donovan and Rivers sites they are found

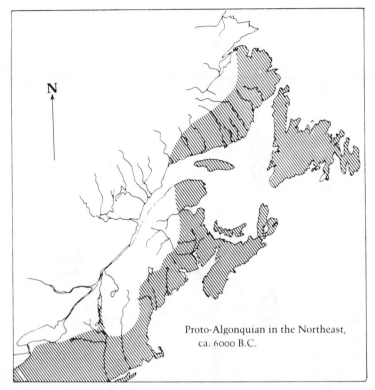

N

Proto-Algonquian in the Northeast,
ca. 6000 B.C.

FIGURE 3–10. The distribution of Proto-Algonquian speakers shown in this map is suggested by the distribution of early and middle Archaic archaeological materials. In New England and the Maritimes, populations seem to have been small, preferring coastal to interior locations. In Maine and the Maritimes, most of these locations were east of today's coastline.

along with typical Vergennes material. At Otter Creek No. 2, Ritchie reports a "definite and intimate" association between nine intact and two fragmentary Vosburg points on the one hand, and the prevailing Otter Creek points on the other. All this, and the lack of anything that could be considered a pure Vosburg assemblage in Vermont, is best explained as the adoption by Vergennes people of foreign styles of projectiles. Consistent with this, most were made of local cherts and quartzites; in one case slate; and only rarely of New York flints.

Three styles of Brewerton projectile points have been identified

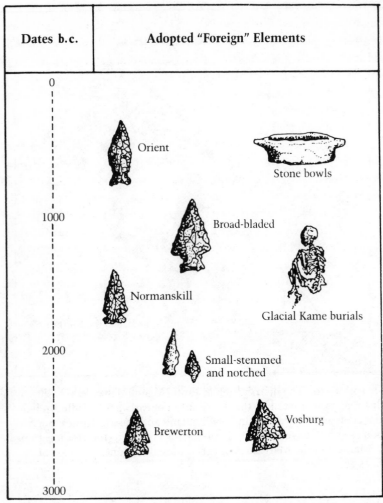

Dates b.c.	Adopted "Foreign" Elements
0	

FIGURE 3–11. Foreign elements adopted by late Archaic peoples in Vermont over the last three millennia b.c.

in the Champlain Valley. Again, they have been found up and down the length of the Valley, most were made of local cherts and quartzite, and they have been found with non-Brewerton materials at the Auclair, Donovan, East Creek, and Ewing sites. All this, and the absence of any identifiable assemblage of Brewerton materials similar to those of central New York, again suggests the adoption of foreign projectile forms by indigenous late Archaic peoples in Vermont.

We do not know for sure when these Vosburg and Brewerton elements were adopted by Vergennes peoples. At the Neville site in southern New Hampshire, what appears to be a small Vergennes assemblage which includes Vosburg and Brewerton projectiles dates somewhere between 4000 and 2400 b.c. Therefore, the modification of Vergennes had to be underway by the latter date at the very latest. In Vermont, use of some Brewerton projectile styles may have persisted quite late. Some of these projectiles have been found at two early Woodland cemetery sites which contained no other Archaic materials, and at a middle Woodland habitation site.

This tendency to adopt elements from foreign sources from time to time suggests to us a partial answer to the question: what caused the eventual disappearance of the Vergennes Archaic? The most likely explanation is that it simply evolved into something else, in response to continued influences from outside, coupled with continued refinement of culture to the changing characteristics of the region. Such an interpretation is supported by three lines of evidence. First, the apparent similarity of the late Archaic linguistic and ethnic situation just discussed to that of the ethnographic present strongly suggests continuity through time. It is exactly what we would expect if the inhabitants of Vermont in the early seventeenth century A.D. were descendants of the late Archaic inhabitants of the region. Second, in spite of different technologies, the way of life of the Vergennes folk was in many ways similar to that of the Abenakis who lived in Vermont in the ethnographic present. The similarity is such that the latter could very well have evolved from the former. We will return to this point in Chapter 5. The third line of evidence relates to environmental changes. Around 2000 b.c., which correlates remarkably well with when we think the Vergennes Archaic came to an end, important changes were beginning to take place in Vermont's forests. Then, hemlock began a major decline, resulting in domination of the forests by hardwoods. While the change was essentially favorable in terms of those resources most useful to hunting and gathering peoples, we would nonetheless expect to see changes in their cultural adaptation as they took advantage of these resources. While some of these changes may have come from within, others may have been borrowed from other peoples.

A number of influences can be identified as coming into Vermont from the outside at a time following some, if not all, of those just discussed. The earliest is represented by several styles of small, narrow-bladed, stemmed, and side-notched projectiles. In the Champlain Valley, such projectiles have been collected from the Canadian border south, but only two out of at least six styles are known north of the Lamoille River, and one other style is known so far only from the Auclair and Ewing sites. This distribution suggests an origin to the south, where similar styles came into widespread use throughout an area extending from the Atlantic coast through southern New England and New York, where they are associated with a variety of other assemblages. Their center of greatest intensity, their presumed origin, lies south of New York; from here they reached southwestern New York by 2500 b.c. Possibly they were brought in by speakers of an early Iroquoian language. From here, they spread to other peoples, becoming common in the lower Hudson Valley and southern New England by 2200 b.c. Presumably they reached Vermont some time after that date, through the lowlands which link the Hudson and the Champlain valleys, and perhaps through the Connecticut Valley as well.

While the Vermont small-stemmed and small-notched projectiles are similar to those to the south, they are not identical to them. Rather, they are regional variants which, as one might expect, were normally made of locally available cherts and quartzite. Rarely are they of exotic flint. Thus, they are not likely to reflect an actual influx of people from the south. Rather, they seem to represent another case of borrowing. This is consistent with their presence at the Auclair, Donovan, East Creek, Ewing, Otter Creek No. 2, and Rivers sites, all of which show evidence of prior Vergennes occupation. In all six cases, the appearance of the new projectiles may be interpreted as one more addition to an already modified technology of indigenous people.

In the Hudson Valley, a new style of projectile, known as Normanskill points, came into use between 1930 and 1350 b.c. These are derived from the earlier small stemmed and notched points; just as they diffused northward into Vermont, so did Normanskill points. In the Champlain Valley, Normanskill points are more common south of the Winooski River than they are north of it. While some are made of New York materials, the bulk are of Vermont quartzite and chert. At the Auclair, Donovan, Ewing, Otter Creek No. 2, and Rivers sites, they are mixed with other late Archaic materials.

In southern New England and New York, small-stemmed, small-notched and Normanskill projectiles eventually gave way after 1500 b.c. to broader bladed styles. In the Champlain Valley, three styles similar, but not identical to, broad-bladed projectiles from New York and Massachusetts have been identified. A fourth style is identical to one further south. They have been found as far north as the Canadian border, but are more common the further south one goes in the valley. Although some were made of New York or other exotic flint, by far the larger number were of local stone. Again, the situation is more easily explained as diffusion from the south than it is as an actual influx of people. And again, the presence of these new projectile styles at the Auclair, Donovan, Ewing, Otter Creek No. 2, and Rivers sites may be interpreted as additions to existing, evolving technologies.

A final set of influences from the south is most clearly seen in the Connecticut River Valley, but it shows up in the Champlain Valley as well. At Sumner's Falls in Hartland a small stratified site was excavated in the 1950s by Howard Sargent, now of Franklin Pierce College in New Hampshire. The site is located on the second terrace of the Connecticut River, about 100 yards north of a series of rapids and falls. Five strata were recognized at the site. At the surface was a cultivated layer of brown sandy loam. Beneath this, an irregular layer of black sandy soil contained various artifacts referable to late Woodland times. A stratum of yellow sand devoid of artifacts separated the late Woodland occupation from late Archaic material in an underlying stratum of sand and clay. The artifacts found in this level consist of a perforator made of felsite, four lance-like projectile points with straight stems, two made of felsite and two of rhyolite, and a large number of flakes. Also observed in this level was a small pit, about 2½ inches deep and 8 to 8½ inches in diameter, which contained a small quantity of charcoal. This has produced a radiocarbon date of 800 ± 80 b.c., or 1001 ± 113 B.C. (*i.e.* 880–720 b.c. or 1114–888 B.C.). Another feature was an arrangement of five stones north of the pit at exactly the same depth, the function of which is unknown.

This deep material from Sumner's Falls is referable to what is known as Orient culture. This terminal Archaic manifestation centers on Long Island Sound, where it dates between about 1050 and 750 b.c. In the Connecticut Valley, Orient materials are present at numerous sites between Sumner's Falls and Long Island Sound. This does not necessarily indicate that Orient peoples moved into Vermont, for the resources available so far north were generally quite different from those exploited by Orient peoples around Long Island Sound. We know that in late Prehistoric and early Historic times the Connecticut Valley was an important north-south trade route, and we shall see shortly that long distance trade was a part of late Archaic life. Therefore, the most likely interpretations of the Sumner's Falls site are either that traders from Long Island Sound stopped off here, or else it was the campsite of local peoples who had adopted a foreign projectile style which they learned of through trade contacts with peoples to the south. Since some of their tools were made of locally available rhyolite, we are inclined to accept the latter interpretation.

The idea of diffusion from Orient peoples receives some support from the presence and distribution of Orient Fishtail points in the Champlain Valley. In the ethnographic present, a route frequently traveled by native people from the Connecticut River followed the Black River, from there across to Otter Creek, and down this to Lake Champlain. In the Champlain Valley, Orient Fishtail points are particularly common around Otter Creek, although they have been found up and down the entire valley. As with the other projectiles we have discussed, most of these Orient Fishtails were made of local stone, and their presence at the Auclair, Donovan, Otter Creek No. 2, and Rivers sites may represent a further modification of indigenous technology.

FIGURE 3–12. Major fragment of a soapstone bowl from the Donovan site, near Vergennes.

In the last millennium b.c. the Orient peoples, in common with their contemporaries in southern New England, adopted the custom of cooking in bowls made of soapstone. A few fragments of such bowls have been found at the Auclair and Donovan sites, and occasionally elsewhere in Vermont, including the Connecticut Valley. Again, the addition of a foreign element to a local, changing technology seems likely. Because soapstone absorbs and retains heat so well, bowls of this substance make effective cooking vessels. However, they are heavy and awkward for a people who must move about from one campsite to another on a seasonal basis. This may be one reason why soapstone bowls apparently were not used in large numbers in Vermont.

Glacial Kame Burials

Not all of the outside influences which affected Vermont in the last two millennia b.c. came from the south, nor were they all of a technological nature. Important influences of an ideological nature entered Vermont from the north via the St. Lawrence and Richelieu rivers. In the period between 1600 and 1000 b.c. in the south central Great Lakes region, there developed an elaborate burial cult known as Glacial Kame. The name derives from the custom of placing the burials in glacial kames, or gravel knolls, which were left by the great ice age glaciers.

In Vermont, Glacial Kame burials were discovered in a gravel pit in Isle La Motte in 1962. The site occupies the west edge of a high terrace, some hundred feet above the level of Lake Champlain. The burials were found by accident in the course of gravel removal (as Glacial Kame burials usually are). After their discovery, various people dug test pits in the area before William A. Ritchie arrived from New York at the urging of Lois Callen of the Isle La Motte Historical Society. Ritchie was able to excavate two graves; two or three others were removed prior to his arrival.

Of the two burials excavated by Ritchie, one was 10 cms below the surface, as stripped of its cover, on a hard deposit of clay and gravel. The grave was shaped like a saucer, and its sandy fill was stained red from ochre to a depth of 10 cms over an area measuring 87 cms by 76.5 cms. The grave contained about 3 quarts of burned adult human bones, which had been cremated elsewhere. In addition, there were the unburned skull and long bones of a child, a burned piece of bone awl, and a fire-cracked flint flake.

The other burial, thirty-five feet away from that just described, was 7.7 cms below humus, dug into firm, tan sand. The ochre mass in this grave measured 38 cms in diameter and 25.5 cms thick. With the ochre were placed the cremated bones of an adolescent and two unburned copper adzes (diagnostic of Glacial Kame, such adzes always occur in pairs in the burials). Probably, these were all placed together in a bag or basket.

The total inventory of materials from the site is presented in Table 5. Overall, it is a pretty typical Glacial Kame situation, although the graves were unusually shallow. The galena crystals, too, are unusual, and while red ochre was usually placed in Glacial Kame burials, it was not invariably so. However, red ochre was prominent in burials of the Maritime Archaic as early as 5500 b.c. and is known from the Vergennes Archaic burial at KI.

It is clear from the distribution of Glacial Kame burials that Glacial Kame influence came into Vermont from the St. Lawrence Valley, which by the second millennium b.c. was part of an important east-west trade route. Even before that we have evidence of copper objects moving east, and an occasional ground slate object moving west. Apparently, by Glacial Kame times,

TABLE 5. *Inventory of Materials from the Isle La Motte Glacial Kame Burials*

Material	No.	Object
Copper	5	Adzes with gouge-shaped bits
	15	Thick beads of rolled copper 1/2 to 5/8 inches long (several found strung on bast fiber)
Shell (marine)	140+	Discoidal beads
	1	Discoidal three-hole gorget
	1	Narrow rectanguloid gorget
	3	Fragments of "sandal sole" gorgets (one repaired by grinding edge, drilling holes, and tieing together)
Chipped stone	1	Finely chipped, thin projectile fragment (Meadowood point?)
Galena (lead sulfide)	125+	Nut-sized lumps, unworked
Leather	Misc.	Pieces, burned
Human bone	Misc.	At least ten individuals represented, including: child, age 5–6 child, age 6–10 child, age 9–12 child, age unknown woman, age 35–45 male, adult others, age and sex unknown

shell was a commodity which also traveled west. Obviously, based on the Isle La Motte finds, Vermont was tied into this east-west trade. Whether or not the individuals in the Isle La Motte burials were midwestern traders who were buried far from home or natives who had adopted foreign burial customs is not known, but we'd bet on the latter. Long distance trade is most likely to have been handled by men, who would leave their women and especially their young children behind in their home village. In any case, in these Glacial Kame burials we get our first glimpse of elements which became prominent in a number of Early Woodland burials of the last millennium B.C. in Vermont: cremation and placement of red ochre; copper beads; shell and imported objects together with the remains of the deceased.

The Archaic as a Way of Life

We have been forced by the unsatisfactory nature of existing reconstructions, and by the availability of new evidence, to devote

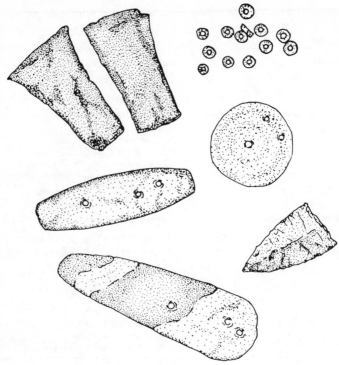

FIGURE 3–13. Representative Glacial Kame artifacts from Isle La Motte. Top: copper adzes and discoidal shell beads, shell gorgets, and fragment of a Meadowood point. Lower left: the sandal-sole gorget has been reconstructed by the artist (not to scale).

much of this chapter to the development of a new reconstruction of how Archaic culture came to and developed in Vermont. Having arrived at a reconstruction which is consistent with available archaeological, linguistic, and paleoenvironmental evidence, and— equally important—our present anthropological understanding of cultural dynamics, we may turn our attention once again to the Archaic as a way of life.

Archaic peoples in Vermont, as elsewhere, subsisted by hunting, gathering, and fishing for a wide variety of wild foodstuffs. Though not emphasized to the degree that it was among the earlier Paleoindians, hunting was still an important source of food, as well as skins for thongs, clothing, and shelter. Hunted animals included deer and bear, as well as a variety of smaller mammals, including beaver and muskrat. Because they were hunted by Maritime Archaic peoples, we might expect their Vergennes Archaic relatives to have hunted fox, marten, otter, moose, and the woodland caribou (where available). The latter were probably rare because they don't live in the same forests as deer and moose. However, the slate bayonet fragment at the Donovan site is of a sort used by Maritime Archaic peoples for killing caribou, and so they may have been occasionally available. But such bayonets are rare finds in Vermont. In the Champlain Valley there is likely to have been some seal hunting. Birds, too, were hunted: in addition to turkeys, which we know they hunted, we would suppose that they hunted ducks, geese, gulls, and loons, as well as any others available which were hunted by Maritime peoples. As with all known hunters and gatherers, the hunting must have been done by men.

The gathering of wild plant foods in season—invariably woman's work among known hunters and gatherers—probably was more important than it was to the earlier Paleoindians. While we do not know for sure what plant foods were collected, they almost certainly included acorns, beechnuts, chestnuts, and any other available mast foods. Such foods are known to have been important in the diets of most other Archaic peoples of North America. In addition, berries and a variety of edible leaves, roots, seeds, and flowers are likely to have been gathered.

Given the connection between the Vergennes and Maritime Archaic, we would suppose that fishing was emphasized to the maximum extent that resources permitted. We do not know specifically what foods, other than turtles, were gotten from Vermont's lakes and streams by Archaic peoples. Salmon was almost surely important, but probably just about anything that could be caught was used.

The equipment employed for the procurement and processing of food included a variety of stone implements, most of which were introduced from various outside sources. Much of the equipment associated with the hunting of land animals seems to have come from peoples living to the south and west, while that used for procuring and processing food from rivers and lakes came from the maritime peoples to the east. Dugout canoes, probably also derived from the east, were used for travel, fishing, and probably some hunting. Given the woodworking skills necessary for canoemaking, it is likely that there were other things made of wood: some containers, for example. Other containers may have been made of animal hides, bark, and basketry. Ultimately, stone bowls came into occasional use.

It is likely that Archaic peoples did not range over such large areas as did Paleoindians before them. A basic riverine orientation is suggested by their use of dugout canoes and the rarity of finds of Archaic materials at any distance from watercourses. Probably, these people carried out most of their activities in specific watersheds, as did Vermonters of the ethnographic present.

Because late Archaic sites and materials are more abundant than those of the Paleoindians, the overall population of Vermont must have been greater than before. Precisely how large or dense late Archaic populations were is unknown. Based on the size of sites such as KI, the groups which lived together seem to have been small. Among most hunting and gathering peoples, such residential groups are normally made up of related families. It is possible that kinship and residence patterns did not differ greatly from those of the sixteenth century in Vermont. As we will see in Chapter 5, such patterns offer certain adaptive advantages to hunters and gatherers.

We know very little about the religious beliefs and practices of Vermont's Archaic peoples. In common with known hunting and gathering peoples, they must have entertained some sort of animistic and shamanistic beliefs, just as we observed for Paleoindians. But we do not know what form those beliefs took. Considering the role played by the Maritime Archaic in the development of the Vergennes Archaic, it is interesting to note that a rich ceremonialism developed on the coast. This is reflected by finely-made animal effigies and an elaborate burial cult. The latter involved the placement of the remains of the deceased in special cemeteries, apart from living areas. With the deceased were placed red ochre and lavish mortuary goods including both utilitarian and exotic items, sometimes in mound burials. This mortuary ceremonialism had its beginnings around 5500 b.c. and flourished in the famous "red paint" burials of Maine and Canada's Atlantic Provinces from 3100 to 1700 b.c. What happened to the beliefs associated with these effigies and ceremonialism as maritime peoples expanded westward we do not know. The only carry-over we can detect in Vermont is the red ochre in the grave at KI. We know that the religious beliefs of a people explain what is otherwise unknown to them about the world in which they live. Their religious beliefs provide them with a means by which they may deal with problems of existence that cause them great anxiety, problems which cannot be dealt with directly through technological and organizational means. Since the world in which the Maritime peoples lived, and the problems they faced, differed from those of the Vergennes people, we would suppose that the beliefs and associated practices of the former were not terribly relevant to the latter.

The Vergennes Archaic, formed by a creative fusion of indigenous and foreign elements, represents the florescence of Archaic culture in Vermont. Following this florescence, continued contact with outsiders, at least in part through trade relationships, continued to bring in outside ideas. In technology, this led to the periodic adoption of such things as new styles of projectiles and stone bowls. In ideology, it led to the introduction of a midwestern burial cult. As these new things were added, old things must have been abandoned or at least modified, but we do not yet have the kind of information which would permit us to say exactly what was abandoned or modified at what time. If we are ever lucky enough to find sites like Auclair and Ewing with a total range of late Archaic materials, but which have not been subsequently disturbed by plowing or other recent activity, then we will begin to have this information.

By some time in the second millennium B.C., enough changes had taken place so that the Vergennes Archaic was no longer a recognizable entity. Yet the basic Archaic way of life itself does not appear to have changed in any really fundamental way. William A. Ritchie has long been a champion of the idea that this late Archaic way of life was quite similar to that of the historic Abenaki peoples. Not only do we agree with Ritchie, but go a step further: in our view, the very roots of Abenaki culture—at least Western Abenaki culture—lie in the Vergennes Archaic. This is a thesis to which we will return, but before doing so, we must bridge the gap between the Archaic and the ethnographic present by discussing the Woodland period in Vermont.

4. THE WOODLAND PERIOD IN VERMONT:
Variations on the Archaic Theme

BY SOME time in the third millennium B.C., while late Archaic peoples were going about their business in Vermont, important changes were beginning to take place in the late Archaic cultures of what is now the midwestern United States. By sometime between the years of 1600–1250 B.C. (1300–1000 b.c.), the cumulative effect of these changes was to bring about a dramatic transformation in the way these early midwesterners lived. As early as 2970 B.C. (2300 b.c.), some of these hunters and gatherers were beginning to plant and cultivate squash, a plant earlier domesticated in Mexico. To this beginning, other domestic plants were added from Mexico: gourds and maize (corn) by at least the last 600 years B.C. (if not earlier), and later on, beans. Although the earliest domestic plants grown were foreign in origin, it was not long before some native plants, most notably sunflower (by 1250 B.C.), marsh elder, and *chenopodium* (goosefoot) were brought under domestication as well. Ultimately, these midwesterners became heavily dependent upon domestic crops for much of their food: as much as 40 percent by 600 B.C., and even more thereafter. Nevertheless, hunting and fishing continued to provide valuable animal protein in the diet, and the collection of wild plant foods was never entirely abandoned.

Along with these changes in subsistence went various technological changes. Among the more important was the widespread manufacture and use of pottery. Although more breakable than containers made of basketry, bark, wood, or animal skins, otherwise pottery is almost indestructible, and so generally outlasts containers made of these organic materials. Moreover, one can cook more easily in pottery vessels, by placing them directly in a fire, than one can in containers made of flammable materials.

Of course one can cook as well in stone bowls, but these are generally heavier and harder to make than pottery vessels. Moreover, the clay from which pottery is made can be found almost anywhere, free for the taking. Indeed, pottery's only obvious disadvantage is that it is less easily portable than baskets, skin bags, or utensils of bark and wood. Thus, it fits in better with a more sedentary, as opposed to highly nomadic, mode of life. This more sedentary life style was made possible by increased reliance on farming.

Another important technological innovation—marked archaeologically by the appearance of generally smaller projectile points —was the bow and arrow. This replaced the spear and atlatl as the primary weapon and generally made for more efficient hunting. Just as a spear can be thrown farther and with more force with an atlatl than without, so can a projectile be launched with even greater force and accuracy, over greater distances, with a bow.

Other changes of an ideological nature took place. By 1250 B.C., elaborate burial ceremonialism was on the rise throughout eastern North America. In the Midwest, this culminated in the construction of log tombs covered by conical earthen mounds. Cremation was common, and with the remains were placed large amounts of red ochre and other elaborate grave goods, often made of exotic materials brought in from some distance. In addition to the burial mounds themselves, earthen enclosures, or sacred circles, and effigy mounds were constructed.

Along with all these other changes, there was a transformation of the social fabric itself. For the most part, Archaic societies seem to have been relatively egalitarian, with no one significantly outranked by anyone else, nor denied equal access to important resources. But in the new order all this changed. Differences in grave construction and differences in grave goods indicative of rank and status show that the new society was one in which distinctions of rank were important. Thus, basic resources along with other rights and privileges were no longer equally accessible to all members of society.

This new, more sedentary way of life is known as Woodland culture. Its earliest elaboration in the Midwest is called Adena, best known as an elaborate burial complex in the Ohio Valley that persisted until about 300 B.C. Adena peoples also were responsible for the Great Serpent Mound in Ohio, which, from the air, resembles a huge serpent. A second Woodland florescence in the Midwest—Ohio Hopewell—dates between about 100 B.C. and A.D. 300. It, too, is marked by the construction of massive earthworks, including burial mounds as well as complex, geometric forms. One of the more distinguishing features of Hopewell mortuary sites, however, is the sophistication of the grave goods which were manufactured from an even wider variety of raw materials than those in Adena burials. Extensive networks of exchange or other forms of interaction made possible the procurement of raw materials from the Rocky Mountains eastward to the Atlantic Coast, and northward from the Gulf of Mexico well into Canada.

Many elements of Woodland culture—itself a product of the fusion of indigenous elements with others borrowed from foreign sources—sooner or later were adopted by other peoples throughout much of the Northeast. In Vermont, both pottery and Adena-like burials made their appearance sometime in the last 500 years B.C., the bow and arrow somewhat later, and native horticulture sometime after A.D. 1000. In Vermont, though, these innovations were not part of a dramatic cultural transformation as in the Midwest; rather, they served primarily to improve an existing way of life which continued to be effective and fulfilling until its ultimate disruption following the arrival of European peoples. Thus, we cannot properly speak of Woodland culture in Vermont, although we can speak of a Woodland period as a span of time during which certain elements of Woodland culture were adopted by Vermonters. The beginning of this period is marked by the appearance of pottery, and its end is marked by the arrival of Europeans.

The Winooski Site

One of the larger and better known sites of the Woodland period in Vermont is the Winooski site, located on the banks of the Winooski River not far from Lake Champlain. The site is of significance for several reasons. First is its size—at least eight acres—which makes it one of the largest sites of its time in the Northeast. Elsewhere in New York and New England, sites contemporary with the Winooski site are generally small and yield scant remains. Second, the intensive investigations conducted at the Winooski site permit a fairly good understanding of the way of life of the people who lived there. The site was first investigated in 1972 by members of the Vermont Archaeological Society's Burlington Chapter. This work, to salvage material which would be lost to river erosion, continued into 1973. Four years later, members of the University of Vermont's Department of Anthropology conducted test excavations for the Winooski Community Development Corporation. These led to the site's placement on the National Register of Historic Places. A year later, the Heritage Conservation and Recreation Service of the United States government funded work by Marjory Power in areas of the site which were threatened by industrial development. In all, she and her field crew excavated 510 square meters and gathered additional information from backhoe trenches excavated as part of the construction activities for a new industrial plant. Much of the site, however, has been preserved for the future.

The Winooski site is situated on the river's east bank, about nine miles upstream from Lake Champlain and one mile downstream from the lower falls of the Winooski. It sits on a level terrace about four meters above the mean water level. On the north and northeast, the site is bounded by a swampy slough, beyond which a steep embankment rises some fifteen meters to a higher terrace. The locale is part of the large floodplain known locally as the Intervale which covers an area of about five square miles. Because it is frequently flooded, the Intervale has remained undeveloped—an anomaly in the Burlington area—and is rich today in plant and animal resources, as it was in the past. The greatest number of fish to be found anywhere in the river inhabit the stretch between the lower falls and the lake. A favored fishing spot, the "Salmon Hole," is located at the base of the falls. Salmon and other migratory fish are available seasonally, as are large concentrations of migratory waterfowl. The variety of birds that nest, feed, or rest in the lake, Intervale, and adjacent habitats include loons, grebes, herons, geese, ducks, rails, gulls, and terns. Migratory shore birds are present from mid-July through late fall. Mammals, too, are abundant. Species found in marsh or valley habitats include deer, cottontail rabbit, woodchuck, raccoon, red

FIGURE 4–1. Two views of the Winooski site. Aerial view by Frank L. Cowan. The view below shows the river bank erosion that led to the site's discovery (Photo by James B. Petersen).

fox, beaver, and muskrat; in the nearby hills and uplands are bear, bobcat, snowshoe hare, and gray squirrel.

Available, too, are a wide variety of plants potentially useful for food, medicine, or other purposes. Trees found near the site today include butternut, hickory, elm, white oak, red and swamp maple, white pine, and cottonwood. Sumac, as well as dense blackberry and raspberry thickets are especially prevalent. The place is therefore a veritable "garden of Eden" with its abundance of riverine, lacustrine, marsh, and upland resources.

While analyses of the data from the 1978 excavations are not yet completed, preliminary results do indicate two major occupations at the site. The first, A.D. 60–350 on the basis of radiocarbon dates (Figure 4–2), is characterized by distinctive pottery decorated with pseudo-scallop-shell stamping throughout (Figure 4–3). This generally well-made pottery is widely but thinly distributed over the site, suggesting repeated short-term occupations by small groups, perhaps some sort of family bands like those known at the start of the Historic period. Actually, this occupation was not the first, for a series of three radiocarbon dates from a deeply buried feature indicate that the site was first visited in late Archaic times some time after 3250 B.C. (ca. 2500 b.c.).

The later occupation of the Winooski site, from about A.D. 500 to 1000, seems to have been the most intensive. Not only are the remains widely distributed, but there are dense middens near the river. Hearths and other discrete features also seem to be more common. This suggests the repeated use of the site by larger groups of people, perhaps comparable to the multi-family bands that are known to have occupied specific watersheds in Vermont at the start of the Historic period.

In all, some seventy-seven features were encountered at the Winooski site; the majority were shallow, basin-shaped hearths containing varying quantities and combinations of charcoal, fire-cracked rock, lithic flakes and artifacts, pottery sherds, and floral and faunal remains. These deposits testify to the preparation and cooking of food, as do carbonized food remains on the interior surfaces of pottery vessels. Patterned clusters of artifacts identify areas where pottery was made and workshops where stone tools were manufactured or finished. Other activities probably included hide processing, woodworking, and possibly bone-work-

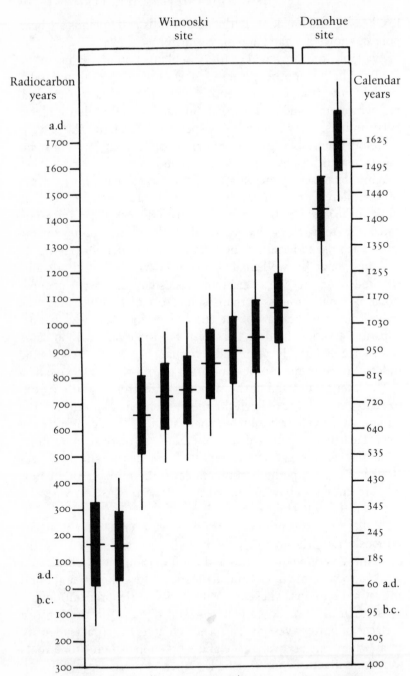

FIGURE 4–2. Radiocarbon dates for middle and late Woodland times.

ing. The range of artifacts and identification of organic remains are indicative of a hunting-gathering-fishing regime, and of mid-summer through late autumn seasonal occupation, at the least.

Two major classes of artifacts were recovered at the site: ceramics and chipped stone tools. Ground stone items are extremely rare; they include celts, four bipitted anvil stones, two perforated pendants of green- and black-banded shale and sandstone, and a polished pipestem fragment, possibly of steatite.

The ceramics from the Winooski site, including those from the earlier excavations, have been analyzed by James Petersen, a graduate of the University of Vermont now pursuing graduate study at the University of Pittsburgh. His study of ceramics from sites throughout Vermont forms the basis for most of what is said about prehistoric pottery in this chapter. Petersen has identified two ceramic complexes at the Winooski site. A sample of at least twenty-five broken pottery vessels, recovered from stratigraphically distinct early occupational contexts, indicates that these were small, well-made, elongate and slightly bulbous in form, with pointed or subconoidal bases (Figure 4–4). The maximum diameter at the mouth is 20 cm, and vessel capacity is estimated to have been from one to two gallons. All were tempered with fine to medium feldspar grit. These vessels were decorated by application of a sinuously-edged stamping tool over the entire exterior surfaces in a zoned pattern, combining simple vertical, drag or push-pull, and rocker stamping techniques (Figure 4–3). Interior surfaces were channeled or striated, with a band of simple or drag pseudo-shell stamping below the square or pointed lip.

This same kind of pottery is widespread in the Northeast, being found throughout the St. Lawrence drainage area from the Great Lakes to the Atlantic Ocean, as well as farther south in New York and New England. This testifies to the close relations that existed between the different peoples in the Northeast, even in the face of major linguistic differences. Radiocarbon dates associated with this pottery outside of Vermont consistently fall between a.d. 1 and 300 (A.D. 60–350). At the Winooski site, two radiocarbon dates from charcoal associated with these ceramics, a.d. 170 ± 155 and a.d. 160 ± 130 (Figure 4–2) are in agreement with this.

The later pottery at the Winooski site is much less standardized in both form and decoration than the earlier pottery. On the basis of a sample of fifty vessels, the general size of the later pottery is larger: mouth diameters range from 20 cms to 35 cms, and vessel capacity ranges from one to four gallons. Two miniature vessels, however, have mouth diameters of only six inches. In general, all of this later pottery is less well-made, having thicker walls and a coarser temper of feldspar grit. Vessels are all cylindrical in form, with slightly rounded subconoidal bases (Figure 4–4). Smoothing of exterior surfaces is common, with some use of cord paddling or a combination of the two treatments. Types of decoration vary widely, but are almost always restricted to the upper portions of the vessels. These include combinations or single use of dentate stamping, wavy line stamping, Z-twist cord impres-

FIGURE 4–3. Pottery sherds from the Winooski site. The sherd on the top left shows the pseudo-scallop-shell stamped decoration typical of the early ceramics. The other sherds show the later decorative styles: *top right*, incised, circular punctate, and small punctate; *far right*, fingernail punctate; *lower left*, cord-impressed, circular punctate, and incised on a low collared vessel; *lower right*, wavy line stamped. All shown one-half actual size.

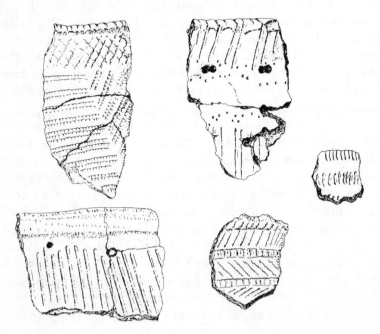

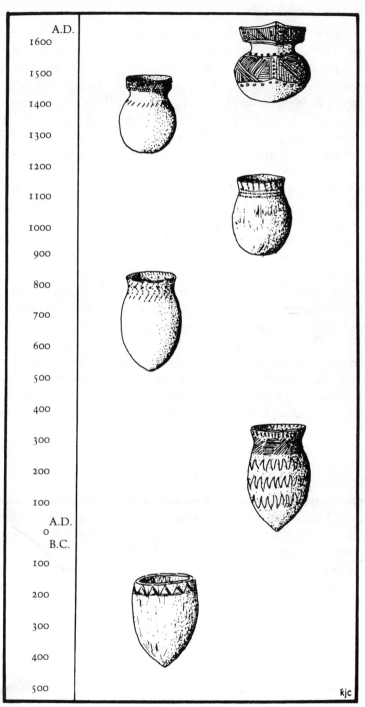

FIGURE 4–4. Changing ceramic styles in Vermont.

sion, incising, trailing, fingernail punctuation, circular punctuation, and other forms of punctate stamping, seemingly applied at random (Figure 4–3). Circular punctuations, simple dentate stamping, and Z-twist cord impressions are the most common forms of decoration employed. Two apparently reliable radiocarbon dates from features containing pottery of this complex are a.d. 750 ± 130 and a.d. 850 ± 135 (Figure 4–2). This kind of pottery has a much more restricted distribution outside of Vermont than that which preceded it. Outside of the Champlain Valley, it has been found at sites on Lake George and in the upper Hudson Valley as far south as the mouth of Fish Creek. Contemporary pottery from sites east, west, and south of this region, although similar in a general sense to the later Winooski pottery, shows enough differences to suggest that regular interaction between peoples throughout the Northeast was coming to an end. This thesis receives some support from other evidence, noted below.

The chipped stone artifacts recovered at the Winooski site include projectile points, preforms (intended for later finishing to produce projectiles), wedges or *piéces esquillées*, end- and side-scrapers, spokeshaves, serrated-edged unifaces, various small retouched flakes, and approximately 7000 unmodified waste flakes. The latter are a by-product of stone tool manufacture. Projectile point types identified from among the 140 points and fragments recovered include 20 corner-notched points, 12 of them the Jack's Reef type, and three pentagonal forms which may also be examples of Jack's Reef points (Figure 4–6). The 108 triangular Levanna-like points (Figure 4–6) occur in two forms: equilateral to broadly isoceles, which predominate; and proportionately longer points. Dates were obtained from two features containing projectile points. One of these—a.d. 655 ± 150—was derived from the dense midden deposits, and contained Jack's Reef and other side-notched points. Artifacts from the second feature—a large hearth—included Jack's Reef points and a triangular point of chert, as well as dentate stamped and rocker cord stamped pottery. The previously cited date of a.d. 750 ± 130 was obtained from this feature.

A major trend which developed at the site was the differential use of raw materials for the manufacture of chipped stone tools. High quality cherts and jaspers, which are foreign to western Vermont, were extensively utilized until sometime around A.D. 800. With a shift from Jack's Reef and other notched projectile point forms to Levanna triangles, locally available stone, specifically quartzite, became the dominant raw material used. This shift appears to be a further reflection of the cessation of regular interaction between peoples in the Northeast that we have already noted. Overall, the impression is one of a kind of retreat to provincialism, or relative isolationism.

While artifact types suggest subsistence activities indicative of a hunting and gathering people, additional information is available, particularly for the later occupation, because specialized techniques were used to recover organic remains from the hearths. Even so, few animal species can be identified among the calcined bone fragments; these include white-tailed deer, fragments of mammalian long bones, possibly including squirrel and dog, a beaver incisor and molars, and a mussel shell fragment. Specimens of sturgeon, bullhead and several unspecified fish vertebrae were recovered, and the location of the site strongly suggests that fishing was an important subsistence activity. Another important activity, and one that can be documeted by the remains, was harvesting of butternuts (*Juglans cinerea* L.). Carbonized nutshells were found in virtually all of the hearths that contained floral remains, and seem to have been important throughout the duration of the site's existence. Butternuts constitute a high-yield resource and are particularly rich in proteins and fats. Their yields do fluctuate, with an abundant crop occurring every two or three years, and constant but somewhat lesser yields expected in the off years. Other nut species may also have been utilized; several examples of hickory (*Carya nutt*) and one possible specimen of black walnut (*Juglans nigra* L.) were also identified.

Seed remains that also indicate gathering include goosefoot (*Chenopodium album* or *hybridium* L.), blackberry and/or raspberry (*Rubus* spp.), hog peanut (*Amphicarpa bracteata* L.), and less commonly, staghorn sumac (*Rhus typinia* L.) and elderberry (*Sambacus canadensis*). All of these plants would have been valuable as foods, and the elderberry has the highest vitamin C content of any of the plants which could have been collected and stored. But, with the exception of goosefoot, they could have served other purposes as well. The ethnographic literature for

FIGURE 4–5. Lithic artifacts from the Winooski site: *upper left*, Pièces d'esquillées or wedges; *middle left*, slate pendant fragments; *lower left*, ground stone celt; *upper right*, range of triangular projectile points of quartzite; *lower right*, Jack's Reef corner-notched chert and quartzite pentagonal points.

North America records their widespread aboriginal use for medicinal purposes. Furthermore, sumac may have been utilized as a dyestuff and as a smoking material. The presence of a seed identified as bullrush or chair-maker's rush (*Scirpus* spp.) might indicate use of this plant for the manufacture of mats or containers. Hickory was often a preferred wood among many aboriginal groups, Abenakis included, for the manufacture of bows. And certainly butternuts, a preferred crop of the historic Abenaki, could be considered as a multipurpose resource. According to the literature, aboriginal use of the tree, in addition to nutmeats, included syrup from boiled sap, a yellow-orange dye from green husks, and, for medicinal purposes, roots and bark.

The total inventory of identifiable plant remains suggests a midsummer through late fall pattern of utilization. In Vermont, sumac and hog peanut are available from the end of July through mid-September; goosefoot from mid-August through early September; blackberry, raspberry, and elderberry from August through September. Butternuts ripen as early as September, but occur through late October as well. Although there are alternate interpretations regarding the postulated seasonal occupation, the lack of storage pits at the site might support the theory that edible plant foods were probably consumed as they were collected. On the other hand, food could have been stored above ground in pots, baskets, or other kinds of containers. Thus, based on current analysis, it appears that an intensive, seasonal subsistence pattern supported the inhabitants of the Winooski site, with butternuts and undoubtedly fish serving as primary staples in a mixed economic subsistence base involving the varied products of hunting, gathering, and fishing.

Middle Woodland Sites in the Winooski Intervale

The Winooski Intervale is proving to be one of the most productive areas for archaeological research in Vermont. A tremendous range both of time periods and types of sites is represented. In addition to the Winooski site, we now know of no less than twenty-two sites, although few have been tested archaeologically. Of those sites which have been tested, five have produced what clearly are middle Woodland materials, while another four have produced less diagnostic material that could be middle or late Woodland, or both.

Apart from the Winooski site, the largest of these middle Woodland sites thus far is the McNeil Generating Plant site. This is located across the river from the Winooski site, in the city of Burlington. Tested by Peter Thomas in 1978, the McNeil site is contemporary with the later occupation at the Winooski site. Within this time span, two more discrete occupations have been identified, separated stratigraphically by flood borne silt. The earliest occupation occurred while Jack's Reef projectile points were in vogue. A large hearth, approximately 6 × 7 feet in size, yielded a wide variety of both organic and inorganic remains, including Jack's Reef points, a drill, scraper, quantities of lithic chips and flakes, dentate stamped pottery with circular punctuations, and fragments of a clay pipe. The organic remains included small fragments of bone from woodchucks, squirrels, unindentified rodents, and young deer. This assortment of animals, and the 5–6 month age indicated by the deer bones, suggests an early fall occupation.

By the time of the McNeil site's reoccupation, Jack's Reef projectile points had gone out of fashion, and triangular Levanna points were in vogue. In association with these points were pottery vessels represented by drag-dentate stamped and cord-impressed sherds. With these, as before, were a drill, scraper, and a large number of lithic flakes. These are primarily of local quartzite, whereas all of the lithic flakes from the earlier "Jack's Reef" occupation were of high quality cherts, a phenomenon already noted at the Winooski site. Animal remains found in a hearth include bones of birds and mammals which cannot be more specifically identified, and the enamel from a beaver's incisor tooth.

Upstream from the McNeil site, still on the Burlington side of the river, are three small middle Woodland sites. Located on a terrace close by the river's lower falls, they are known collectively as the Chace Mill sites. The most westerly of the three is represented by a subsurface scatter of lithic flakes, and two sherds; the second, directly across a small brook, yielded similar materials. At the third, located adjacent to the "Salmon Hole," artifacts diagnostic of early Woodland (for example, the basal portion of a Meadowood point) and, more commonly, middle Woodland were recovered. These include a Levanna point and the basal section of what in New York would be called a Steubenville Stemmed or Fox Creek point, (Figure 4–6) as well as quantities of sherds, decorated with techniques and elements that appear to bridge the gap between the early and late ceramics at the Winooski site. None of the three sites appears to have been used for habitation, but rather seem to represent limited activities carried out by a few individuals at any one time. These individuals most likely lived at the Winooski, McNeil, or Lague sites, which were but a short distance away.

The Lague site, another important Intervale site, is located downstream from the Winooski site, on a high terrace near the river's mouth. Known only from surface collections, the Lague site is of particular significance because of its long history of aboriginal use: artifacts in the collection of Jim Lawrence, an amateur collector, and the anthropology department at the University

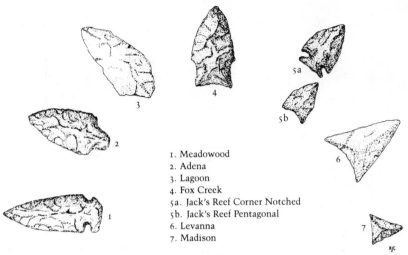

1. Meadowood
2. Adena
3. Lagoon
4. Fox Creek
5a. Jack's Reef Corner Notched
5b. Jack's Reef Pentagonal
6. Levanna
7. Madison

FIGURE 4–6. Projectile points of the Woodland period.

of Vermont, attest to occupations in Archaic, middle and late Woodland times, and even into the seventeenth century. The middle Woodland ceramics from the site exhibit characteristic early and late decorative elements. Two vessels represented among the sherds, however, combined decorative elements characteristic of both ceramic assemblages. This may mean that the site was occupied for a period of time between A.D. 350 and 500 when the Winooski site may have been temporarily deserted, just as the Winooski site continued to be occupied during the brief period between the two occupations at McNeil. This is an important point, for it indicates that although any particular Intervale site might be abandoned for varying periods of time, the Intervale itself clearly was not. Exactly this sort of pattern was common in northeastern North America in early Historic times. For example, here is a description given by Anthony Wallace of the dynamics of eighteenth century Seneca villages in New York:

Now a village was simply an area within which individual families and kin groups built or abandoned their cabins at will; such focus as the area had for its several hundred inhabitants was provided by the council house (itself merely an enlarged dwelling), where the religious and political affairs of the village were transacted. Year by year the size of a village changed, depending on wars and rumors of wars, the shifts of the fur

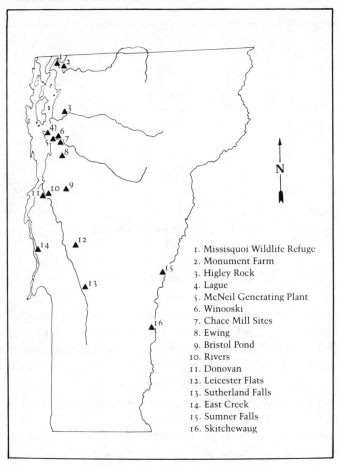

FIGURE 4–7. Middle Woodland sites in Vermont.

1. Missisquoi Wildlife Refuge
2. Monument Farm
3. Higley Rock
4. Lague
5. McNeil Generating Plant
6. Winooski
7. Chace Mill Sites
8. Ewing
9. Bristol Pond
10. Rivers
11. Donovan
12. Leicester Flats
13. Sutherland Falls
14. East Creek
15. Sumner Falls
16. Skitchewaug

trade, private feuds and family quarrels, the reputation of chiefs, the condition of the soil for corn culture, and the nearness of water and firewood. The same village might, over a hundred years' time, meander over a settlement area ten or fifteen miles square, increasing and decreasing in size, sometimes splitting up into several little settlements and sometimes coalescing into one, and even acquiring (and dropping) new names in addition to the generic name, which usually endured.

Now the middle Woodland people of the Champlain Valley were not Senecas, nor did they grow corn. Otherwise, allowing for differences of time and place, there is no reason why their settlements would not have shifted about in a similar manner in response to similar considerations.

Other Middle Woodland Sites in Vermont

Rich though the Winooski Intervale may be in middle Woodland sites occupied between A.D. 50 and 1000, there is no dearth of contemporaneous sites in other parts of Vermont. These range from small sites where people carried out specialized collecting activities, to large villages like the Winooski site. In the Champlain valley, middle Woodland sites are found along the lower reaches of the three other major rivers that flow into the lake (the Missisquoi, Lamoille, and Otter Creek), on smaller tributary streams, and on inland ponds. Many of these sites were not occupied for the first time in the middle Woodland period. For example, the Ewing site on Shelburne Pond, which we discussed in Chapter 3, seems to have been occupied more or less continuously since Archaic times; both the Donovan and Rivers sites (also discussed in Chapter 3) as well as the Winooski site were first occupied in late Archaic times. While this is suggestive of continuity of populations through time, if we allow for settlement shifts of the sort we have just discussed, the greater abundance of middle Woodland sites suggests that populations were substantially larger after A.D. 1 than they were in late Archaic times.

On the lower Missisquoi, in what is now a National Wildlife Refuge, dense concentrations of middle Woodland materials probably representing something like the Winooski site were located in 1979 by Peter Thomas of the University of Vermont. Like the Winooski Intervale, this is a region where there are extensive wetlands, where both plant, fish, and other animal resources are especially abundant. Quantities of artifacts and hearths found along the river levee testify to several occupations. Identification of a bullhead (*Iotalurus nebulosus*) spine recovered from a hearth suggests warm season occupation. The artifacts include late middle Woodland pottery fragments with dentate rocker stamping, cord impressions, and circular punctations. Lithic flakes identified by types of raw materials were mostly of good quality cherts, with lesser amounts of orange jasper. Sampling resulted in the delineation of potential site areas ranging from small areas, where individual families might have carried out their activities, to large villages.

The Monument Farm site, located a short distance upstream from the refuge, has been surface collected but not professionally excavated. Sherds from the site include those from at least two vessels decorated in characteristic middle Woodland fashion. Similarly, sherds representing a single middle Woodland vessel have been surface collected at the Higley Rock site on the lower Lamoille River. This site also produced a middle Woodland Jack's Reef corner-notched point.

Further south, in the Winooski watershed but outside of its intervale, middle Woodland materials are abundant in proximity to Shelburne Pond. At the Ewing site, the uppermost 5–21 cms over the site produced ten times as many triangular (Levanna) as stemmed points; similarly, the ratio of quartzite to chert artifacts was ten to one. Deeper down, between 23 cms and 36 cms, the ratio of triangular to stemmed points was one to three, with quartzite and good quality chert being used in equal quantities. Again, the trends through time noted at the McNeil and Winooski sites seem to be evident.

Most of the pottery recovered by Ken Varney in his original excavations at the Ewing site, recently donated to the University of Vermont's anthropology department, come from the 23–36 cm level. This, along with the bulk of the pottery later excavated by the Burlington Chapter of the Vermont Archaeological Society, related primarily to late Woodland times. However, some sherds are decorated in the typical late middle Woodland manner, with dentate and dentate rocker stamping, circular punctations, and cord impressions. Sherds from two vessels recovered on the limestone ridge back from the shore of Shelburne Pond clearly relate to the earlier part of the middle Woodland period.

South of Shelburne Pond, middle Woodland materials have been found in at least five sites in Addison and Rutland counties: on the shores of Bristol Pond, the Leiscester Flats site near Salisbury on a tributary of the Otter Creek, the Donovan and Rivers sites on Otter Creek itself not far from the lake, and the Sutherland Falls site on Otter Creek in Proctor. Early middle Woodland materials are present at all but the Rivers site; in fact, all 200 sherds from Sutherland Falls, a site discovered by the amateur collector Bert Olsen and tested in 1976 by professional archaeologists, are just like the early middle Woodland ceramics from the Winooski site. While some sherds are undecorated, most show pseudo-scallop-shell, and some rocker dentate, stamping. Artifacts include a gorget, pendant, corner notched projectile of Onondaga (New York) chert, and flakes of both local and foreign cherts.

Later middle Woodland materials are known from both the Donovan and Rivers sites. The latter has been more extensively excavated: by John Bailey in 1938–39, Edward Brooks and Leaman Hallett in 1946, Brooks in 1951, and Louise Basa in 1972. For all this work, though, no adequate reports have ever been published, nor are the few available summaries particularly useful. However, a summary account of the occupation of this important site can be given. Although occupied first in late Archaic times, the Woodland occupation seems to date between about A.D. 800 and 1100 (according to Basa). Thus, we are dealing with late middle Woodland and early late Woodland times.

The Rivers site was clearly a living site, where people went about their ordinary day to day activities. Some notion of what those activities were is provided by an analysis of fourteen of the thirty-nine refuse pits discovered by John Bailey. On the basis of the artifacts found within them, all fourteen pits pertain to middle Woodland times. This analysis was done by Russell Barber, now with the Peabody Museum at Harvard University, as a senior honors project at the University of Vermont. Working with Bailey's field notes, and the artifacts recovered by Bailey which are housed in the Fleming Museum, Barber started with the assumption that objects were likely to fall or be dumped into pits near to where they were used. He then examined the wear patterns on seventy-seven stone tools such as blades, scrapers, drills, and so on, to determine as best he could exactly how these tools were used. Other refuse from the pits was then studied in order to confirm, if possible, the postulated activities.

The contents of ten pits suggested that specific kinds of activities were indeed carried out nearby: woodworking near five pits, stone-working near four, skin- or hide-working near three, food preparation near three, bone-working near two, and heavy butchering near one. The combined inventory of organic remains in the pits include nutshells, cherry pits, clamshells, and quantities of bone, including deer. Other species reported by Bailey, Brooks, and Basa include bear, beaver, dog (butchered, apparently), elk, fish (mostly catfish with some perch), fisher cat, moose, muskrat, porcupine, and turtle.

At least eighteen postholes have been discovered at the Rivers site, but they are unpatterned, and so the dwellings whose post they held cannot be reconstructed. They do suggest, along with the abundance of other remains, that Rivers was more than just a hunting and fishing camp. More likely, it represents the same sort of seasonally occupied village site along the Otter Creek as does the Winooski site along the Winooski River. Added support for this interpretation is provided by the five burials discovered at the Rivers site. These include a child between 3 and 7 years of age; two women, one aged between 30 and 40 years, the other between 45 and 55 years; and a man aged between 30 and 40 years.

These burials from the Rivers site stand in marked contrast to the elaborate burials of early Woodland times (see page 115). The bodies were all placed on their sides, in flexed positions, in shallow refuse pits in the village itself, rather than in a special cemetery. Except for incidental refuse located in the fill, none were accompanied by special grave goods. This is a far cry from the elaborate mortuary ceremonialism that first appeared in Vermont at the end of Archaic times.

The adults buried at Rivers were a short, robust, muscular people. In height, the two women stood at 154.36 cms and 157.35 cms, respectively (just under 5 feet 1 inch and 5 feet 2 inches). The man was a bit taller, at 166.27 cms (just over 5 feet 5 inches). Heads were long to round, and noses broad. The younger of the two women had bowed legs and was troubled by more than the usual arthritis for her age. Even more of a problem, though, were her teeth and gums. The latter were severely diseased, fourteen teeth had been lost before death, and of those that remained, four were extensively decayed, and one was broken off at the gum. The others were heavily and unevenly worn, one of them right down to the gum. Degeneration of the supporting bone was so advanced that, had the woman lived, she would not long have retained her remaining teeth.

The dental health of the older woman was no better. Six of her lower teeth, and all but two of her upper teeth had been lost. Degeneration of the bone was so advanced that the two remaining uppers would soon have been lost; moreover, because the teeth below them in the lower jaw were gone, effective chewing for this woman was impossible. The remaining teeth were all severely worn, especially in the front. By contrast, the man had suffered no tooth loss, showed only moderate wear, and only slight decay on one tooth. If these three adults are representative of the Rivers population as a whole, which they may or may not be, it would suggest that, in addition to chewing their food, the women were using their teeth for some task that the men were not. Just what that task might have been is not known, but the difference seems much too great to be accounted for solely on the basis of different diets for men and women.

In view of the abundance of middle Woodland sites in the Champlain Valley, it is probably significant that middle Woodland materials are comparatively uncommon in southwestern Vermont. An extensive collection of artifacts has been amassed by Gordon Sweeney from sites along the Hoosic and Walloomsac rivers in Pownal and Bennington; this collection was studied in 1979 by Peter Thomas. He reports that it includes a fair quantity of late Archaic, but not much recognizable early or middle Woodland material. But middle Woodland pottery is not altogether absent, and Levanna points, which became popular in late middle Woodland times and continued in use thereafter, are fairly common. Apparently this corner of Vermont was deserted, or nearly so, near the end of late Archaic times. People did not return in any substantial numbers until near the end of middle Woodland times.

The differences between the middle Woodland occupations of southwestern Vermont and the Champlain Valley becomes meaningful when considered in conjunction with other information. The Hoosic and Walloomsac rivers together are a part of the upper Hudson drainage system. In early Historic times, the upper Hudson, along with the upper Housatonic River in western Massachusetts, was occupied by Mahicans. Their major settlements were on or near the upper Hudson itself, but at certain times of the year they hunted the uplands of southwestern Vermont and western Massachusetts. Thomas notes a close similarity in both the chronological periods represented and the types of raw materials between Sweeney's collections and collections from the upper Housatonic region. He therefore suggests that in early Woodland times, the people operating in southwestern Vermont had withdrawn to their homes in the upper Hudson Valley. This may have been a response to a climatic trend toward cooler temperatures which began about 3000 years ago, and which in upland regions had an adverse effect on the wild plant and animal resources utilized by humans. It was not until perhaps 800 A.D. that peoples from the upper Hudson began returning in any substantial numbers to their haunts in the uplands of southwestern Vermont.

The problem with this theory is that no one has yet found the homes along the upper Hudson to which people from southwestern Vermont would have withdrawn. According to New York State Archaeologist Robert Funk there is scant evidence for any early middle Woodland occupation anywhere in the entire Hudson Valley. But this would still indicate that southwestern Vermont had more in common with the Hudson Valley in middle Woodland times than it did with the Champlain Valley. Thus, it seems reasonably certain that the close cultural connection between southwestern Vermont and the Hudson Valley, which existed in early Historic times, existed in middle Woodland times, too.

East of the Green mountains, one, if not two, middle Woodland sites are known in the Connecticut Valley. Some thirty years ago, Maurice and Gordon Crandall amassed a large collection of artifacts from an area extending for a distance of about three miles along the river in Springfield, Vermont. Known as the Skitchewaug site, it may represent a continuous series of small sites, all located on a terrace above flood level. The middle Woodland materials come from a relatively restricted locale on the eroding riverbank. Although the bulk of the materials are pottery sherds, they include a small stemmed point of white quartz, a triangular point of black chert, and more than a dozen cache blades of a type known in New York as Petalas Blades. All are consistent with a middle to late middle Woodland occupation.

Twenty-four vessels represented by sherds in the Crandall collection show a wide variety of decorative elements, sometimes used singly, and sometimes combined with others. Examples of the former include a net-impressed vessel and one that had been incised. Among eight cord-impressed vessels, three combined either circular punctations, rocker cord stamping, or net impressions with the cord marking. Seven vessels show a combination of dentate and rocker dentate stamping. Finally, seven vessels were wholly undecorated.

In the discussion of the Archaic occupation of the Sumner Falls site in Hartland, the presence of overlying late Woodland materials was noted. While not denying the reality of such an occupation, it is possible that it actually began late in middle Woodland times. Four triangular points of chert and quartzite were recovered from the surface layer, a quartzite triangle from the second level down, and nineteen cord-impressed sherds from both levels. One, incised with lines suggestive of chevrons, would not be out of place in the late middle Woodland. The site appears to have been a small campsite.

Unquestionably there are middle Woodland sites in Vermont other than those that we have surveyed here. For example, a pottery vessel from a village site at the mouth of East Creek, illustrated in John Huden's book *Archaeology in Vermont*, appears to be an example of the middle Woodland dentate stamping technique. Warren K. Moorehead, in a 1922 report of his investigations on Isle La Motte, refers to conoidal-based cord-marked pottery.

In her study of projectile points from the Champlain Valley, Mariella Squire reports on the distribution of three types which were in use in middle Woodland times. Limited numbers of Jack's Reef forms have been found along the lakeshore and inland on the major rivers from the Lamoille southward to Barnes Beach in Addison County. Stemmed broad-bladed Steubenville or Fox Creek points, the characteristic type in early middle Woodland sites in the Hudson Valley, are much more restricted in their distribution. With the exception of one found at one of the Chace Mill sites, they are known only along the Poultney River in West Haven and along the Little Otter Creek. By contrast, Levanna Points, which continued in use through late Woodland times, are commonly found along every major stream from the Canadian border to the southern end of Lake Champlain, on the shores of ponds such as Shelburne, Bristol, and Monkton, and on subsidiary streams in the Otter Creek drainage.

To sum up our present knowledge of the middle Woodland period in Vermont, and allowing for gaps in the data, sites of various types appear to have been located along the Connecticut River and the major rivers of western Vermont which flow into Lake Champlain (Figure 4–7). Some of these—the Missisquoi Refuge, Winooski, Rivers, and Higley Rock(?) sites—appear to have been large villages located not far from the mouths of major watercourses; a similar village may have been developing in southern Vermont on the Connecticut River. All were occupied in late middle Woodland times, although the beginnings of the Winooski site clearly go back at least to early middle Woodland times. The same seems to be true for the Rivers site, which is located directly across Dead Creek from the Donovan site. Its Woodland occupation picks up just where that at the Donovan site ends, and so we can reasonably consider one to represent a continuation of the other. The beginnings of the other villages may be equally old, but insufficient work has been done to allow us to confirm this. As we shall see, though, the presence and nature of early Woodland materials on the lower Missisquoi does suggest that a village was developing there by the very beginning of middle Woodland times.

The association of middle Woodland sites with rivers, streams, and ponds suggests that fishing, along with hunting and the gathering of wild plant resources, was an important subsistence activity; and of course this has been confirmed by the recovery of fish remains from those sites where care has been taken to recover such refuse. But the association suggests as well that canoe travel may have been an important mode of transportation, as indeed it was by early Historic times, and as it is thought to have been as early as 4375 B.C. (3500 b.c.). Finally, the overall pattern of middle Woodland sites in the Champlain Valley, large villages on the lower reaches of the four major rivers not far from the lake with smaller sites located in a variety of micro-environmental settings, such as high terraces, pond fringes, and small tributary streams, is suggestive of an overall way of life not very different from that followed by native peoples in the Champlain Valley in the early seventeenth century A.D.

Early Woodland Cemetery Sites

Having surveyed the wealth of archaeological materials in Vermont dating from middle Woodland times, we must now turn our attention to the early Woodland period so as to bridge the gap from late Archaic times. The difficulty here is that in Vermont, as in much of eastern North America, the bulk of the evidence relating to the early Woodland period comes from cemetery sites. We simply do not have, or at least have not been able to recognize, the kinds of living sites that we have for middle Woodland, and even late Archaic times.

Four early Woodland cemeteries have been discovered in Vermont, all of them in the Champlain Valley (Figure 4–8). The first one was discovered in 1868 and has variously been referred to as the Swanton, Frink Farm, or Hemp Yard site. Materials from here are pretty well scattered; some of them are housed in the Smithsonian Institution, as well as the Fleming Museum in Burlington, the Historical Society Museum in Montpelier, and the R. S. Peabody Foundation in Andover, Massachusetts. The most recently discovered cemetery is the Boucher site in Highgate, which was excavated in 1973 by Louise Basa for the University of Vermont. The collection from this cemetery was generously donated to the university by the Bouchers, owners of the site; it represents the only reasonably intact collection from an early Woodland cemetery in Vermont, as well as much of the Northeast. Both Boucher and the Swanton cemetery are located along the lower Missisquoi River, the Boucher site but a short distance upstream from the previously mentioned Monument Farm site.

The other two cemeteries, the East Creek and Bennett sites, are located in Orwell. The East Creek cemetery was excavated in the 1930s for the Museum of the American Indian Heye Foundation in New York, where much of the material is still housed. Unfortunately, proper field records detailing these excavations do not exist. The Bennett site was unfortunately pillaged in the early 1940s, although one burial was excavated by the now defunct

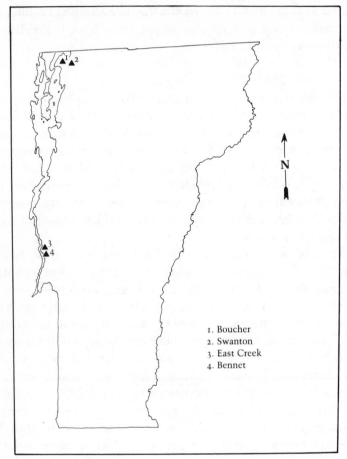

FIGURE 4–8. Early Woodland cemeteries in Vermont.

Champlain Valley Archaeological Society. There may have been yet another early Woodland cemetery near Burlington; George Perkins, one-time State Geologist, reported the finding of a blocked-end tube fragment with several spear points made of materials similar to those used for objects in the Swanton cemetery.

Although these cemeteries show some variation, they all share a number of features in common, indicative of ritual activity as well as far-ranging trade or other contacts. Pottery, which defines the beginning of the Woodland period in Vermont, is present in two of the cemeteries: East Creek and Boucher. The Swanton cemetery produced the only round discoidal stones, and the Bennett site produced a shell pendant and some other objects absent at the other cemeteries, not to mention an unusual variety of bone objects. East Creek produced none of the shell beads so numerous in the other cemeteries, but it has produced the only tubes of unfired clay.

Before describing these Vermont cemeteries in somewhat more detail, it is useful to summarize briefly what is known about early Woodland materials in New York State; this will help in understanding the situation in Vermont. What William Ritchie has called the Meadowood phase was defined on the basis of burial sites in central, western, and northern New York. Sites consist largely of small cemeteries, located in spots along streams and lakes potentially favorable for fishing. Meadowood sites are particularly common in what, in later Woodland times, was Iroquois country. This includes the Susquehanna and Mohawk watersheds, as well as southern Ontario and eastward into southern Quebec. Outside of Iroquois country, in the Delaware and Hudson valleys, Meadowood materials have been found, but sporadically. Similarly, typical side-notched Meadowood projectile points and cache blades have sometimes been found in New England, including Vermont. Possibly the Meadowood peoples of New York spoke early Iroquoian languages, while the people of eastern New York and New England did not, even though they occasionally made use of objects borrowed from Meadowood peoples.

Certain practices in Meadowood burials are reminiscent of Glacial Kame and related mortuary cults of the upper Great Lakes region; the use of red ochre, the practice of cremation, and the placement in graves of artifacts such as shell beads, gorgets, celts, adzes, beads and awls of copper, and birdstones. Although rare in Meadowood sites, pottery is present. Known as Vinette I, it is represented by grit-tempered, thick-walled vessels with more or less pointed bases. Lips are rounded or pointed, and the inner and outer surfaces of the vessels were given their final shape with a cord-wrapped paddle prior to firing. Commonly, the cord markings on the outside have a vertical orientation, horizontal on the inside. The timespan represented by Meadowood, based on radiocarbon dates, is about 1000–560 b.c. (1250–600 B.C.).

TABLE 6. *Major Traits of the Middlesex Phase*

Artifacts	Mortuary Practices
Blocked-end tubular pipe	Extensive use of red ochre to cover remains
Large leaf-shaped and lanceolate knife	
Projectiles with lobate or straight stems, or side-notched	Burials flexed, extended (rare), bundled, or cremated
Ovoid and trianguloid cache blades	Grave goods of ritualistic significance
Copper celt	
Copper awl	
Boatstone	
Bar amulet	
Truncated birdstone form	
Gorget	
Pendant	
Cylindrical copper beads	
Discoidal, barrel-shaped, and cylindrical shell beads	
Marginella shell beads	

What Ritchie in New York has called the Middlesex phase really should be regarded as an Adena burial cult temporarily grafted onto local traditions. Known only from burial sites, Ritchie has described Middlesex as "Adena in the North," based on the significant number of commonly shared traits, both burial practices and artifacts, that occur in the two regions. These latter items include classic Adena artifacts manufactured of Ohio Valley raw materials such as chalcedony, flint, slate and Ohio fireclay. The major shared traits (of a total of ninety-two Middlesex traits) are listed in Table 6.

The original site in central New York at which Ritchie first recognized Adena relationships was identified in 1937, with the blocked-end tube—thought to be a smoking pipe—providing the common denominator. By 1959, nineteen Middlesex sites were known in the eastern United States, including, in New England, three in the Champlain Valley, three in the Connecticut Valley up into Massachusetts, and one on the Maine coast. The discovery of the Boucher site in 1973 brings the total up to twenty.

In Vermont, both Meadowood and Middlesex influences and in some cases materials can be identified in the cemeteries as well as among surface-collected projectile points. Unfortunately the cemetery data are for various reasons incomplete. Thus only general descriptions of sites and site contents will be attempted here.

The Swanton cemetery is located about five miles from Lake Champlain on a sandy ridge above the Missisquoi River. It was discovered quite by accident in 1861 in the course of tree-clearing operations, when blowing sand exposed depressions containing burials in red-stained soils. These were excavated by amateurs, and although the exact number is unknown, at least twenty-five and possibly as many as thirty-five burials were represented. Poor bone preservation is probably one source of the confusion; only a few green-stained fragments remained, preserved by the presence of copper artifacts. The red-stained soils are undoubtedly due to the liberal use of red ochre. Evidently all but two burials were accompanied by this "red paint." The two that were not appear to have been cremations.

The original artifact collection from the site consisted of approximately 150 artifacts; by 1873, 100 were still available for examination by Vermont State Geologist George Perkins. Major classes of artifacts by material of manufacture were copper, shell, and both flaked and ground stone. Among the copper artifacts were some small, chisel-like celts, one with the remnant of a wooden handle. An awl was found between the teeth of one corpse. Also included in the graves were about half a dozen bi-pointed, pencil-shaped objects of copper, and a number of beads made by rolling up thin sheets of copper. Over thirty other beads, cylindrical in shape, were made from snail shell, mostly *Columella*, with one or two identified as *Marginella*.

A variety of ground stone artifacts were found in the graves, including at least twelve blocked-end tubes. These ranged from 12 cm to 25 cm in length, and were blocked by small pebble plugs, some of them specially shaped for the purpose. If drawings we have of artifacts are accurate, one tube was engraved with a Thunderbird figure, with three line-and-dot units engraved below the figure. Other ground stone materials included drilled slate pendants and/or gorgets, some with one and some with two holes. Most were roughly rectangular, but some were diamond-shaped and some were circular; some were thick, some were thin, and some were beveled. Of five known axes, two small ones were made with slight notches on the side, presumably for hafting. The other three were unnotched, short, and very well polished. Five objects may have served as atlatl weights—three boatstones of red slate, gray slate, and steatite; and two pop-eyed birdstones of red slate and marble. The latter is currently housed in the museum of the Vermont Historical Society in Montpelier. Other ground stone objects included several bar amulets; one if not two discoidal stones of white quartz about three inches in diameter, with concave sides; a smooth, water-worn pebble of white quartz, oval in shape and weighing about a pound; and two fossiliferous stones of which only one—of sandstone—was actually shaped by being squared and smoothed. The discoidal stone is virtually identical to gaming stones which were used by southeastern peoples to play a game called Chunky. Such Chunky stones are quite uncommon in the Northeast. The white quartz pebble was heavily stained by ochre on one side and may have been used to grind hematite so as to make the "red paint."

We do not know how many chipped stone tools were included in the graves, but we do know that they included several spear points, large knife blades, and numerous triangular or leaf-shaped cache blades. While some were made of what appears to be Monkton quartzite and St. Albans chert, several pieces were made from exotic flints from as far away as the Midwest. These include both the classic Ohio Adena lobate-stemmed points and corner-notched Meadowood points (Figure 4–6).

In his interpretation of the site, Perkins stated that the Swanton artifacts were comparable to those found in the burial mounds to the west, particularly in the Scioto Valley of Ohio. On this basis, he suggested that peoples from the Ohio area wandered eastward into Vermont, probably following the St. Lawrence into the Champlain Valley. This migration hypothesis was restated almost a hundred years later by two professional archaeologists, only the proposed route of entry was changed.

Approximately one mile west of the Swanton site, the largest of the early Woodland cemeteries, the Boucher site, was excavated under salvage conditions by Louise Basa in 1973. The site was discovered by a bulldozer operator who was excavating a basement for a new home. The owners of the property, the John Boucher family, permitted excavations to continue at considerable inconvenience to their building plans and subsequently donated the collection to the University of Vermont. Analysis of the data has not yet been completed, but on the basis of several short articles and public talks by Basa, a few general comments can be made.

Boucher was located on a terrace above the Missisquoi in Highgate, approximately four miles from Lake Champlain. At least eighty pit burials ranging from one to six feet deep were found, many lavishly sprinkled with red ochre. Subsequent to their filling, fires were built over some of the graves. Identifiable burial types included forty inhumations and twenty cremations. Other pits were devoid of human remains, but did contain artifacts. These were deliberately placed; otherwise, the fills were barren of artifacts or other living debris. It is not unlikely that these pits once contained human remains, but they subsequently decayed completely.

The wide variety of ornamental, ceremonial, used and unused utilitarian grave goods recovered at Boucher included many items manufactured of raw materials indigenous to areas other than Vermont. Those identified by Basa are copper from Lake Superior; stone from the Hudson River Valley, central and western New York, northeastern and southeastern Ohio, and possibly northeastern Kentucky; and *Marginella* and *Columella* shell beads from the Atlantic Ocean.

Among all artifact classes, two clearly demonstrate ties with Adena mortuary complexes: sixteen blocked-end tubes, some of Ohio fireclay; and the classic Adena lobate-stemmed projectile points, a few manufactured of Ohio materials. Other objects of stone consist of bifacial knives and scrapers, flat sandstone, and red slate tablets, the only objects invariably made of stone from Vermont. These tablets were found in association with red ochre and graphite. Traces of rotary grinding suggest that they may have served as tools for the preparation of pigments. Use marks also occur on one-hole banded slate pendants. These marks appear to be similar to grooves that might be produced by sharpening bone needles or awls. A single-banded, slate-keeled boatstone was recovered, but its context is unknown. Celts and adzes, which never were used, are also part of the collection.

According to Petersen's examination of the Boucher pottery, at least four small subconoidal based vessels are represented. All were stained with ochre, and carbonized deposits on their interior surfaces attest to their use as cooking pots. Cord marking typical of Vinette I consists of horizontal cording on interior surfaces, vertical and oblique cording on exteriors. Occasionally the exterior surfaces are heavily smoothed, almost obliterating the cording. One vessel was decorated with incised lines and triangles around the rim, treatment which is a departure from Vinette I wares. Further, that this vessel was considered "special" is indicated by the differential ochre staining on the sherds: it was deliberately broken (ritually "killed") before inclusion in the burial.

Especially abundant in the graves were beads of copper. Strings of up to 300 beads were frequently placed with each body, generally near the head but not necessarily around the neck. In all, there are some 4000 beads in the collection. Because the copper salts have acted as a preservative, bones and other organic remains are unusually well preserved. From their skeletons, we can

FIGURE 4–9. Artifacts from the Boucher cemetery: *upper left*, ground slate pendants; *upper right*, Adena points; *center*, chert blade; *bottom*, blocked-end tube of Ohio fireclay; *lower right*, copper awl fixed in portion of wooden handle.

FIGURE 4–10. One of the four pottery vessels from the Boucher cemetery. The incised line decoration near the rim is unusual for Vinette I
pottery. Diameter of the pot at the opening is 12 cms. Photo by John D.
Owen, Courtesy Fleming Museum.

describe the Boucher folk generally as of moderate stature with
markedly round heads, high vertical foreheads, wide noses and
faces, and some slight prognathism. Infant mortality was high:
about 15 percent of the skeletons are of individuals who had died
by the age of 2; another 10 percent were dead by the age of 6; an
additional 15 percent dead by the age of 11. Things appear to have
been better for teenagers: only 5 percent of the skeletons are
those of people who died between the ages of 11 and 21. But then
the mortality figures rise again: 10 percent died between ages 21
and 35, 30 percent between ages 35 and 55. Only about 15 percent
of the population lived to a really old age.

Health-wise, the Boucher folk suffered their share of arthritis,
although no more than is usual in human populations. A few of
the skeletons show evidence of traumatic injury: breaks or other
effects of severe blows. And some show bone pathologies that
may have been caused by a vitamin C deficiency. Consistent with
this, the dental health of the adults who show this condition was
quite poor. Otherwise, though, the dental health of these people
was fairly good into early adulthood. But the teeth of adults between the ages of 35 and 55 were very heavily worn, with occasional caries. Tooth loss was on the increase in this age group,
with about 16 percent gone, accompanied by some loss by resorption of supporting bone. In adults over 55 years of age, tooth wear

was extreme, with extensive tooth loss: 66 percent and up; with this went extensive resorption of supporting bone. Generally, lower teeth were lost before uppers, and front teeth before rear teeth.

Preserved by the copper salts along with the human remains were a number of other organic substances, including beechnuts and acorns, several examples of textiles, portions of cordage on which the copper and shell beads were strung, thong fragments used for suspension of a one-hole banded slate gorget, and portions of a wooden handle for a copper awl. Identifiable animal remains include deer (bone awls), beaver incisors (one hafted in a bone handle), cut bear jaw, mink, fox (or dog), and a fully articulated snake skeleton, placed over the face of one individual.

According to Basa, the Boucher cemetery was used for a relatively brief time, perhaps a century. Judging from the lack of superimposed burials, these were remembered spots. The presence of cremations as well as inhumations, along with evidence that some of the latter involved bodies that were not fresh at the time of burial, suggests that the bodies of people who died over the course of a year were saved for burial until such times as the ground was no longer frozen, in the spring. Those who died over the summer, by contrast, could have been buried almost at once. This, and the size of the cemeteries, suggests a people returning on a regular basis to the same spot, year after year. This, of course, implies the existence of a nearby settlement which was permanent in the sense that its location was fixed, and it was deserted at most for only part of the year. Such a settlement could well be the precursor of the middle Woodland settlement located only a mile downstream, on the wildlife refuge. On this basis, it is reasonable to suppose that the people buried at Boucher, and in the Swanton cemetery, were the ancestors of the people who, in middle Woodland times, lived at least part of the year in what now is the Missisquoi Wildlife Refuge.

The Bennett site, like the two just discussed, was discovered by accident in the course of gravel removal. One burial, that of a child, was excavated in 1942 by Payson Hatch of the Champlain Valley Archaeological Society, and this is the only adequate report we have. The child was buried in a flexed position and was accompanied by a blocked-end tube, a copper awl, a thin, side-notched point of jasper, and two *Columella* shell beads. Other artifacts known to have come from this cemetery include at least four other blocked-end tubes; several other thin, side-notched points (up to 4 inches long); two boatstones; two celts; and more than twenty ochre-stained cache blades. Organic remains consist of numerous awls, three broad gouges, and a barbed fishhook, all manufactured of bone; many split and ground beaver teeth, as well as seven beaver tooth knives with handles of antler; several conical projectiles of antler; pieces of flat, perforated "netting needles"; many beads of *Marginella* and *Columella*; and a thin, round, centrally perforated pendant of shell.

The East Creek cemetery, unlike the other three, is known to be immediately adjacent to a village site that was first occupied in late Archaic times, and was utilized through later Woodland times. One might suppose that that the village was occupied as well in early Woodland times by the people responsible for the cemetery. Unfortunately, the material from the village is so thoroughly mixed, as well as incompletely reported, that this cannot be proven beyond a reasonable doubt.

There is no question that East Creek was a sizeable cemetery. Just how large cannot be determined; conflicting reports range from forty to fifty-two burials. No intact skeletal remains were recovered; seemingly the majority of burials were cremations or bundle burials. Most occurred in basin-shaped pits, often lined with bark, with a thin layer of hard clay beneath the bark. Profuse amounts of red ochre were found in all of the burials. A possible crematory was also identified at East Creek. This feature was a pit approximately 3 × 5 feet in diameter at the top, which was filled with charcoal. It may have been used to cremate a series of individuals, whose remains were redeposited elsewhere. Included in the pit were nearly 100 cache blades and a particularly handsome birdstone. The entire situation is reminiscent of, without being quite like Meadowood cremations in New York.

With a few exceptions, the range of grave goods reported from the site is similar to that represented at the other cemeteries. Copper artifacts included awls and celts, some with fragments of wooden handles, and strings of beads of two types, both fashioned of rolled sheet copper. The first and most common type was a thin cylindrical tube, approximately .5 cm in length and .4 cm in width. The second type was formed by rolling the sheet several times into a flat, heavy bead, 1.5 cm in width and ranging in length from 1 cm to 2 cm. Among the chipped stone tools were numbers of Meadowood cache blades, most manufactured of local chert, probably from Mount Independence. They accompanied burials in quantities ranging from 5 to 87. Many of the blades and points have disappeared, but records indicate the presence of large stemmed points, generally made of exotic flints and jaspers. One of these, an Adena point apparently manufactured of Flint Ridge (Ohio) flint, is approximately 14 cm in length. Also indicating ties with the Ohio Valley in the form of raw materials are inclusions of groups of tiny pressure flakes in several burials, perhaps suggesting that resharpening had been accomplished in conjunction with burial activities. Other chipped stone artifacts include a few side-notched points of local chert, some scrapers, and three celts, one made of imported chalcedony.

Obvious Adena relationships are indicated by blocked-end tubes. Eight of Ohio fireclay were reported, along with twenty-one counterparts made of unfired clay. Many contained carved, steatite plugs. In addition to tubes, other ground stone items include atlatl weights in the form of three bar amulets, the bird-stone already mentioned, and two boatstones. One of the latter is of banded slate and is keeled. The second is triangular in form and exhibits a knob on the top. Red slate gorgets are also reported, along with an unusual ground stone artifact, a slate spear point. The point is now missing from the collection, but based on a photograph, Stephen Loring describes the process of manufacture as follows: the point was first shaped by flaking, then ground and polished, and finally pressure flaked along the edges. While the general description suggests a Vergennes Archaic point, finishing the edges of slate points by means of pressure flaking was not practiced by Archaic tool makers.

Other objects of stone from the graves include sharpening stones, hammerstones, and fire-making kits of flint and iron pyrites. Organic remains include several beaver teeth, but objects of shell are conspicuous by their absence. Whole shells and fragments of what probably were quahog shells were found at the village site, but we do not know whether or not they are from an early Woodland context.

From a study of such artifacts and records pertaining to East Creek which survive today, Stephen Loring has in some cases been able to identify the specific artifacts from specific burials. One of these, Burial 31, is unusual in the inclusion of artifacts not found with any of the other burials. These include an unworked quartz crystal, a stone plummet (commonly found in Archaic contexts), and the most significant artifact, a small pottery vessel. This pot is described as steep sided with a broad rounded base. It is 15 cm in height and 22 cm in diameter. Decorative elements consist of incised line-filled triangles that occur below the rim. Louise Basa believes that the vessel's incised decoration is similar to the Boucher incised pot, except that the decoration does not extend to the lip.

Despite the obvious problems involved in assessing all these early Woodland mortuary data—lack of radiocarbon dates for temporal control and the differential rates of preservation, to name but two—the four cemeteries by necessity form the basis for interpreting the early Woodland occupation in Vermont. Of value also is Mariella Squire's study of projectile point types and distribution. Included in her work were two major early Woodland types: Meadowood side-notched and Adena lobate-stemmed; a third type, which may be a variant of the Adena point, is similar to what are called Lagoon points elsewhere in the Northeast and which are contemporaneous with Adena (Figure 4–6). Squire's research was confined to the Champlain Valley, and the majority of points examined were surface finds. Some, however, did occur at previously known sites such as Donovan and Auclair (see pages 54, 65). More recently, a fragment of a Meadowood point was found at one of the Chace Mill Sites in Burlington. The thin, corner-notched Meadowood projectiles, characterized by their fine workmanship, are generally smaller than their New York counterparts. The dominant type of raw material used in their manufacture is western Onondaga flint from New York, and less commonly, local cherts and quartzites. These points are widely distributed in the Champlain Valley from the Canadian border southward to the Poultney River. All have been found on rises within a quarter of a mile of navigable streams, but tend to cluster at the mouths of rivers and creeks. In contrast to Meadowood points, the majority of the lobate-stemmed Adena points are flaked from local black chert, such as that found at Mount Independence; but local quartzite, Onondaga flint and Flint Ridge, Ohio raw materials are also identified. These points are found most commonly along open rivers and marshlands in the northern portion of the valley. A similar distribution pattern is suggested for Lagoon-like points, with frequencies decreasing as one moves from north to south. These, too, are also made primarily of local cherts, but are differentiated from Adena points on the basis of their cruder workmanship and wider range of variation in form.

Early Woodland Culture

Combining the available data, then, our current perceptions of this prehistoric period can be briefly summarized as follows. First, evidence of early Woodland peoples is concentrated in the Champlain Valley, although they might have been present in the Connecticut Valley as well. Early Woodland cemeteries have been found along the Connecticut in Massachusetts, and Stephen Loring reports that a blocked-end tube is known from Woodstock, which is most accessible from the Connecticut Valley, via the Ottauquechee River; more investigation of the Connecticut Valley is needed.

In the Champlain Valley, both cemeteries and concentrations of surface-collected points are found within easy access of the lake. This distribution may well reflect reality, rather than sampling error. Among the numerous "indeterminate" Woodland sites known outside the Champlain Valley, none of the diagnostic early Woodland markers—either Vinette I pottery or projectile point types—have been recognized. Also, the size and composition of the cemeteries tend to suggest larger aggregations of people than were identified during Archaic times, perhaps the beginning of a settling-in process as small groups of people regularly came together at the same spots along rivers for a common purpose. The ceremonialism associated with such ritual activities involved many elements that were seen in the earlier Archaic cultism, such as the use of red ochre and the procurement of exotic raw materials. More specifically, it is in the Glacial Kame burials from Isle La Motte that we see the first practice of cremation and burial in special cemeteries apart from settlement sites, as well as placement in graves of copper adzes, beads of copper and shell, gorgets, and a Meadowood-like projectile. Early Woodland people, evidently, expanded upon earlier beliefs and practices, judging from the quantity and quality of their burial goods and by the even more elaborate modes of burial.

And what can be inferred about daily life from the utilitarian items found in mortuary contexts? Burial inclusions suggest that generalized hunting, fishing, and gathering activities continued from Archaic times. Hunting practices included the use of the spear and atlatl, indicated by large projectiles and a variety of atlatl weights, and deer, bear, beaver, mink, and fox remains document at least some of the animals that were utilized. Two by-products of hunting, thongs and skin containers, as well as the presence of awls, scrapers, and knives, denote hide and skin processing activities, probably for clothing as well as for containers. Evidence for fishing and collecting is provided by fishhooks and by edible wild plant remains (beechnuts and acorns). Wild plants were also used for textiles and cordage. The acorns may have been roasted over hot stones in pits; such an acorn roasting pit is known from the East Creek Village site. As was the case during Archaic times, heavy woodworking activities were important; the presence of celts, adzes, and gouges might attest to the manufacture of dugout canoes. Wood was also fashioned into handles for piercing and incising tools. Tubular pipes were most likely associated with ritual rather than with secular smoking activities.

Taken together, the early Woodland data strongly suggest an *in situ* development from late Archaic times. To the general continuities already identified might be added a few instances of Archaic artifacts found in the cemeteries. These include the plummet and ground slate point at East Creek; Brewerton projectile points at Boucher, East Creek, and Swanton; and an Orient Fishtail point identified at Swanton. There is evidence, too, that when foreign elements were introduced, they appear to have been adopted with some local variation or elaboration. Vinette I pottery, for example, is typically undecorated in New York, yet lines and triangles were incised on two vessels in the Vermont cemeteries. Similarly, elaboration of a blocked-end tube in the form of an incised bird occurred at Swanton. Local lithic resources were often used in the manufacture of all three early Woodland projectile points. Although Onondaga chert is identified as the dominant raw material used in the manufacture of Meadowood points, it is significant that the local versions are smaller in size than the New York forms. Also of significance is the fact that both Adena and the Lagoon-like points were more commonly made of local cherts than of exotic materials.

Early and Middle Woodland Trade Networks

The presence in the Champlain Valley of blocked-end tubes of Ohio Valley fireclay, Flint Ridge lithics, and other raw materials and items indigenous to the Adena heartland has been of particular interest since the Perkins era; indeed, the nature of the "Adena connection" is the source of continuing debate. One of the theories to account for this material in the Northeast is through an actual migration of peoples from the Ohio Valley into the region. The earliest champion of Adena migration was, of course, Perkins; more recent proponents are Ritchie and Don Dragoo, who propose a south to north dispersal pattern. Their hypothesis was formulated by means of a statistical analysis of Adena-Middlesex traits and the distribution of Middlesex sites throughout the Northeast. The results of their work suggested to them a route of travel from the Ohio Valley via the Monongahela and Potomac valleys to Chesapeake Bay; from this center on the Atlantic coast, Adena groups moved northward through Delaware and New Jersey and into New York and New England via the Delaware, Hudson, and Connecticut rivers. Pointing out specific groupings of Middlesex burial sites in the Champlain, Mohawk, and Connecticut valleys, they suggested that in these areas, Adena peoples, by whatever means, "obtained tenure" and ultimately merged with the resident populations.

Ritchie and Dragoo's conclusions have been criticized on statistical grounds, and indeed Dragoo himself no longer holds to the migration hypothesis. Moreover, the kind of deliberate, long distance migration pattern originally proposed by Ritchie and Dragoo is certainly uncommon among historically known peoples who rely on hunting and gathering for a significant percentage of their subsistence resources. This is not to say that such a migration could not have occurred; merely that it seems unlikely, particularly if one can find a more economical explanation of the evidence. In view of what we know about the prominence of trade in the early Woodland cultures of the Great Lakes region and the Ohio Valley, the role of the Great Lakes–St. Lawrence Corridor as a trade route both in late Archaic as well as early middle Woodland times, and the distribution of Glacial Kame and early Woodland materials in the Champlain Valley, the most likely explanation is that there was no significant influx of outsiders into Vermont in early Woodland times. Rather, native Vermonters were participants in an extensive long distance trade network, and this brought midwestern goods as well as ideas down into the Champlain Valley from the St. Lawrence Valley in the north.

With the early Woodland period, participation in long distance trade reached its peak in Vermont. By early middle Woodland times, there were fewer imports of exotic ceremonial and ornamental objects. Nonetheless, flints and cherts from foreign sources continued to be used for the production of some tools, and the close similarity of Vermont's pottery to that made throughout much of the Northeast indicates that wide ranging contacts were still maintained. Nevertheless, these apparently continued to decline, as reflected by the increasing regional differentiation and technological decline of pottery (though more varied in form and shape, late middle Woodland pottery is much less well made than before). Finally, by very late middle Woodland times, regular exchange with peoples at any distance seems to have ceased altogether as native Vermonters turned almost exclusively to local raw materials for the production of their tools.

We do not yet know what brought about the decline of long distance trade in Vermont and the Northeast. It does not seem to have been brought about by any local crisis, for the evidence indicates that conditions were favorable enough to support continued and steady population growth into and through middle Woodland times in the Champlain, and possibly Connecticut, valleys. Probably the causes are related to the decline of Hopewellian culture in the Midwest. If, as seems likely, Hopewellian peoples played a key role in controlling and maintaining long distance trade throughout much of eastern North America, then the decline of their influence could easily have led to a breakup of that trade.

Decline of Ceremonialism

In Vermont, as in much of the Northeast, cultures took on a more secular emphasis as long distance trade declined. This is perhaps not surprising since early Woodland burial cults clearly had their inspiration in the Midwest, and many objects and/or materials associated with burial ceremonialism were themselves imported from the Midwest. In any event, by middle Woodland times, ceremonial and ornamental items generally were much less prominent than they had been, and mortuary ceremonialism had been abandoned in favor of relatively simple disposal of the dead in living sites or other convenient places, rather than special cemeteries. Possibly this reflects a greater sense of security on the part of middle Woodland peoples, for it is an anthropological truth that most of a people's ritual activities are attempts to impose their control on aspects of nature which cause them anxiety, and which do not yield to more direct organizational and technological control. Thus, ritual activity tends to be more marked in times of crisis than otherwise. Perhaps the same improvement in subsistence resources which permitted peoples from the upper Hudson Valley to return to southwestern Vermont towards the end of middle Woodland times played a role as well in the decline of interest in elaborate burial ceremonialism. The rise of that ceremonialism in the first place seems to correlate pretty well with the climatic changes which are thought to have been responsible for the withdrawal of peoples from southwestern Vermont by early Woodland times.

The Late Woodland Period in Vermont

However isolated people in Vermont may have been by the end of middle Woodland times, they were not altogether cut off from what was going on elsewhere in the Northeast, and it was not long before they were once again selectively borrowing ideas and innovations from outside sources. Many of these were of a minor sort, comparable to the periodic changes in late Archaic projectile point styles that were described in Chapter 3. But in late Woodland times (after A.D. 1000) it was not so much projectile point styles that changed. Indeed, Levanna points continued to be the "standard" projectile points throughout the period, and they continued to be made of local stones, mostly quartzite, but also chert from places like Mount Independence and St. Albans. However, collections from the Champlain Valley appear to include a few small, triangular Madison points. In New York State, Madison points were the exclusive Iroquois projectile style, but are rare in the Hudson Valley and around Lake George. This and their rarity in Vermont no doubt relate to an absence of any late Woodland occupation by Iroquoian peoples of regions which, at the dawn of Historic times, were occupied by speakers of Algonquian languages.

Unlike projectiles, pottery in Vermont underwent a number of changes in late Woodland times: in vessel shape, techniques of manufacture, and decorative modes (Figures 4–4 and 4–11). These paralleled developments elsewhere in the Northeast, which in New York State culminated in the ceramics of the Five Nations Iroquois (Seneca, Cayuga, Onondaga, Oneida, and Mohawk). For this reason, late Woodland pottery from Vermont has often been referred to as "Iroquoian," with the implication of an actual Iroquoian occupation of the state. More recently, it has been well-documented that "Iroquoian" ceramics were made by non-Iroquoian peoples as well. For example, the Algonquian-speaking Mahicans of the upper Hudson Valley made and used pottery not unlike that of their Mohawk neighbors to the west. Because a number of elements characteristic of late Woodland pottery in New York appear to be later in Vermont, it looks as if most, if not all, the similarities between late Woodland pottery in Vermont and New York are the result of diffusion in generally south and west to north and east directions.

In New York State where they are known best, these changes began with what is known as Owasco pottery, in vogue between about A.D. 1000 and 1300. Owasco vessels show a gradual change from the conoidal bases of late middle Woodland pottery to globular, round-bottom forms. Midway through Owasco times, thickened, squarish, or everted lip forms were replaced by collars, sometimes with castellations. Decoration took the form of cord impressions, linear stamping in geometric motifs, and occasional

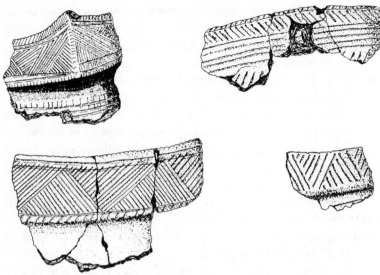

FIGURE 4–11. Late Woodland pottery sherds from Vermont. On the upper left is a sherd found somewhere along the Missisquoi River that shows incised decoration on a high collared rim in the style of the St. Lawrence Iroquois. The other sherds, all from the Ewing site, show Owasco-like corded decoration on a rim (*upper right*); Chance-like incised decoration on a low collared rim (*lower left*); corded decoration on a low collared rim similar to New York's Oak Hill Corded style (*lower right*). All are shown one-half actual size.

incising confined to the upper portions of the vessels, but cord-paddled exterior surfaces also occur.

After A.D. 1300, the globular form continued, as did decoration of thickened rims or collars with cord impressions. This latter technique was gradually replaced by incising, with lines oriented in horizontal, oblique, and chevron designs. At about the same time, a change in the method of manufacture occurred: coiling was replaced, at least in New York, by the paddle and anvil technique. Exterior surfaces were no longer cord-malleated, but smoothed. The application of incised decorative motifs occurred most commonly on collars; however, necks and shoulders were occasionally decorated. Castellated and notched collars became more frequent toward the end of late Woodland times.

The one really substantive innovation that seems to have been adopted by Vermont's peoples in late Woodland times was limited horticulture. In what is now New York State, people were planting and harvesting corn, beans, and squash by A.D. 1100 (with a good possibility that they were doing so by as early as A.D. 900 in the Mohawk Valley). In Vermont, the earliest evidence for corn, if not beans and squash, comes from the Donohue site in Burlington's Intervale, excavated in 1978 by Peter Thomas. Thomas's excavations were limited, and the protection of the remainder of the site has been ensured by its nomination to the National Register of Historic Places.

The Donohue Site and the Adoption of Horticulture

The Donohue site is located on a sandy levee along the western edge of a slough, itself just west of the Winooski River. The effects of floodplain dynamics were observed by Thomas and his assistant, Pamela Bumstead; there is some evidence that a portion of the site has eroded, while heavy silty loam flood deposits have built up over the site, protecting it from disturbance by plowing. The site today is approximately 125 m × 75 m in size, but to the east and across the slough at a slightly lower elevation, testing revealed the presence of another site, known simply as Vt-Ch-95. Similarities in the cultural remains and in stratigraphic characteristics suggest that both sites were occupied at the same time. If they were jointly occupied, total site size would be approximately 110 m × 287 m. Two radiocarbon dates from Donohue (Figure 4–2) indicate that the site was occupied at least twice, if not continuously, between at least A.D. 1470–1480, if not A.D. 1360, and sometime in the seventeenth century.

Some twenty-two features were identified at Donohue, including multiple hearths and globular-shaped storage pits. In addition to food preparation and storage, the artifacts and organic remains indicate that hunting, gathering, fishing, and horticultural activities took place at the site, as did the manufacture of stone tools. In addition to numerous lithic flakes, the majority of quartzite, the stone tools included five Levanna projectile points, biface cutting tools and scrapers, and a stone tabular rod which may have been used as a pestle for the preparation of nuts. Another possible food processing tool is an unburned deer mandible.

Such mandibles have been referred to in early archaeological literature as "corn graters," and were apparently used to remove kernels from the cobs by some historic peoples.

At least ten pottery vessels were identified among the sherd collection. These resemble Owasco ceramics from New York and exhibit squarish lips and smoothed interior surfaces. Exterior surfaces were smoothed or smoothed-over cord paddling. Rim and collar decorations consist of cord impressions, incising, dentate, and parallel linear stamping.

The inventory of organic remains clearly indicates a varied diet. In addition to three corn cobs and a number of individual kernels, other species include the remains of fish and deer (one specimen is the toe bone of an immature animal), butternuts, grapes, and acorns. Simultaneous use of some of these resources, such as butternuts, corn, and grapes, is documented by their association together in the same hearths. This particular example would suggest an early fall occupation. However, because some of the pits, presumably used for storing corn or nuts, were emptied and subsequently used as hearths, a longer occupation may be the case. It is assumed that a gap between the period of harvest and consumption is thus represented, which could extend the occupation well into the winter season. People must also have been at the site at least as early as late spring, in order to plant the corn. They may have fished as well, for spring fishing is good in the Winooski. However, there is no proof for this. The fish remains which were recovered at Donohue all were in association with butternut remains, so the fish from which they came were caught later in the year.

We do not yet have sufficient evidence to be sure about just when native horticulture came to Vermont, but the dates from Donohue suggest that it may have been a lot later than New York. Throughout the Northeast, native people were accustomed to storing their corn, along with other foods, in pits similar to those seen at the Donohue site. In New York, food storage pits appear occasionally as early as A.D. 400 to 500, and became common thereafter. Presumably they were first used for the storage of wild foods, but became common as horticulture caught on. In Vermont, storage pits are conspicuous by their absence at both the Winooski and McNeil Generating sites, and so it seems that people in Vermont did not begin storing their food in such pits until five or six hundred years at least after people began doing so in New York. Of course, this doesn't prove that native horticulture came later to Vermont, but it is suggestive. Moreover, it is consistent with other evidence of conservatism on the part of people in Vermont that we shall review shortly.

Of course, the growing of corn and other crops in Vermont had to wait until strains had developed which could cope with the short growing season. On the other hand, once crops could be grown in the Mohawk Valley, it shouldn't have been long before they could be grown in the Champlain Valley. It would seem that Vermont's people were in no hurry to become farmers.

The apparent reluctance of Vermont's people to take up farming may come as a surprise to those accustomed to thinking of this mode of subsistence as superior to hunting and gathering. But evidence from various parts of the world indicates that hunters and gatherers do not necessarily see things this way. The invention of farming in the first place, at least in southwest Asia and Mexico, seems to have been an accidental by-product of an intensification of existing hunting and gathering subsistence patterns. Even at that, it took several thousand years for these people to become full-time farmers. In some other places, such as coastal South America, farming may even have been a subsistence strategy of last resort, which hunters and gatherers took up only because they had no real choice. Indeed, some people in the world did not abandon hunting and gathering as a way of life until the past few decades; there are even cases of people who have abandoned farming in favor of hunting and gathering.

FIGURE 4–12. This photograph shows one of the corn cobs found at the Donohue site. Photo courtesy Peter A. Thomas.

The reluctance of hunters and gatherers to become farmers is understandable, so long as these activities continue to provide them with all the food they need. The hunter is free from tedious routine, and his daily activities are more exciting. He hunts when he needs food, which, except in the harshest environments, does not require long hours, day after day, as does farming. In the Kalahari desert, for example, Bushmen hunters work no more than twelve to nineteen hours a week. Thus, hunters have ample time to relax and enjoy themselves. Gathering is somewhat more tedious, but there are times when the whole family can camp under a tree that bears tasty and nutritious nuts in abundance. It is an eminently satisfactory way of living together in small, intimate groups. Farming, if practiced full-time, brings with it a whole new system of human relationships that offers no easily understood advantages, and disturbs an age-old balance between humans and nature and among the people who live together.

It seems likely that Vermont's peoples finally adopted such farming as they did only because it fit in very well with what they were already doing. Ignoring, for the moment, the corn, the organic remains from Donohue indicate that its late Woodland inhabitants lived there at the same time of year, and ate the same kinds of foods, as did their middle Woodland forebears at the Winooski and McNeil Generating sites. Their villages seem to have been located in places which, purely by chance, were admirably suited for the growing of crops. Furthermore, they could be planted, tended, and harvested without too much interference with traditional spring through fall hunting, fishing, and gathering activities. Finally, the cultivation of crops did not necessarily mark a significant departure from traditional subsistence activities. To one degree or another, hunters and gatherers actively manage the wild food resources on which they depend, and part-time horticultural activities could easily have been viewed as no more than an intensification of resource management techniques.

Other Late Woodland Sites

Another site occupied in late Woodland times was the Ewing site. This seems to represent a continuation of the previously discussed middle Woodland occupation (see page 108). The bulk of the more than 2000 pottery sherds recovered in the course of all excavations at this site are typically late Woodland types. The majority of the ninety-two vessels identified in Varney's collection exhibit features characteristic of Owasco ceramics. Over half have square lips and smoothed interior surfaces. One-third of these vessels are decorated with variable applications of cord impression, confined primarily to rims and necks. Among the collared vessels, incising is the prevalent decorative technique, appearing primarily on necks and rims, and less commonly on body surfaces. Petersen's assessment of the ceramic sequence is that of an intensive, if not continuous, occupation by late Woodland peoples throughout Owasco times and well into what in New York is called the Oak Hill phase, dated there between A.D. 1300 to 1400 and beyond. The presence of a vessel reminiscent of Chance pottery from New York, in vogue after A.D. 1400, would represent the latest ceramic expression in the long sequence that occurred at Ewing.

The flotation of soil samples by Vivian Catania, a student at the University of Vermont, has provided some information regarding resource utilization. Samples were derived from what is presumed to be the late Woodland occupation, and analysis suggests that fishing (as would be expected) and hunting were of primary importance. Bone constituted the highest percentage of remains in the samples, which also included lithic flakes, sherds, charcoal, and small amounts of Chenopodium seeds, butternut shells, snail shells, and fish scales. Among the species identified are perch, bullhead, northern pike, and muskrat. Quantities of small mammal bones, possible bird bone, and a fragment of turtle carapace were also recovered. In addition to Catania's study, other animal species have been identified in the past. Some of these may, however, represent earlier occupations as well as late Woodland. The inventory includes deer, moose, beaver, bear, mussel, and possible fisher. Remains of three dogs, two apparently butchered and exhibiting some charring, were encountered during the excavations of the Burlington Chapter of the Vermont Archaeological Society. Information on relative frequencies is not available, but the plethora of fish bone certainly suggests summer, if not spring and fall activities; the presence of Chenopodium seeds and butternuts surely verifies fall activity. Thus, summer/fall can be considered as the minimal period of seasonal occupation.

An example of a different type of site occurs at Chipman's Point in Addison County. A long, low, stratified rock shelter, excavated by John Bailey in 1938, is of particular interest on account of the presence of human burials. The site is located on a limestone bluff, with the base of the talus approximately thirty-six feet above Lake Champlain. The rock overhang extends about 120 feet along the bluff and ranges in depth from ten to thirteen feet. Two occupational strata were identified by Bailey. On the basis of projectile point types and the absence of pottery, he concluded that the earlier midden represented the activities of a small Archaic group who utilized only about one-third of the shelter, apparently at the western end. Evidence of a late Woodland group was encountered in both eastern and western portions of the shelter in a stratum ranging in depth from eight inches to two feet. He described the later inhabitants as "bringing with them a good grade of pottery and arrows tipped with triangular points. They also used bone awls, fishhooks, and harpoons, and appear to have turned cannibal on at least one occasion."

That these people engaged in hunting, collecting, fishing, and fowling is documented by the artifacts and animal remains identified in the refuse. Stone artifacts include a corner-notched chert point and three black chert triangular forms, one with a corner removed by flaking. Bone-working activities are inferred by the presence of split beaver incisors and a worked bear canine, all of which may have been used as gravers; among the bone tools are two awls, a complete unbarbed fishhook, grooved at the end of the shaft to facilitate the attachment to a line, the "harpoon," represented by two fragments, each with six shallow barbs, and a thin rectangular object, identified by Bailey as a spatula for pottery manufacture. The pottery descriptions and illustrations of castellated collars and cord-impressed and incised decorations are indicative of both Owasco and Oak Hill ceramics.

The range of animal species found in the midden is impressive: in addition to food, many could have provided skins, raw materials for tools or served other purposes. These include white-tailed deer, bear, beaver, muskrat, porcupine, raccoon, mink, red squirrel, bobcat, small wolf or dog, woodchuck, and fox. Fragments of turtle shell were present, as well as two caches of mussel shells, one containing more than 300 specimens, resting on a bed of

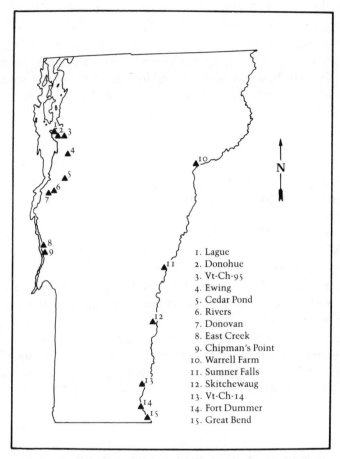

FIGURE 4–13. Late Woodland sites in Vermont.

1. Lague
2. Donohue
3. Vt-Ch-95
4. Ewing
5. Cedar Pond
6. Rivers
7. Donovan
8. East Creek
9. Chipman's Point
10. Warrell Farm
11. Sumner Falls
12. Skitchewaug
13. Vt-Ch-14
14. Fort Dummer
15. Great Bend

limestone. Numerous fish bones were unidentifiable by species; bird included heath hen, Canada goose, thick-billed guillemot (a species of auk), and barred owl. Obviously, those who made use of the rock shelter were accomplished hunters.

The remains of two humans were located at the eastern end of the shelter. The first, an 18-year-old girl, had been badly disturbed by pothunters. The second, a 45-year-old woman, was represented by deposits in three locations. Two vertebrae were recovered from a hearth at the back wall; nearby, a pile of badly shattered scapulae (shoulder blades), ribs, and long bones, along with six mussel shells and a chert chip were encountered. The third deposit, a few feet away, had been covered with a limestone slab. The skull, complete with mandible, was found on top of the bones. All of the long bones had been split lengthwise; animal bones, treated in the same fashion, were also found intermixed with the human remains, a situation that suggested cannibalistic practices to Bailey.

It is hard to know what to make of this apparent cannibalism. Ritual cannibalism has been well documented for the Iroquois, and evidence for the practice appears in late Woodland sites in Iroquois country. In New England, by contrast, archaeological evidence for cannibalism is next to nonexistent. Moreover, people like the Mahicans and western Abenakis referred to their Mohawk neighbors by names considered to be something less than complimentary, and which meant "maneaters." One possibility is that we have here at Chipman's Point a victim of an Iroquoian raid across the lake. The victim may be described as having a head neither particularly round, nor long and narrow, but something in between. She had a high vault, high narrow face, high rectangular eye orbits, and a nasal opening of medium size.

Apparently, there was a substantial late Woodland occupation of the East Creek Village site, previously mentioned in connection with the early Woodland cemetery (see page 125). Both Owasco and post-Owasco pottery seems to be present. A somewhat enigmatic "Iroquoian Pot," illustrated by John Huden in his book, *Archaeology in Vermont*, was decorated with broad, parallel incised lines, crudely executed, running in zig-zag fashion from the rim to the base.

Bailey's reports on the Donovan and Rivers sites suggest that both were occupied in late Woodland times. At Donovan, over 200 triangular projectile points were recovered, the majority manufactured of quartzite. At least eleven collared pottery vessels are represented in the collection of over 600 sherds, with cord impressions, smoothed interior surfaces, and horizontal, oblique, and vertical incised decorations indicating Owasco and Oak Hill influences. A reconstructed vessel, recovered from a pit, has a notched, castellated collar, decorated with horizontal and oblique incised lines. The presence of ten drilled holes shows that the

vessel had been broken and attempts made to repair it. In addition
to Bailey, both Brooks and Basa also identify late Woodland occupations at Rivers, with Brooks's temporal placement encom-
passing early and late Owasco.

Numerous other sites are known in the Champlain Valley, but
for the most part they are represented by sparse materials suggestive of camps or other short-term occupations. An exception is
the Lague site in the Winooski Intervale, which may have been a
sizeable village. Levanna and other late Woodland variants have a
wide distribution, occurring along the lakeshore, on the lower
reaches of virtually all of the major rivers, and on the shores of
inland ponds and larger lakes, such as Lake St. Catherine. This is
the same pattern—large villages on the lower reaches of the
larger rivers, with a variety of smaller hunting, fishing, and gathering sites in a variety of environmental settings—that we saw
for middle Woodland times.

Some of the Champlain Valley materials indicate relationships
with the St. Lawrence Iroquois to the north. The famous Colches-

FIGURE 4–14. These two vessels were found in Bolton, Vermont in the
nineteenth century. The one on the right, found lying on the floor of a
rock shelter near Bolton Falls resembles pottery in vogue in New York
in the sixteenth century A.D. When full, it had a twelve-quart capacity.
The vessel on the left, which held about fourteen quarts when full,
shows some resemblance to New York's Chance pottery, in vogue after
A.D. 1400. Photos by John D. Owen, courtesy Fleming Museum.

ter Jar (Figure 5-9), discovered in 1825 and housed in Fleming Museum, as well as several unprovenienced sherds from the Missisquoi area, are similar in design elements to pottery produced by these peoples who lived along the lower St. Lawrence between Montreal and Quebec City. Their ceramics are distinguished from contemporaneous materials in New York on the basis of a high degree of vessel elaboration, particularly in design motifs. A ceramic chronology established at the Beaumier site, located on the St. Maurice River approximately 24 km down the St. Lawrence from the mouth of the Richelieu, suggests that the Colchester Jar and similar pottery in Vermont fits most comfortably into a timespan of A.D. 1400 to 1550. It appears that influences were moving both ways; Roger Marois has recognized relationships with Vermont at Beaumier, as well. The St. Lawrence Iroquois disappeared by 1603, most likely dispersed (or annihilated) by the Mohawks, Hurons, or Algonquians. It has been suggested by Bruce Trigger and James Pendergast that some refugee groups may have been absorbed by other peoples, including the Abenaki. While the presence of pottery similar to St. Lawrence ceramics is not necessarily an indication that St. Lawrence Iroquois were in the Champlain Valley before 1603, the possibility exists. More likely, the ceramic similarities merely represent the last prehistoric manifestation of interaction between peoples of the Champlain and St. Lawrence valleys which began during Archaic times.

As previously discussed, the presence of late Woodland artifacts in the southwestern portion of the state has been documented by Thomas. Based on his assessment of the Gordon Sweeney collection, Levanna points and castellated pottery are common at a number of sites on the Hoosic River in Pownal. A mile-long stretch of the Walloomsac River in the Bennington area may have been extensively used, perhaps in the form of a series of base camps, during late Woodland times. Thomas further reports parallels between this area and the southern end of Lake Champlain, particularly late Woodland manifestations on inland bodies of water such as Lake St. Catherine, which may suggest utilization of the region by peoples of the upper Hudson drainage. It should be remembered that southwestern Vermont was considered Mahican territory at the start of Historic times.

Compared to the middle Woodland period, more sites are known in the Connecticut River Valley, but most have been identified only on the basis of surface collections. One exception is the Warrel Farm site, which is located on the east bank of the Passumpsic River in East Barnet, approximately one mile from the river's mouth at the Connecticut. During the course of contract work associated with a highway project, three small areas of refuse were identified along an area approximately 100 m in length. Each consisted of charcoal, calcined bone, and small sherds. The dispersed nature of the sparse remains, indicating transitory camps, in conjunction with the proximity of a series of small waterfalls, strongly suggest that the function of the Warrel Farm site was that of a portage. The small ceramic assemblage is seemingly Owasco-related, with cord-paddled exterior surfaces and cord-impressed decorations. One sherd, representing a collar decorated by notching and horizontal incised lines, is probably indicative of a post-Owasco occupation. Similarly, the bulk of the ceramics recovered at the Sumner Falls site, discussed previously, appears to fall within the Owasco pottery complex.

Further south in the Connecticut Valley, late Woodland ceramics have been identified by Petersen at four additional sites. While the predominant occupation at Skitchewaug is middle Woodland, two sherds, each representing a single vessel, may be late Woodland. A rimsherd with an everted lip is decorated with cord impressions characteristic of Owasco, while an incised pattern exhibited on the second sherd may represent a Chance incised motif.

Still further south, in Windham County, seven sherds were collected by Walter Needham at a site known simply as Vt-Wd-14, on Dummerston Island, opposite Catsbane Island in Dummerston. All seven are from a single vessel that had been repaired with the aid of drilled holes. The cord impressions and incised decorations present on the collar are suggestive of Oak Hill decorative techniques. Oak Hill is also suggested by the decoration on a single aboriginal sherd excavated at Fort Dummer in Brattleboro, the site of the first British settlement in Vermont (1724 to 1760). The association of the sherd with historic debris could reflect the fact that the fort also operated as a trading post, or merely that a prehistoric occupation was disturbed by British activities.

A wide variety of European trade materials, as well as sherds representing twelve aboriginal vessels was collected in the Great Bend area of Vernon by Walter Needham in 1936. This site is located on the west bank of the Connecticut near the mouth of the Ashuelot River. All vessels were smoothed on their interior surfaces, all had collars, and the majority of these were notched. Castellations occurred in two cases, and both were incised, most combining vertical, horizontal, or oblique orientations. The ceramics are clearly post-Owasco, and Petersen believes they relate to the early Historic period, a determination suggested by the trade goods as well as the site's location, across the Connecticut from the Sokoki Fort Hill site at Hinsdale, New Hampshire (a village we will discuss in chapters 5 and 6). Furthermore, historic accounts refer to a large, important village at the Great Bend occupied by Sokoki peoples and refugee groups. This being so, then it seems that the evolution of ceramics in Vermont, while following the generalized New York sequence, may have proceeded at a different pace. That decorative motifs may have persisted for a longer period of time than is true for their counterparts in New York may also be suggested by the late dates at the Donohue site in the Champlain Valley. It is further confirmed by evidence from the Ewing site, where pottery continued to be made by coiling long after the paddle and anvil technique had been adopted in New York. In fact, potters in the Connecticut Valley were still making pottery by the coiling technique as recently as the winter of 1663/64, for the coils for such pots have been found at Fort Hill.

Summary

With our discussion of the late Woodland period, we have reached the end of prehistoric times in Vermont. By then, a way of life which emerged thousands of years earlier, in late Archaic times, had been significantly refined and enriched, often by the borrowing of outside ideas and innovations. But in their borrowing, Vermont's peoples did not slavishly imitate any of their neighbors. Rather, they were selective about their borrowing, went about it in their own good time, and put their own distinctive stamp upon the things that they did borrow. The result was a rich and varied culture, not unlike those of other peoples in the Northeast, but not quite like them, either. In the next chapter, we shall take a closer look at what this culture had become by the time the French and British arrived in northeastern North America.

5 · LIFE IN VERMONT ON THE EVE OF EUROPEAN PENETRATION

WHEN the first French and English settlers came to North America, they were singularly ill prepared to secure their own survival. Among other problems, they were incapable of providing for their own subsistence and so were dependent on the regular shipment of basic commodities from their homelands across the sea. For example, ploughing and planting at Quebec did not begin until twenty years after its founding in 1608. So long as supplies from the home country continued to arrive in good time, the existence of European settlements was assured; any interruption placed their existence in jeopardy. Given the hazards of ocean voyages, and the indifference of suppliers back home, it is not surprising that the French and British in North America were frequently faced with desperate situations which brought them to the brink of starvation. If they managed to survive, it was only because of assistance offered by the native peoples.

The Western Abenakis and their Neighbors

One such desperate situation was faced by French settlers at Quebec in the winter of 1628. Food supplies were running short when, in the nick of time, some Montagnais arrived with news of a people to the southeast—the direction of the winter sunrise—who were willing to furnish aid. The Montagnais' name for these southeasterners was "Dawn Land People," and Abenaki is a corruption of the Montagnais word.

The Abenakis of whom the Montagnais spoke lived in what today is the state of Maine, and by 1637 it had become the custom among the French to refer to all those Maine natives who traded at Quebec as Abenakis. Much later, the term was extended to cover all those peoples native to the lands extending from the Penobscot River watershed westward to Lake Champlain and the

Richelieu River, from the St. Lawrence River south to a boundary which ran, approximately, from Lake Champlain west and south of Otter Creek to the height of land in the Green Mountains, south into northern Massachusetts, and over to the coast north of the Saco River passing somewhere near Deerfield and Northfield, Massachusetts and Manchester, New Hampshire (see Figure 5–1). It is ironic that these people should be known today by someone else's name for them, for they had a perfectly good name for themselves. In western Abenaki dialect it is *Alnôbak*, which means "ordinary people," as opposed to monsters, giants, and all other peoples.

In the early seventeenth century, the Abenakis consisted of several independent groups of people who, at various times, for various reasons, and in various combinations, occasionally entered into loose political alliances with one another and with their eastern neighbors, the Passamaquoddies and Maliseets of eastern Maine and New Brunswick and the Micmacs of Nova Scotia. Collectively these Wabanakis, as the Abenakis and their eastern neighbors are called today, show considerable linguistic and cultural unity when compared to their neighbors, the Iroquoian-speaking Mohawks to the west, the central Algonquian-speaking Cree-Montagnais-Naskapi north of the St. Lawrence, and the various Algonquian-speaking peoples of the Hudson Valley and southern New England. However, there are sufficient linguistic and cultural differences among the Wabanakis to justify making certain distinctions among them. Among the Abenakis, a distinction must be made between easterners and westerners. The easterners, who actually differ very little from the Passamaquoddies and Maliseets, include the Amarascoggins, Kennebecs, and Penobscots of Maine. Westerners include the Penacooks and Winnipesaukees of the upper Merrimack; Sokokis (known to the British as Squakhaegs) and Cowasucks on the middle and upper Connecticut; and the *Mazipskoiák* (Missisquoi) and others on the rivers of western Vermont. It is not clear whether or not the Pigwackets, of the upper Saco River, were westerners or easterners. Culturally, the westerners did more in the way of farming than did the easterners, who, for their part, devoted more attention to the utilization of coastal resources. Linguistically, westerners and easterners spoke different dialects of Abenaki language. There is a nice illustration of the difference in Thoreau's book, *The Maine Woods.* In the Moosehead region, he and his Penobscot guide ran across a native from St. Francis who was clearly a western Abenaki. The two natives were able to converse quite well in their native tongue, but they were aware of dialectical differences. At one point they sat down and compared these differences, much as a contemporary "down-easter" from the coast of Maine and someone from the middle Atlantic region might compare dialects.

It is generally agreed that the Abenakis are the descendants of the late Woodland peoples who inhabited the same region prior to the arrival of Europeans. Therefore, Abenaki culture at the time of European contact gives us a glimpse of what late Woodland culture had become by then. Unfortunately for us, since it was western Abenakis who lived in Vermont, much more has been written about the culture of the easterners. They were the first ones contacted, beginning officially with Verrazano's voyage of 1524. Unofficially, Verrazano was preceded by boatloads of European fishermen who had some contact with the indigenous peoples. The first contact with western Abenakis may have come in 1605, when Champlain visited a village at the mouth of the Saco River. A few years later, in 1616, Ferdinando Gorges, to whom King James had given most of what now is the state of Maine, spent the winter at the mouth of the Saco River. While there, he at least heard of western Abenakis, probably Sokokis and Winnipesaukees. Direct contact with Abenakis living in or near Vermont, however, did not take place until 1642, when the French rescued a Sokoki captive from his Montagnais tormentors. By then, possibly, native Americans were no longer the novelty they once had been. But whatever the reason, early French and English accounts contain a good deal of information on the eastern Abenakis of Maine and their neighbors in the Maritimes, but the French, who knew the western Abenakis best, had surprisingly little to say about them.

Early in the twentieth century, trained ethnographers did valuable work among the few eastern groups which had managed to stay put in their original homelands, recording what was remembered of traditional culture. Here, the work of the late Frank Speck among the Penobscot ranks as outstanding. Unfortunately,

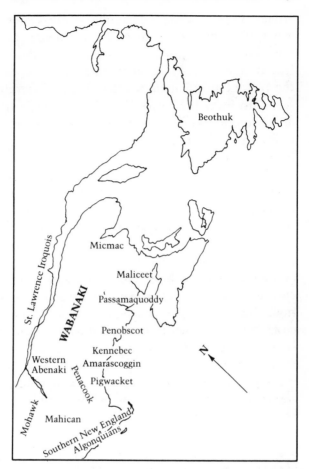

FIGURE 5–1.
The Wabanaki
peoples and
their neighbors.

comparable work was not done among western Abenakis: They
were an almost forgotten people to anthropologists until Gordon
Day, in the 1950s, began his extensive archival and informant
work. It is his work, fleshed out where appropriate with material
from other sources, which forms the basis for our description of
western Abenaki culture as it was in the ethnographic present of
the early seventeenth century.

Western Abenaki Settlement and Subsistence

In Vermont, there were several major bands of western Abenakis,
each of which was associated with a substantial village. These

villages were located on canoeable streams near a major body of water: the Connecticut River on the east and Lake Champlain on the west. Historic sources mention an important Cowasuck village at Newbury, in the Cowas Intervales (*Kowasék*, or "Place of the White Pines"); and a Sokoki village at Northfield, Massachusetts, just south of Vermont (see Figure 1–1). In 1663, the Sokokis (from *Sohkwahkíak*, "The People Who Separated") established a new village at Fort Hill, north of the Ashuelot River a quarter to a half mile from the Connecticut. In western Vermont, villages seem to have been located near the mouths of Otter Creek, the Winooski, Lamoille, and Missisquoi. Two of these survived late enough to be mentioned in historic sources: *Winoskík*, for which the Winooski River was named, and *Mazipskoík*, which was corrupted to Missisquoi. *Winoskík* means "At Wild Onion Land," probably because the land nearby is suitable for the growth of the onion-like wild leek *Allium canadense*. *Mazipskoík*, which eventually became an important collecting point for refugees from elsewhere in New England, means "At the Flint." Day suggests that this refers to an aboriginal chert quarry a few miles south towards St. Albans Bay, but large nodules of flint-like chert are to be found along the lower Missisquoi River itself.

Favored locations for villages were high bluffs, where one could see what was going on in the countryside nearby, and where a sharp lookout could be kept for enemy raiders. The east side of a stream was preferred; this put the stream between the villagers and their traditional enemies, the Iroquois; it also took advantage of the prevailing westerly breezes to blow away summer insects. Palisades which surrounded villages provided further protection from attack. These were built by digging trenches and then burying in them the ends of vertically set logs. They imparted a castle-like quality to the villages, which is why early Europeans often referred to them as "castles." Inside the palisades were built rectangular houses with long arched roofs and round, dome-shaped sweat lodges. The houses, from 20 to 100 feet long and 20 to 30 feet wide, were constructed of two layers of birch or other bark over a frame of poles. Holes in the centerline of roofs permitted the escape of smoke from fires inside the houses.

In Historic times, the Missisquoi village held about 300 people; Thomas estimates about 500 for Fort Hill. It was customary for

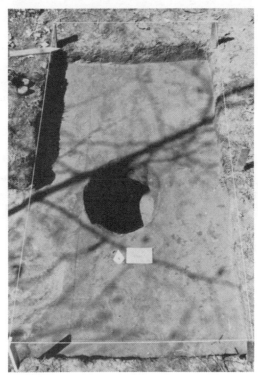

FIGURE 5–2. Two
food storage pits at the
seventeenth-century
Sokoki village at Fort
Hill. One is shown as
it would have appeared
when empty, and the
other is shown filled
with garbage and other
living debris. One
quarter of this pit has
been excavated away,
to show its outline
and the layers of de-
bris in it. Photos cour-
tesy Peter A. Thomas.

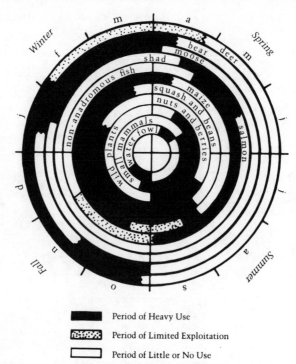

Period of Heavy Use

Period of Limited Exploitation

Period of Little or No Use

FIGURE 5–3. Reconstruction of major dietary con-
stituents in the early seventeenth-century Sokoki
subsistence cycle. From Thomas 1979b, by permission of author.

all these people to spend the deepest and coldest part of the winter in their village, living on food which had earlier been put by
for this purpose. This included dried and smoked meat, maize,
and wild plant foods such as sumac, dried raspberries, blackberries, elderberries, grapes, chokecherries, chestnuts, and butternuts. Thomas estimates that between 3200 and 4000 bushels of
maize were put by at Fort Hill for the winter. Much of this was
stored in mat, basket, or bark-lined pits, each of which held about
four or five bushels. Once emptied of food they served as garbage
pits. During this cold-period sojourn, a special midwinter feast
was held.

Basic to western Abenaki life was a cyclical pattern of subsistence activities, which varied according to the season of the year. Four seasons, calculated by "moons," were recognized. Sometime after the midwinter feast, depending on the severity of the weather and the extent of remaining food reserves, the main hunting season began. Usually, this was sometime in February, at which time everyone except the old and infirm left their village for their upland hunting territories. For the average village of about 500 people, there were roughly twenty-five such territories, each one averaging about twenty miles square. This permits a very rough estimate of population density in that part of Vermont inhabited by Abenakis, ca. A.D. 1600, on the order of one person per square mile. This is considerably lower than population densities in southern New England, which had a native population on the order of 72,000 to 90,000 people at the time of contact. This works out to between 4.97 and 6.22 persons per square mile, although densities are known to have been as high as 109 per square mile in some places (Block Island).

Hunting territories, contrary to popular belief, were not just vaguely defined tracts of wilderness over which people wandered and hunted at will. Rather, they were clearly defined, although not in terms of precise boundaries. The principles involved are the same as those that we discussed for Paleoindians, even though western Abenaki hunting territories certainly were not just like those of the earlier Paleoindians. But they were defined in terms of their core features, which in this case consisted of a system of trails related to watercourses. In the center of each hunting territory was a tributary stream of a larger river, such as the Connecticut or Missisquoi. When not frozen, the tributary served as a transportation artery, from which one could gain access to all parts of the territory. One may think of them as analogous to the exits from modern interstate highways, with the major rivers analogous to the highways themselves. When streams were frozen, one either walked on the ice or on clearly marked trails which ran nearby. Usually, there was a main trail associated with the principal tributary stream. A second main trail ran at right angles to the first, bisecting it and dividing each hunting territory into quarters. Boundaries corresponded more or less to the divides between watersheds, but were not precisely defined. This allowed them to fluctuate, which they did from time to time, primarily in response to the amount of sedentary game species, such as beaver, available within them.

Each hunting territory was controlled by a particular family band, whose trusteeship was indicated by the blazes employed to mark trails within the territory. No one else could hunt there, or even trespass, without the permission of the controlling family band. But such permission really could not be denied to those members of other family bands who were relatives of those in the controlling band. Indeed, it is not really accurate to say that a family band actually owned its territory, at least in the modern sense of ownership. There could be no buying or selling of land; indeed, it might almost be said that the members of the band belonged to the territory, so close was their identification with it. The "sense of place" of these peoples seems to have been a good deal stronger than that of modern North Americans, who for the most part show far more tendency to move about from one place to another than did Abenakis prior to the Historic period.

Even within their territories, people did not simply hunt wherever they wished. Rather, it was the custom to manage game resources by hunting only one quarter of the territory at a time. This not only allowed animal populations in previously hunted quarters to make a comeback, it also reduced the wariness that is characteristic of animals which are under more or less constant pressure from hunters. This practice of hunting only one quarter of available territory at one time suggests that the western Abenakis maintained their populations at about 25 percent of actual carrying capacity. It is characteristic of hunting and gathering populations throughout the world to stabilize at about 25 percent of carrying capacity, if the possibility of expansion into neighboring regions does not exist, as it generally has not for the past several centuries. By keeping their populations so far below what the land might actually support, they provide themselves with a margin of safety against potential hard times; it is unlikely that they would ever face starvation, as might have been the case had their populations been closer to carrying capacity. The western Abenakis, as we will see, were not exclusively hunters and gatherers. However, even though there were sufficient frost-free days in the average year for the growing of corn, beans, and squash in the Champlain and Connecticut valleys, unpredictable late spring and early fall frosts occurred often enough to prevent full reliance on native horticulture. Thus, one could never be sure when an unusually short growing season would ruin the harvest for the year, and so it seems fair to say that horticulture, though playing an important role in the western Abenaki subsistence cycle, functioned as a supplement to hunting and gathering. This contrasts with the people who lived south of them in what is now Massachusetts, Rhode Island, and Connecticut. Some of the difference probably relates to a slightly higher carrying capacity in southern New England than in Vermont, especially in coastal areas. But the native peoples of southern New England were more fully horticultural than were the Abenakis of Vermont, with hunting and gathering as supplements. Among horticulturalists, population densities are normally greater than among hunters and gatherers, frequently reaching or even exceeding carrying capacity. This, we think, explains most of the differences between population densities in Vermont on the one hand and southern New England on the other.

The animals hunted by Abenakis in late winter were primarily moose, but deer were taken as well. Both have a hard time getting around in deep snow and were easy prey for a man on snowshoes, armed only with a spear. Other game was hunted as chance afforded: bear, beaver, mink, muskrat, otter, and porcupine. Usually, more meat was obtained than family members could eat at the time. This surplus was left to freeze in troughs made of pine or basswood, to be retrieved later on. All of the hunting was done by men, either as individuals or as partners. While the men hunted, the women tended to the household chores of cooking and making clothing and utensils out of such materials as hides and furs, birch bark, and spruce root, ornamented with porcupine quills, moosehair, and paint.

Frequently accompanying the hunters were dogs, which served to indicate the proximity of game. They also helped hold animals at bay in the deep snow. Dogs had other uses as well: they could be eaten, when, for whatever reason, meat was in short supply. In the winter of 1663/64, substantial numbers of them were consumed at Fort Hill. It is also likely that they performed an important scavenging function in the villages.

FIGURE 5–4. Women's work among
the Abenakis included food preparation and the making of clothing.

As the milder weather of spring approached, subsistence activities shifted back to the villages. Here, the women and children tapped the maple trees. To do this, a diagonal slash was made on the tree, into which was inserted a hollow elderberry twig. Birchbark pails collected the sap, which was processed by boiling in containers of both pottery and birchbark. Once the collection and processing of maple sap was completed, the women turned their attention to the task of collecting ground nuts (*Apios americana* and *tuberosa*) and spring greens. To help relieve the monotony of the task, they were accustomed to singing their own personal gathering songs, which were also thought to be imbued with supernatural power.

While the women tended to the collection of maple sap and wild plant foods, the men were engaged in fowling and fishing, which provided close to 100 percent of the spring diet. Before their extinction in the early part of the twentieth century, passenger pigeons flew through Vermont in large numbers. When this happened every spring, the people would knock low flying birds out of the air, net them in flight, or shoot them as they roosted. When the spring runs of shad, salmon, and alewives began they, too, were harvested. For this, men stationed themselves in rapids with their three-pronged fish spears and nets. Basket traps and weirs were also used to get fish. This fishing provided more fish than could be eaten immediately, even though they were consumed to the near exclusion of all else. The large surplus was preserved by smoking. So productive was the spring fishing that villages were often located near good rapids. For example, Sokoki villages were located near some of the best fishing rapids on the entire Connecticut River. Here, five men in two days are reported to have landed 75 bushels of fish in the year 1875. Earlier, in the eighteenth century, there are reports of seine hauls at the same spot of 1000 to 3000 shad and salmon, many of the salmon weighing over 35 pounds apiece. In the Champlain Valley, *Winoskík* seems to have been located near the lower falls of the Winooski, at the base of which is the "Salmon Hole," well known to local fishermen.

The spring season ended in late April or May with the planting of crops—corn, beans, and squash—in alluvial fields near the villages. Although farming was defined as women's work, the men were involved to the extent of tending the tobacco crop, which was grown in separate gardens. Native Americans generally regarded tobacco as endowed with special powers which facilitated communication with spirit beings. Therefore, it was usually dealt with differently than ordinary food crops.

The summer season was frequently spent in or near the main villages, although those who were able often moved to camps on the shores of lakes and ponds. Here there was less of a problem with mosquitoes and blackflies. At the same time, the fishing was good, and so there was much lake fishing from canoes. For this, dugout canoes of white pine were frequently left on the shores of inland ponds ready for use. The fishing was done either by day, or by night by means of torchlight, which attracted the fish to the fisherman. Hooks of bone, stone, or wood on a handline were used, as were fish spears and nets. Along with their fishing, the men did some local hunting, especially of muskrats. By closing off their tunnels, digging into them from above and driving the muskrats out to be clubbed, up to thirty or thirty-five could be gotten in a half-hour's time. Summer was also a time for travel, so that one could visit and trade with peoples living at some distance.

While the men hunted, fished, and traveled, the women tended the gardens and gathered berries and fruits as they ripened. Such things as blueberries, cranberries, raspberries, and blackberries were eaten fresh, stewed, baked in breads, or were dried for winter use. The ability of the people to utilize efficiently and to their advantage wild plant resources is especially well illustrated by the cattail: the young shoots were eaten in the spring, dried to be made into flour or eaten in the winter, and boiled to make a syrup. The pollen was used for flour, the small flowers and seeds were eaten, the down was used to wrap around infants for warmth, and the stems were used to make mats, darts, and knives.

Native Americans generally made use of a wide variety of plants and herbs for medicinal purposes, more than 200 of which at one time or another were later included in the *Pharmacopeia of the United States* or in the *National Formulary*. All but a handful of native American vegetable drugs known today were used by native peoples, and the Abenakis were no exception. Medicinal plants were thought to be at the height of their powers late in the summer. It was then that they were gathered by women, who always were careful to take only "one family" of plants from a given colony, and to shake a few seeds from other plants into the holes that they left. Medicinal plants were dried, and eventually processed by grinding with stone mortar and pestle.

Some green corn and green beans were also gathered in late summer, but the main harvest was carried out by women in September. Ears of corn were then hung to dry; once shelled, the corn was stored in bark-lined pits. The women also gathered nuts as they were available: beechnuts, black walnuts, butternuts, chestnuts, and hickory nuts. Acorns, too, were important as they had been earlier in Woodland times. White ones were eaten raw; those from red or black oaks were roasted, or baked after the tannic acid has leached out. Nuts, along with dried berries, were stored for winter use along with corn and other crops.

The final season of the subsistence cycle saw a return of small family groups to their upland hunting territories. Left behind in the villages were the aged and infirm, with some younger people to care for them. The object of the hunt was to get sufficient meat to preserve by smoking and drying for winter, as well as for immediate consumption. Skins, too, were important. In the fall of the year, the moose were in their prime, and so the best skins were available. It was also the rutting season, so that moose calling could be effectively employed by the hunters. Moose calling

FIGURE 5−5. Summer fishing was one of the summer activities of Abenaki men.

FIGURE 5–6. In the summer, Abenaki women gathered wild plant foods and worked in the gardens.

FIGURE 5−7. An important activity in the fall was the moose hunt.

was developed into a fine art in the Northeast, and the way this was done in Vermont seems to have been identical to the way the Penobscot went about it. Long before dawn, a hunter would station himself in his canoe in a likely spot, giving a few preliminary calls through a cone of rolled birch bark. As time passed, he would begin to make more calls, varying these considerably. By daybreak, a practiced moose caller could expect to hear a bull moose thrashing about in a rage of passion. Then, all of the hunter's skill came into play. He would give his most appealing calls, also using his birch cone to pick up and let run some water, in imitation of a cow moose's expectant urination. Shortly thereafter the bull would appear to see not the object of his affection, but rather the hunter who, if he didn't want to get hurt, rapidly killed the bull with his bow and arrow.

Deer were also hunted in the fall by individual men stalking or waiting in ambush. As fall moved into early winter, fur-bearing animals were trapped by means of snares and deadfalls for their prime pelts. Following the formation of sufficient ice, beavers and muskrats were gotten by the simple procedure of taking them directly from their lodges. Other animals hunted—especially if food was at all short—were porcupines and spruce grouse, both of which were taken with sticks. Finally, as winter really set in, everyone returned to their village and the period of midwinter slack.

Technology

The equipment required by men in pursuit of their subsistence activities included, for hunting, stout-handled spears and bow and arrows. The Abenakis used a long bow, preferably made of hickory but often of maple or ash instead. It was strung with animal sinew. Arrows were feathered and had points of stone or bone. Given the proper kind of stone, a good sharp arrow point could be made in fifteen or twenty minutes. Effective though these points were, by the 1660s the Sokoki, if not all Abenakis, had become totally dependent on European brass and iron for their points. Arrows were carried in a quiver on the hunter's back. Each hunter also carried a knife, in a sheath suspended around the neck, and his personal tool kit. The latter, a pouch held by his belt, included some smoldering punk held in clam shells so that fire could be quickly obtained, a fire-making kit in case the smoldering punk went out, a pipe and tobacco, and a small effigy of the hunter's animal helper. Snowshoes were worn with double moccasins over a foot wrapping of tanned skin or rabbit fur. The moccasins, like those of all Abenakis—eastern as well as western— were made from three pieces of animal hide: one piece for the sole and sides, another for the tongue and top, and the third a wraparound ankle flap. In winter, hunters also used boots made of moose hocks, which were nearly waterproof.

For clothing, the hunter wore a breech clout and belt wrapped two or three times around the waist. This was often all that was worn in summer, but for winter, more was required. Skin leggings were worn, tied to the belt and gartered below the knee. The belt also held the hunter's personal tool kit. The hunter's upper gar-

FIGURE 5–8. With a good piece of flint or similar stone, Abenaki men could make a good, sharp arrow point in fifteen or twenty minutes, at most.

ment was a robe, preferably of beaver fur, worn belted and with the arms bare. Sometimes a sleeveless shirt made of two moosehide panels was used. When needed, separate sleeves were worn on the arms, tied to each other at the middle of the chest and back. The hunter often went bareheaded, but sometimes wore a conical birchbark cap, a cap made of the shoulder hide of a moose, or a cap made of the skin from a buck's head, complete with antlers.

For shelter in the woods, hunters built bark-covered lean-tos, facing south away from the north wind. The back was banked with snow; in front was a log fire, and on the floor fir boughs covered by bearskin. A more permanent winter camp often resembled two lean-tos facing each other, with the fire built at the center. The lower walls of these were built of logs chinked with moss, with upper walls of poles and bark insulated with evergreens.

To transport his game in the winter, the hunter made use of a toboggan made of smooth strips of white ash or yellow birch. He pulled this himself, by means of a strap across his chest, leaving his hands free. Game was also backpacked, in a skin bag or pack basket of basswood, with a tumpline around the forehead. The preferred means of travel was by birch bark canoes, which were used extensively except when ice prevented. These canoes were well-suited to the region, with its abundant lakes and streams. They were durable craft, yet light enough—under 100 pounds— to be easily carried when necessary. And, they would carry a substantial load. The eastern Abenaki canoe which carried Thoreau across Moosehead Lake in the nineteenth century carried two other men plus 166 pounds of luggage, about 600 pounds in all. This kind of eastern Abenaki canoe is the prototype of today's canvas, fiberglass, and aluminum models; the western Abenaki canoe had lower sides and ends, and thinner lining, than the eastern canoes. They were better for the shallower streams of the region, and easier to carry. Emergency canoes were sometimes made of spruce bark; for example, hunters often returned from the late winter hunt in such craft. Also, dugout canoes were left "parked" conveniently on lakes and ponds for fishing. But spruce bark canoes were makeshift affairs, and dugouts were heavy and of less shallow draft; only in birch bark canoes could people get about over long distances with relative ease and dependability.

Canoes were made from the bark of birch trees larger than those which are customarily found in forests today. The bark was gotten in the winter when it is hardest, toughest, and separates easily into layers. The way the Penobscot went about building a canoe probably didn't differ too much from procedures in Vermont. First a large tree, two feet in diameter and knot-free for a length of twenty-two feet, was felled so as to lie across two other logs. A slow fire was built beneath to keep the bark pliable, which was slit and peeled off with a chisel of fire-hardened wood. The bark was placed on the ground, outside up, and inside rails of spruce or birch wood were sewn with spruce root to the two edges of the bark. Following this, logs and rocks were placed on the bark, which was then shaped by raising the sides and driving stakes all around the outside to hold things in place. As the bark was shaped, slits were cut as necessary, at the two ends, and cross pieces of larch or maple were sewn in place between the rails. The entire inside of the bark was coated with pitch, and then lined with strips of cedar shaved to a thickness of less than 1/2 inch. Any leaks were plugged with spruce gum.

It took about three weeks to complete a canoe which when properly cared for would last about ten years. The tools used consisted of a stone axe, adze, drills made from rejected projectile points or knives, a crooked knife, and any convenient stone for hammering. Crooked knives are thin-bladed, eight or nine inches long, curved to a hook, and used by drawing the blade toward the user. They are derived from a beaver tooth prototype and were part of every man's equipment.

Canoes were simply equipped with paddles of maple or ash, a long staff for poling, and a bark container full of pitch, for patching leaks.

Women's tasks, as we have seen, were different from men's and so their equipment differed, too. Interestingly, women's equipment did not change over from native to European items as quickly and thoroughly as did the men's after contact. In the 1660s when the men were tipping their arrows with metal and using guns when they could get them, the women were still using traditional pottery, which they made themselves, rather than iron or brass kettles. For processing hides, every woman's tool kit included awls, needles, and scrapers of stone, wood, and bone. For processing corn and other vegetable foods, hollowed-out hardwood stumps were used as mortars, with large hardwood pestles. For cooking, in addition to pottery, there were birch bark and wooden containers. While pottery was particularly useful in the villages, it was heavy and breakable, and so less convenient than bark containers when families went off to their hunting territories. Cooking in bark vessels was accomplished by heating stones and dropping them in with the food. Or, they could be used over a fire, so long as they were not placed directly in it. However, this did tend to shorten the life expectancy of such vessels.

The clothing worn by women did not differ greatly from that worn by men. In the summer, they went about in breechclout and belt worn with a kneelength skirt of tanned buckskin. Their hair was worn long and loose, or secured by a headband, or in two braids with a flat coil on the crown of the head, tied by a thong with its ends hanging down. Men wore theirs differently. If he were young and unmarried, a man wore his hair long and loose or with a headband. A married man wore his coiled or knotted on the crown of his head, held by a thong.

FIGURE 5–9. The famous Colchester Jar, shown left was found in 1825 by a Captain Johnson, a Burlington surveyor. Made in the style of the St. Lawrence Iroquois, who lived in the St. Lawrence Valley at the time of Cartier's visit but who were gone by the time of Champlain's, we do not know whether Abenakis obtained the vessel in trade, or made it themselves in imitation of a foreign style. It may now be seen in the University of Vermont's Fleming Museum. Height of the jar is 19 cms, with a maximum capacity of 9 pints. Photo by John D. Owen, courtesy Fleming Museum.

The Cowasuck Jar, shown half size, was found in Newbury, Vermont where the Cowasucks had their main village. Similar pottery was being used by the Sokokis as late as 1663. The Cowasuck Jar is currently in the possession of Armand Beliveau of St. George, who graciously allowed us to photograph it.

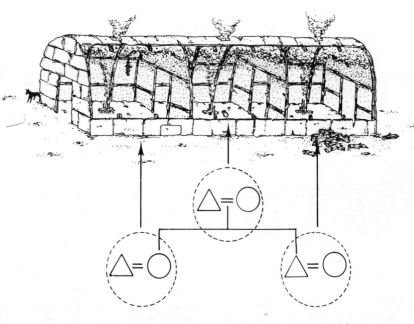

FIGURE 5−10. The western Abenaki household consisted of from one to four nuclear families that lived together in a single house. The composition of a "typical" household would be something like that shown here. In the diagram, men are represented by triangles, women by circles. Vertical lines indicate descent, horizontal lines a sibling relationship, and equal signs (=) a marital tie.

Western Abenaki Social Organization

The organization required for the western Abenaki way of life was relatively simple, but effective. The important functional units were families and family bands. Every individual was a member of a nuclear family—husband, wife, and dependent children—and several related nuclear families together constituted a household. Each household occupied a single large house, and each nuclear family within the house had its own fire, with its living space on either side of the fire. If a household was made up of four nuclear families, for example, then there were four fires in a line down the center of the house.

In anthropological parlance, residence was ambilocal, with a

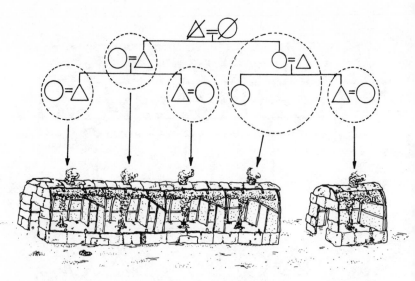

FIGURE 5–11. When a western Abenaki couple married, they went to live in either the household of the bride's parents or the groom's parents (ambilocal residence). Usually, the household of the groom's parents was chosen (patrilocal residence, as opposed to the alternative, matrilocal residence). In the example here, three of the couples are living patrilocally, and one matrilocally. The ancestral couple is deceased, and one of the younger couples has taken over their space in the house. If the houses of both the bride's and the groom's parents were already full, the newly married couple could establish a new house close by the existing one with which they wished to be associated. In the example here, the couple in the new house are living patrilocally.

patrilocal bias. This means that when a couple married they chose to live either in the household of the bride's parents or in that of the groom's parents. Although the tendency was for the couple to live in the household of the groom's parents, the actual choice was made on the basis of the relative prestige of the two households and the resources available to them. If a couple's prospects looked best as members of the bride's household, then that is where they lived, establishing their own fire. If both houses happened to be full, then the couple could build a new house, usually close by that of the bride's or groom's parents. More usually, if one household was full, there was room in the other, in which case there was no need to build a new house.

Given this pattern of residence, a distinctive pattern of relationships developed within each household. The core members of each were people who had grown up within it, and so were "blood" relatives of one another. Under strict patrilocality, core members would all be men. Under ambilocality, however, core relatives normally included some women as well as men (Figure 5–12). The in-marrying spouses, though not blood relatives of the core members, nonetheless became full-fledged members of the household. Because new members were being born into them as old members died off, households had continuity over time and a

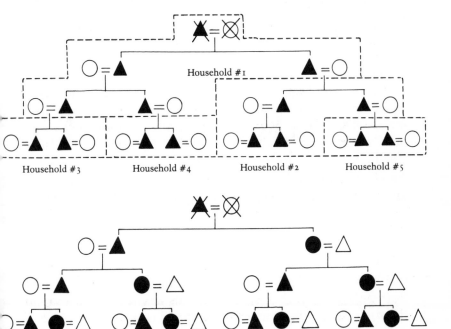

FIGURE 5–12. The process of family growth, as generation succeeded generation, would have led to the periodic establishment of new households nearby established ones, as described for Figure 5–11. The members of such related households all would have been members of a single family band. These members consisted of a core of people who were "blood relatives," with their in-marrying spouses. Under strict patrilocality, the core relatives all would have been men, as shown above. More usual, under ambilocality, would be core relatives along the lines shown below. Core relatives are shown in black; deceased relatives are shown with an X through them.

permanence that independent nuclear families could not achieve.

Each household was associated with a particular animal, examples being bears, beavers, hummingbirds, muskrats, otters, partridges, raccoons, and turtles. It seems that households associated with the same animal were closely related and, together, constituted single family bands. Thus, two Bear households together, for example, would constitute the Bear family band. Family bands consisting of more than one household would come about in situations where the parental households of a newlywed couple were already full, and so the newlyweds would have to establish their own household. Each family band controlled its own upland hunting territory, which was marked by the band's animal emblem. If new households did not maintain their association with an existing family band, they would not have access to resources vital for survival.

Here, we can begin to see the adaptive advantage of ambilocal residence over strict patrilocality. With populations below carrying capacity, and the boundaries of hunting territories able to expand or contract somewhat owing to their imprecise definition, a small amount of growth in the membership of a family band could be absorbed. But too much growth would inevitably produce a band membership too large to be sustained by the resources available to it. This kind of overgrowth would have been more likely under strict patrilocality; it would have taken but a few generations of a higher than normal incidence of live male births. Under ambilocality, by contrast, members of overly large family bands could be encouraged to leave, upon marriage, to join the family bands of their spouses. In this way, relative stability in the size of family band membership could be achieved.

There has in the past been a good deal of confusion over the association between family bands and their animal emblems. Lewis Henry Morgan, a nineteenth-century scholar often regarded as the founder of American anthropology, regarded these emblems as totems, indicative of the presence of clans. Full-fledged totemism involves the idea of descent from a plant or animal ancestor, with associated ritual observances and taboos. It is frequently associated with clans, which are social groups to which people belong by virtue of descent from a common ancestor, usually reckoned exclusively through men (patrilineal) or women (matrilineal). This is the kind of situation found among the Iroquois, for example, with whom Morgan was most familiar.

The western Abenaki situation seems to have been different. There is no evidence of any food or other restriction in connection with the animals associated with the family bands. Nor is there any evidence that descent as such was a formal criterion for group membership, succession to positions of authority, or the like. Furthermore, residence patterns did not produce patrilineal or matrilineal alignments of kin with any consistency, as we have seen. In short, these animals seem to have been purely emblematic. Particular animals may have been chosen as emblems by particular family bands because they were especially common in that group's hunting territory, or because they were thought to embody the group's characteristics. Bears, for example, were thought to be particularly wise, and members of the Bear family might also like to be thought of as wise. Beyond this, the use of animals for emblematic purposes is indicative of their importance to a people who placed great importance on hunting. This shows up in other ways, as we shall see later (see pp. 190, 197).

The organizational structure of western Abenaki households and family bands was reflected in their kinship terminology, which in some respects was more precise in its labeling of relatives than is that of most North Americans today. As we have seen, the core members of family bands consisted of "blood" relatives, some of whom were related in the male, and some in the female, line. In human societies where such groupings of kinfolk occur, kinship terminology usually makes important distinctions by generation; relatives on the parental generation are called by different terms than those on one's own generation, and so forth. In western Abenaki kinship, different sets of terms were used for grandparents, relatives on the parental generation, relatives on one's own generation, relatives on the generation of one's children, and relatives on the generation of one's grandchildren. With the exception of the latter (grandchildren, grandnieces/nephews), the terms distinguished the sex of the relative: women and girls were called by different terms than men and boys.

No further distinctions were made on the grandparental generation, but on the parental generation, distinctions were made between maternal and paternal, as well as collateral and lineal relatives. Thus, there were separate terms for one's father, father's brother, and mother's brother; similarly, separate terms applied to one's mother, mother's sister, and father's sister. This is called by anthropologists bifurcate collateral terminology; it is particularly common in aboriginal North American societies which do not have matrilineal or patrilineal descent groups, such as clans, further evidence that clans were not a part of aboriginal western Abenaki social organization. Because different terms apply to the members of different nuclear families, such terminology seems particularly appropriate for a society in which nuclear families, though parts of larger family bands, still had a degree of independence in that they could choose which family band they would be a part of.

In western Abenaki society, one grew up in a household which included the children of some of the siblings of one's mother or father. Thus, if one's parents were living patrilocally, one grew up in a family which was likely to include the children of father's brother and/or father's sister. Conversely, if one's parents were living matrilocally, one grew up in a family which was likely to include the children of mother's sister and/or mother's brother. In either case, there wouldn't be much difference between them and one's biological brothers and sisters. This sort of situation favors what anthropologists call Hawaiian terminology, in which the terms used for brother and sister are used as well for the children of father's brother, mother's sister, father's sister, and mother's brother. In a behavioral sense, all are actual or potential "brothers and sisters."

Although it was not important for the western Abenakis to make a terminological distinction between biological brothers and sisters on the one hand and cousins on the other, or between cross and parallel cousins, they did make other terminological distinctions. Not only was the sex of the relative specified by the use of different terms for males and females, but the sex of the speaker was also distinguished. Thus, the terms used by a man to refer to his "brothers" and "sisters" differed from those used by a woman. In addition, there were suffixes which were added to the end of the kinship term to indicate whether the "brother" or "sister" referred to was older or younger than the speaker.

There was some tendency for a dual organization of western

Abenaki villages, but not, so far as we know, on the basis of descent. Thus, villages were divided in half for competitive sporting events, such as canoe tilting, wrestling and racing, or games of lacrosse. It was also done for certain ceremonies and funerals.

Family bands of particular watersheds were loosely organized into what some have called tribes, others have called bands, and what we refer to as major bands, to distinguish them from family bands. Thus, all of the family bands of the Missisquoi watershed, for example, constituted a single major Missisquoi band. Equivalent, but independent groups occupied other watersheds. Because most marriages took place within the same major band between individuals from different family bands, all members of a major band were relatives of one another. Thus, each major band constituted what some anthropologists call an endogamous deme, a community of people related to one another through both men and women, who normally marry within their own community. Because the members are relatives of one another, the deme can function as a large kinship group, rather than some sort of politically organized group.

Political Organization

In societies with high degrees of social and economic diversity, complex systems of government are necessary to manage the diverse and often conflicting interests of groups within the society. Since western Abenaki society at the start of the seventeenth century was relatively egalitarian, with minimal diversity of interests, there was no need for a complicated system of government. Family bands for the most part took care of their own affairs, but each major band did have a governing council, composed of family elders along with a war chief. This was presided over by a civil chief, who was selected for the position on the basis of his personal prowess and prestige. There was no fixed rule of succession; what was important was that the man inspire confidence by being an especially good provider. This required wisdom, strength, fortitude, and generosity. A chief held his position until he died, unless he were deposed for bad behavior. When he became old, people began thinking about possible successors. So by the time the old chief died, people usually had a pretty good idea as to who his successor would be.

Tradition has it that the raising of a western Abenaki chief was accomplished with much pomp and ceremony, in the course of which he received a new name. How far back in time this pomp and ceremony goes, however, is an open question. Nicholas N. Smith has suggested that most Abenakis had no significant chief-making celebration in pre-contact times. While not unimportant earlier, chiefs do seem to have become more important with the rise of the European fur trade and the accompanying shifts in tribal alliances, and this may have been reflected in chief-raising ceremonies.

Although a chief enjoyed much prestige, he actually had very little authority. Influence, rather than authority, was the key to a chief's success. Such obedience as he commanded was purely voluntary; no one was actually obliged to do as he requested. If he could manipulate people so as to achieve his desired ends, that was acceptable, but he could not force people to do what they chose not to do. A chief had to be careful about this; whatever he could get away with was acknowledged as legitimate, and his great personal prestige gave him a certain amount of leverage. Although most chiefs seem not to have had unusual supernatural powers, a subject to be discussed shortly, some of them did, and this gave them added influence. But if a chief went beyond what people were willing to put up with, and persisted in doing so, then he lost followers and could be replaced.

The actual duties of the chief were rather commonplace and largely ceremonial in nature. Besides presiding over meetings of the band council, he served as the major band's representative at gatherings with other bands and tribes.

The war chief, like the civil chief, was selected for his position on the basis of his personal prowess and prestige. His ability as a war leader stemmed particularly from his reputation as a warrior. Such special authority as he had came into play following a declaration of war, at which time he would rise with his ceremonial war club, and ask for volunteers. Other men of reputation would do the same, and ten warriors led by such a man constituted a war party. The actual declaration was made by a general council of men, women, and children, all of whom were entitled to speak.

War seems to have been more prominent among the western Abenakis than among those further east. As a general rule, farmers—those "gentle tillers of the soil"—tend to be more warlike than hunters and gatherers. Among the western Abenakis though, there seems to have been little reason for aggressive warfare. For one thing, Abenakis generally seem to have believed that one could not operate successfully in someone else's territory, since one didn't control the necessary supernatural powers. Furthermore, operating far below carrying capacity, they had no need to go after the resources of others. The main problem seems to have been the Iroquois; we have no indication of troubles between western Abenakis, at least those in Vermont, and their Algonquian-speaking neighbors until the 1620s. The Iroquois, in common with many slash and burn horticulturalists around the world, engaged in predatory warfare against their neighbors. Their main motive in going to war was to achieve dominance, by making their neighbors acknowledge Iroquoian superiority. This was acknowledged periodically by payment of tribute. But the relation between victim and victor was one of subjection, rather than outright subordination. The payment of tribute purchased "protection" from the Iroquois. But the price of that protection was not only tribute payment; it included constant and public ceremonial deference to the Iroquois, free passage for their war parties through the subjugated group's territory, and the contribution of young warriors to Iroquoian war parties.

Although undertaken primarily to establish their own preeminence, economic considerations were probably important in Iroquoian warfare. Archaeological evidence indicates that significant environmental degradation took place around Iroquoian settlements in late Woodland times. This suggests overutilization of resources, and the exaction of tribute from others probably helped cover the deficit. However that may be, it is a fact that the western Abenakis and Iroquois—especially the Mohawk—were engaged in intermittent wars with one another from at least A.D. 1570 on.

Among the western Abenakis, the formation of a war party was celebrated by feasting and dancing. Warriors prepared themselves by painting their faces red and their bodies with marks symbolic of past accomplishments in war and depictions of their animal helpers, so that friends would recognize them and not kill them by mistake. The leader of the war party, as well as the war chief, commanded by reputation, persuasion, and example. He did not enjoy the absolute authority of a modern military commander. The men under him followed by choice, because of the leader's proven ability and reputation. Tactics employed included surprise, stealth, and trickery. Weapons used were the bow and arrow, spear, knives, clubs, and—very important—magic. The objective, sensibly enough, was to do the most harm to the enemy with the least harm to themselves. Whatever gave promise of accomplishing these ends was tried.

Western Abenaki Life Cycle

Growing up in western Abenaki society was a relatively easy business, not marked by elaborate rites of passage such as one finds among many of the world's peoples. The birth of a child seems to have been marked more by practical than ceremonial considerations; the newborn child was cleansed, well wrapped, and placed on a cradle board. If the mother died in childbirth, or thereafter, a potential stepmother was always at hand, in the form of a grandmother, the mother's or father's sister, or the wife of the father's brother, one of whom was bound to be a member of the family band. If at some point both of the infant's parents died, it was usually the father's brother and his wife who took charge. Sometimes, of course, infants died. If this happened, a special grief was felt, for an infant was thought to be incapable of caring for itself in the "other world." As an expression of this grief, presents were given to the dead infant's parents, who would later give a feast for their friends.

There is no reason to suppose that infant mortality was any higher among the Abenakis than it was among Europeans of the time. Those infants that survived spent their days on a cradle board, or in a hammock-like affair made of blankets and cord. There were probably a number of acts thought to be beneficial to the proper growth and development of children. Among Vermont peoples it was thought that if a child bit through a rattlesnake from its head to its tail, the child would grow up to have sound teeth.

Child rearing after infancy was fairly permissive. Children were rarely handled in authoritarian ways, or subjected to slapping, spanking, or beating. They were, however, subjected to the frequent telling of tales with morals. One example is the tale of the swamp creature, who can be heard calling, trying to lure children into swamps, where they will drown. The moral of the story is quite simple: swamps are dangerous places, stay away from them. When told well, the story is probably a lot more effective at keeping children away from swamps than just telling them "don't go near swamps." This is not to say that Abenaki children never misbehaved. Sometimes they did, and if a child persisted in misbehaving and was really bad, it was isolated from the family and exposed to public disgrace. This was done by blackening the child's face and putting it outside the house.

Little girls began early to learn about women's work. They were given simple chores to do, such as tending the baby if there was one, and gathering firewood. Later, they learned more skilled tasks, like how to web snowshoes, and how to ornament clothing with paint, dyed quills, moosehair embroidery, and beadwork. Her father's brother's wife functioned as a kind of tutor if the girl's parents were living patrilocally.

Boys, too, began to practice at an early age the skills they would need as men. Around the age of 5 or 6, they were given small bows and arrows and began to practice hunting. Archery was an obsession with them, for good reason, and archery practice and contests took up many hours, even in adulthood. By the age of 10 to 12, a boy was taken into the woods by his father or father's brother, who frequently served as a boy's tutor. In the woods, he learned other skills of woodcraft and endurance.

Wrestling and other physical contests, too, began early and continued through adulthood. The ability to run was particularly esteemed, and footraces, as well as games with running starts, began early. There is some suggestion that special status was attached to being the fastest runner in the family band. Among the eastern Abenakis, the job of the fastest runner was to run down and kill game in its tracks. Although he was highly honored, the runner had to observe strict sexual and food taboos; a significant price was paid for the honor.

At puberty, it was the custom for a boy to go in quest of a guiding vision and spirit helper; this was an individual undertaking, unmarked by any public rites of passage (see page 185). By 14 a boy was "of age" and counted as a warrior. Girls went into seclusion at first menstruation, for women in such a state were considered poison to men. With this event they became women, again without any public rites of passage.

After puberty came marriage, and anyone of the same generation not covered by the kinship term for brother or sister was eligible as a marriage partner. In our own terminology, this means that close cousins, along with actual siblings, were covered by the incest taboo. There were no other formal rules of exogamy requiring, for example, marriage outside of one's own family band. But since age mates not regarded as brothers and sisters were less likely to be found inside one's own band, most marriages were to people from other family bands, though still within one's own major band.

Proposals of marriage were usually handled by an elder man from the family of the prospective groom. To propose marriage, this go-between would take a present to the prospective bride. In the eighteenth century, the present included a string of wampum; whether this was so at the beginning of the seventeenth century we do not know. To reject the proposal, the girl had only to send the gift back. If she accepted, however, her suitor then had to present the girl's mother with his next game kill. Following this, he went off by himself on an extended hunt, to return only when he had a suitable present for the girl herself. All of this, of course, established his potential as a provider.

The Abenakis took family life very seriously and did not enter into marriage lightly. Not only did the prospective groom have to demonstrate his ability to provide for his wife-to-be, but the couple had to show that they could get along living together. Therefore, when the prospective groom returned from his hunt, he and his intended bride entered into a trial period of living together with her family. During this time they slept head to foot, for no one wanted children until they were sure that the marriage would work. If the couple could not get along, then the deal was off, and the unsuccessful suitor forfeited all of the presents he had given to the girl and her family. Since these presents represented a substantial investment of time and effort, a man didn't propose marriage in the first place unless he was serious, and wanted it to work. Therefore, most of these premarital trials were probably successful. When success was assured, the marriage was "certified" by feasting and dancing in the presence of chiefs and parents.

Although the life expectancy of Abenakis at the start of the seventeenth century was undoubtedly below today's standard, it does not seem to have been below that of Europeans of the time. We do not have figures for the Abenaki, but the life expectancy for North American peoples generally in late prehistoric times was 37 ± 3 years, according to the physical anthropologist W. M. Krogman. Even as late as the end of the eighteenth century, the life expectancy of Euroamericans—Europeans and their descendants in North America—was only 35 years. But life expectancy figures tell only a part of the story; the late Aleš Hrdlička of the U.S. National Museum once observed that the proportion of Native Americans 80 years of age and above was far in excess of that among Euroamericans. Among the Abenakis, it appears that a large number of those who survived early childhood or, in the case of women, the rigors of childbirth, lived to very ripe old ages. Even recently, Gordon Day has known several Abenakis who reached ages in the 90s, and around 1900, there were three or four who lived past 100. The eighteenth-century war chief Grey Lock who led many a raid against northern Massachusetts settlements from Missisquoi, lived until he was at least 85, if not as old as 92. Elderly persons were well-respected and cared for, unless hard times made this impossible. But then everyone's survival was at stake, and abandonment of the elderly was an extreme measure of last resort. Overall, one has the impression that the elderly were better cared for in traditional Abenaki society than are many of the "senior citizens" of modern North America, who are so often consigned by their offspring to the limbo of "old peoples' homes."

When death occurred, the remains of the deceased were buried whenever possible, for otherwise their spirits were thought to hang around the living. Of course this could not be done when the ground was frozen, so the bodies of people who died in the winter were placed on scaffolds away from scavenging animals, there to await spring burial. If the deceased was a hunter off in the woods, his partner placed the corpse on a scaffold near the place of death, and the first person who came by in the spring was obliged to bury it.

For burial, the deceased was dressed in his or her best clothes, wrapped in a role of bark, and tied with a cord. Some food was placed with the corpse to sustain it in its journey over the Milky Way. Utensils—probably the appropriate personal tool kit depending on the sex of the deceased—were also placed with the corpse for its support in the afterlife. The grave itself faced east and was covered with a tent-like structure of wood slabs. At one end a wooden slab was set upright, and on it was painted the mark of the deceased. If it was a chief's grave, then it was planted around with tree seedlings. A graveside ceremony was held at which people gave way to long, unrestrained mourning. After all, the people of a major band were relatives of one another, who knew each other well, and the death of one generally affected all the rest very deeply. The widow of a dead man spent a year in mourning. During this time she wore a hood, could not join in any festivities, nor could she remarry. The widower of a dead woman marked himself with black paint and could not engage in pleasurable activities.

Western Abenaki World View

The subject of death, with its associated idea of an afterlife, brings us quite naturally to the subject of western Abenaki world view. Before delving into this, though, some background is necessary. Humans are, by their very nature, social creatures. As such, their behavior has to be orderly and predictable; people cannot live together, work together, and cooperate with one another unless they know exactly how each will act in particular circumstances. This orderliness and predictability is provided by culture, which sets the standards for acceptable behavior. Since culture is created and learned rather than biologically inherited, each generation must learn these standards anew.

This learning begins with the development of self-awareness—the ability to identify oneself as an object, to react to oneself, and to appraise oneself. It is this that permits individuals to assume responsibility for their conduct, to learn how to react to others, and to assume a variety of roles. But in order for this to emerge and function, each individual must learn about a world of objects other than self. The basis of this world of other than self is what we would think of as the objective environment of things. This, though, is never perceived in completely objective terms. Those aspects of the environment that a particular culture defines as significant are singled out for attention and labeled; the rest are ignored or else lumped together into broad categories. But culture doesn't just describe the environment in particular ways, it also explains it. By doing so, it provides the individual with an orderly, rather than chaotic universe in which to act. Such an orderly universe seems to be essential as a setting for orderly behavior.

In the absence of modern scientific knowledge, conceptions of the self and behavioral environment, which we can lump together under the heading of "world view," are apt to be quite supernaturalistic in nature. This was certainly true of the world view of the seventeenth-century western Abenakis, who invoked the actions of a variety of supernatural beings and powers to explain the world in which they found themselves. To the early Europeans, such explanations were regarded as false and shot through with superstition—an ironic attitude, given that the world view of Europeans at the time was really no less supernaturalistic than that of the Abenakis. Let us not forget that Europeans were hanging witches in Salem in 1692, and Salem was exceptional only in the number of "witches" involved (of interest is the fact that the last of the Salem witches was not exonerated by the Massachusetts legislature until 1957). As Francis Jennings has put it, "The Indians were not superstitious because they had a ritual for persuading divinity to make rain; their superstition lay in sending their prayers to the wrong address."

No matter how different, or even strange, a world view may seem from our twentieth-century vantage point, if examined closely it will always be found to be logical and basically "sensible" in terms of the knowledge available to those who subscribe to it. Moreover, without an understanding of the world view of a particular culture, one cannot fully understand the behavior of individuals within their society. For the fact is that the behavioral decisions which people make are always strongly affected by their cultural conception of themselves and the world in which they live.

Returning now to the western Abenakis, it is unfortunate that we have no published information on their traditional concept of "self." However, there is no reason to suppose that this differed significantly from that of the Penobscot, for whom we have much good information. The Penobscot concept of self was associated with a number of personality traits which the anthropologist A. Irving Hallowell showed were common among Algonquian-speaking peoples throughout the Northeast. Moreover, the process of growing up, in the course of which concepts of the self are learned, was pretty much the same among the western Abenakis as it was among the Penobscot. Therefore, we should be able to reconstruct with a fair measure of assurance the western Abenaki concept of self, at least in broad outline.

Each individual was thought to be made up of at least two parts—the body and what may be called the "vital self." The latter was dependent on the body, yet was able to disengage itself from the body and travel about for short periods of time to perform overt acts and to interact with other "selves." It was activity on the part of the vital self that was thought to occur in dreams. So long as the vital self returned to the body before the passage of too much time, there was no problem. But should the vital self be detained, the individual would sicken, and, if the vital self didn't return, die. Along with this dual nature of the self went a potential for every individual to wield supernatural powers, with which every living thing was endowed. Theoretically then, it was possible for anyone's vital self to be lured away from the body, resulting in sickness and eventual death.

These characteristics of the self stand out most clearly in the case of shamans, usually men, but occasionally women, whose powers were greater than those of most people, and who were able to exert a considerable measure of control over the spirit world. Shamans enjoyed the reputation of being clairvoyant, able to see what is taking place afar and foretell the future. They were also credited with the ability to locate game through divination, usually by heating the shoulder blade of a deer or moose over a fire and interpreting the cracks and smudges as a map of the hunting territory. They effected certain cures by dint of their mental powers, and they were thought to be able to walk so powerfully that their feet sank into the very rock. Last but not least, their sexual appetites were regarded as above normal. Because of this, some shamans seem to have kept multiple wives.

One did not become a shaman because of any particular desire to be one. Indeed, one might not even have wanted to be one.

Rather, one became a shaman by virtue of possession of special powers. Anything about an individual suggestive of the abilities just enumerated indicated possession of such powers, and to renounce them was to court death by supernatural means. Thus, any unknown person might be a shaman, and even though they weren't supposed to do it, they had the potential to use their great powers against the best interests of others. In fact, any misfortune tended to be attributed to the work of such individuals.

Although a shaman was born with more than the ordinary amount of supernatural power, to actually be a shaman that power had to be cultivated. Of the utmost importance was the gaining of power over an animal helper. Although all men customarily sought such a helper, a shaman was more skilled at its use. A shaman was able to transfer his vital self into the animal's body at will, his own body remaining inert for the duration. There was a certain danger in this, though, for if the animal was killed at this time, the shaman also died. But then, the job of killing was complicated by the ability of the shaman to metamorphose into something else, like a bird or a swift-footed animal, and get away. A shaman might also send his animal helper off to run errands, without actually transferring his vital self to it. Animals reputed to have served as animal helpers include the bear, beaver, various birds, the dog, eel, otter and porcupine. It is interesting that what could be birds, eels, and a dog are depicted in petroglyphs on a rock along the Connecticut River in Brattleboro. These may be depictions of shamans' helpers, for there seems to be a connection between rock art and shamanism in northeastern North America. An especially powerful shaman could have more than one helper; one famous Penobscot shaman had seven. The way one gained control over an animal helper was to go out into the woods by oneself and sing for it. The first animal which came close enough to be stroked was thereby bound to the shaman's service. From that time on, its flesh was taboo to the shaman.

A shaman's power also derived from his drum, which gave him the power to communicate with the spirit world. The efficacy of this is conveyed by this statement, from a Passamaquoddy:

Storms hearken to the sound of my drum . . . the wood spirit ceases chopping to listen to my drum . . . lightning, thunder, storms, gale, for-

FIGURE 5–13. Photograph of the Petroglyphs at Brattleboro, Vermont, taken in the nineteenth century. By permission Peabody Museum, Harvard University; photo © President and Fellows of Harvard College.

est spirit, water spirit, whirlwind, spirit of the night and air are gathered together and are listening to my drum.

In the eastern Abenaki region and on up into Labrador, the shaman's drum was a wooden hoop with a head of green deerskin. Over this were two rawhide strings which produced a buzzing sound, thought to represent singing.

In addition to his drum, the shaman has his cedar flute. This gave him the power to call game, lure enemies, and attract women (there was a bit of the libertarian about most shamans). Finally, there was the shaman's ability to perform tricks. Normally, he was adept at fooling people with sleight of hand, ventriloquism and similar arts. This sort of thing is typical of shamanism, wherever found, and is one of the main reasons why "nonbelievers" often take a rather dim view of it. The fact of the matter is that a shaman is usually quite sincere about the job and regards his ability to perform tricks as proof of his superior powers, just as Puritans in the late seventeenth century believed that commercial success was a measure of God's favor.

To repeat what we said before, the western Abenaki beliefs about the self, as we have reconstructed them, are apt to seem a bit strange to many modern-day North Americans. But to the Abenakis themselves, in the seventeenth century, their concept of self made sense, given the unavailability of scientific knowledge; it adequately accounted for their experience, regardless of its "rightness" or "wrongness" in any objective sense. Furthermore, their concept of self is relevant for anyone who wishes to understand Abenaki behavior. For one thing, it caused an undercurrent of suspicion and distrust of strangers and a secretiveness about oneself. This individual secretiveness made it hard for a potentially malevolent stranger to gain control of one's vital self. Also, the belief that dreams were real experiences, rather than expressions of unconscious desires, could impose burdens of guilt and anxiety on individuals who had dreamed of doing things not accepted as proper. Finally, individuals might indulge in acts that would strike people today as quite mad. Probably there were cases rather like that of the Penobscot who spent the night literally fighting for his life against a windfall, a big log that fell on him. To the man, the windfall was a metamorphosed shaman who was out to get him, and it would have been madness not to try to overcome his adversary.

The behavioral environment in which the western Abenaki self operated consisted of a flat world, in which rivers served as points of reference as well as being the main arteries for canoe travel. These rivers flowed through forests abounding with game. Like humans, these animals were also composed of a body and a vital self. Although humans hunted and killed animals to sustain their own lives, they clearly recognized that animals were entitled to proper respect. For example, when one killed beaver, muskrat, or waterfowl, one couldn't unceremoniously toss their bones into the nearest garbage pit. Proper respect demanded that their bones be returned to the water, with a request that the species be continued. Similarly, before eating meat, an offering of grease was placed on the fire to thank *Tabaldak*, "the Owner." More generally, waste was to be avoided, so as not to offend the animals. Failure to respect the rights of animals would result in their no longer being willing to be killed.

Not just animals, but indeed all living things, were endowed with the ability to act in ways beneficial or detrimental to human beings. An example is afforded by the Abenaki corn legend, as related by Stith Thompson:

A long time ago, when Indians were first made, there lived one alone, far, far from any others. He knew not of fire, and subsisted on roots, barks, and nuts. This Indian became very lonesome for company. He grew tired of digging roots, lost his appetite, and for several days lay dreaming in the sunshine; when he awoke he saw something standing near, at which, at first, he was very much frightened. But when it spoke, his heart was glad, for it was a beautiful woman with long light hair, very unlike any Indian. He asked her to come to him, but she would not, and if he tried to approach her she seemed to go farther away; he sang to her of his loneliness and besought her not to leave him; at last she told him, if he would do just as she should say, he would always have her with him. He promised that he would.

She led him to where there was some very dry grass, told him to get two very dry sticks, rub them together quickly, holding them in the grass. Soon a spark flew out; the grass caught it, and quick as an arrow the ground was burned over. Then she said, "When the sun sets, take me by the hair and drag me over the burned ground." He did not like to do this, but she told him that wherever he dragged her something like grass would spring up, and he would see her hair coming from between the leaves; then the seeds would be ready for his use. He did as she said, and to this day, when they see the silk (hair) on the cornstalk, the Indians know she has not forgotten them.

Along with plants and animals, the western Abenakis shared the world with various quasi-human supernatural beings which frequented the forests, bodies of water and the air. On a number of occasions, some of these would enter into active association with humans. Frequent relations of such incidents are contained in Abenaki mythology. In these myths, some of these quasi-humans have their origins explained. But the existence of others seems to have just been taken for granted.

One of these quasi-humans was *Odzihózo*, "He Makes Himself

from Something." This being seems to have created himself out of dust, but since he was not the real Creator, he wasn't able to accomplish it all at once. At first, he managed only his head, body, and arms; the legs came later, growing slowly as legs do on a tadpole. Not waiting until his legs were grown, he set out to change the shape of the earth. He dragged his body about with his hands, gouging channels which became the rivers. To make the mountains, he piled dirt up with his hands. Once his legs grew, Odzihózo's task was made easier; by merely extending his legs, he made the tributaries of the main streams.

Gordon Day has described Odzihózo's last act of landscape transformation as follows:

It was Odziozo who laid out the river channels and lake basins and shaped the hills and mountains. Just how long he took is a subject which Abenakis, only recently deceased, used to discuss over their campfires. At last he was finished, and like Jehovah in Genesis, he surveyed his handiwork and found it was good. The last work he made was Lake Champlain and this he found especially good. It was his masterpiece. He liked it so much that he climbed onto a rock in Burlington Bay and changed himself into stone so that he could better sit there and enjoy the spectacle through the ages. He still likes it, because he is still there and used to be given offerings of tobacco as long as Abenakis went this way by canoe, a practice which continued until about 1940. The rock is also called Odziozo, since it is the Transformer himself.

It is too bad that the rock as it appears on maps today is labeled "Rock Dunder," it really ought to be called by its proper name. Odzihózo's wife, incidentally, sits on another rock, off the southern tip of Grand Isle.

What we have in Odzihózo is the western Abenaki version of the transformer who, in one form or another, shows up in the mythology of all Algonquian-speaking peoples. Whatever the transformer's specific attributes, he is always instrumental in shaping the face of the earth, modifying the elements, and altering animal species, usually reducing them from giants to their present size. As a result of his activities, things are much more suitable on the face of the earth for human beings than would otherwise be the case. Besides explaining the origins of major features such as the rivers, lakes, and mountains of Vermont, transformer tales explain the origin of places like Rock Dunder, Split Rock, or the lower falls of Otter Creek.

FIGURE 5–14. Odzihózo's last work was Lake Champlain. So pleased was he with this masterpiece that he climbed onto a rock and changed himself into stone so that he could sit there and enjoy it through the ages. Photo courtesy Jane Mowe Gibbons.

Odzihózo was not the only transformer recognized by the western Abenakis. Another was *Bedgwadzo*, "Round Mountain." Bedgwadzo was described as a great shaman who lived long ago, although not so long ago as Odzihózo. In his personal characteristics he was much more human than Odzihózo and was much more concerned about humans and their welfare. Though Bedgwadzo's acts of transformation included the taming of a whirlwind and subduing the thunders, they generally were less grandiose than those of Odzihózo.

Although he created himself and altered the face of the land, Odzihózo was not the western Abenaki creator. That status belongs to *Tabaldak*, "the Owner." He created all living things, with the sole exception of Odzihózo. Man and woman he made out of a piece of stone, but he didn't like them, so he broke them up. Then he tried making them of living wood, and from them came all later Abenakis. Here, we seem to have an expression of the idea of a closeness between all living things.

Quasi-human beings also included several varieties of underwater creatures, all of which were natural enemies of humans.

Stories were told about them only in winter, when they were safely confined beneath the ice. One variety was some kind of giant lizard, about whom Gordon Day has been unable to elicit information. Another variety was a great serpent, about which Gordon Day provided the following information for the film, *Prehistoric Life in the Champlain Valley*:

There are many stories of his being seen in different places. In one of my best stories he figures in the common theme of a girl being seduced by a snake. He often has been mistaken for a log over which someone walks or drags a canoe, then discovers it was a serpent's body. His presence in quiet bog ponds is detected by a boiling of mud and trash up from the bottom. There are several places which are pointed out as former dens of this serpent and from which he went out. The draining of several former ponds is accounted for in this way. In one detailed story, he was first thought to be the head of a deer swimming at a distance, since he had horns, later as he got closer he was seen to have a head not like a deer, more like a horse. Some thought him to have been a great shaman who only sometimes took this form.

A third kind of underwater creature was the swamp spirit, which we have already mentioned in connection with child rearing. This spirit was more mischievous than malevolent, but never helpful. It tried to lure children into swamps, from which they would never return. It could be heard crying when one was alone by a swamp.

A fourth kind of underwater creature consisted of the *Manôgemassak*, or "Little People," who lived in rivers. Shy rather than malevolent, they had thin faces like ax blades and spoke in small, squeaky voices. Sometimes they worked at night making round concretions, such as those found on Lake Champlain at Button Bay. Similar mudstone concretions were found by Thomas in the course of his excavation at Fort Hill, occupied by Sokokis in the winter of 1663/64. When surprised by humans, these little people submerged in their stone canoes, disappearing from sight.

Mannigebeskwas was a young woman who embodied personal independence. At times she was willfully ugly and dirty, at others beautiful and neat. She often disappeared for long periods, traveling over the mountains teaching each bird its proper song.

The western Abenaki trickster, a figure prominent in the oral traditions of most all native North Americans was *Azeban*, "the

Raccoon." Trickster tales were meant to be entertaining and in-structive. In the tales, no locale was specified, or else could be changed to suit the pleasure of the storyteller. Azeban's pranks were always carried out in a spirit of mischief or curiosity, and usually resulted in some kind of disaster for him.

A flying creature of immense power was *Pmola*. Though dan-gerous, Pmola could on occasion be called to a hunter's assis-tance. Dean Snow has cautiously suggested that some bird forms known from prehistoric rock art in the eastern Abenaki region may be representations of this quasi-human flying creature. If so, then the six bird-like figures in the Brattleboro petroglyphs, some of which are almost human in shape, may be depictions of Pmola.

The most dreaded of quasi-humans was a cannibal giant known as "the Forest Wanderer." His tracks were sometimes seen in the woods by hunters, which we may suppose caused the immediate evacuation of the area. At least the Penobscot reacted this way. The Penobscot thought that some of these cannibal giants were dead shamans, others were ordinary men with a piece of ice shaped like a human in their stomachs. All were capable of being killed, but only if cut up into little pieces. Cannibalism is a motif which crops up frequently in the lore of northern Algonquian peoples and is expressed most dramatically as the Windigo psy-chosis. This is a mental disorder known to occur only among northern Algonquian peoples, and which is greatly feared by them. The victim of the psychosis experiences an increasingly strong craving for human flesh, which may ultimately lead to ac-tual cannibalistic behavior. To our knowledge, though, no in-stance of Windigo psychosis has ever been reported for Abenakis, eastern or western.

A final class of supernatural beings recognized by Abenakis consists of personifications of natural phenomena. One of these is the "Wind Bird," generally regarded as dangerous. Another is the "Earth Grandmother," producer of all life when warmed by the sun, which also is personified. So, too are the "Thunders." These seven brothers have great powers, but fortunately are friendly to humans. Apparently, they were once subdued by Bedgwadzo somewhere between an island and the west shore of Lake Cham-plain. Less cosmic in scope were various local spirits associated with local places too numerous to keep track of. An example of these are the "Spreaders," who frequented a dangerous campsite on the St. Maurice River in Quebec, a region hunted by western Abenakis after 1830. They would prop open with sticks the eyes, mouth, and fingers of any traveler foolish enough to stop over there.

This, then, is the nature of the world in which the western Abenakis lived, as they perceived it early in the seventeenth century. To those who expect the world to be explained scientifically, it will seem to have a fairy tale quality about it. It was, though, real enough to those who lacked the scientific knowledge which is available to us today. Storytelling was a favorite pastime, and so every child growing up heard over and over the myths and tales detailing the exploits of all the various supernatural beings. These were consistent enough with the world as they experienced it, in which they could hear, when off alone by a swamp, what sounded like the cry of the swamp creature. Or a lone hunter crossing a pond on the ice might hit an unexpected and unpredictable soft spot in the ice; in the middle of winter, when the ice should be strong, such soft spots are sometimes to be found on pond ice. In cases like this, it would be easy enough to believe in malevolent underwater creatures. Or if something happened to a hunter off by himself so that he never returned, a reasonable explanation would be that he ran afoul of some malevolent being which got him. In short, the actions of supernatural beings neatly explained otherwise unexplainable phenomena. The apparent ability of one's vital self to travel about while the body slept, interacting on occasion with various of these supernatural beings, not to mention other people, lent further credibility to the whole construct.

Social Control in Western Abenaki Society

The subject of western Abenaki world view is not only fascinating in its own right, an understanding of it is essential if we are to know how order was maintained in this society. These people did not live in a state of anarchy, for they had a well-regulated society, as we have already seen; sanctions were consistently applied to ensure that people's behavior conformed to what was regarded as acceptable. Unlike modern peoples, however, they did not rely on formal sanctions, enacted into law and administered by governmental officials, for the maintenance of order. Instead, they relied heavily on such devices as fear of supernatural retribution and direct retaliation by grieved parties to keep people in line.

Unfortunately, little has been written about the operation of sanctions in western Abenaki society. The few bits of information we do have, though, suggest that sanctions worked in much the same way as they did among the Penobscot. This being so, it seems legitimate to extrapolate, with caution, from the Penobscot to the Abenakis who lived in Vermont. On this basis, it is likely that disputes between different family bands, if they were not too serious, could be arbitrated by the chief and council of the major band. In such cases, neither chief nor council had the power to decide a case and then force both parties of the dispute to abide by their decision. But given their combined prestige, they were in a strong position to persuade the disputants to accept a reasonable solution. As with the Penobscots, decisions handed down probably were designed in large part to satisfy the feelings of the grieved parties.

In the case of serious problems—murder, for example—the victim's family most likely had not only the right, but the duty to pursue and apprehend the offender. If the Penobscot are an accurate guide, then family members could do this with or without the sanction of either chief or council. It was, though, a matter of form to let them know what action the family band was taking. Such notification, in a sense, made their action legal. The power to act, then, really lay with the family bands. The chief and council could arbitrate if asked to do so, but their powers were those of persuasion, and most definitely not those of coercion. This seems to have been the extent of "governmental" involvement in the maintenance of social control.

Based upon the way sanctions worked among the Penobscot, the bulk of western Abenaki sanctions almost certainly involved the operation of supernatural powers. One can divide these into two groups: those involving the practice of shamanism, and those simply following from the act, with no necessity for human action at all. Both served as powerful deterrents to crime.

Each family band included among its members someone who was a shaman, and it was the shaman's job to protect the other

members from certain kinds of crime. One such crime was trespass. Each shaman supposedly had the ability to detect the presence of anyone in the band's hunting territory who was not authorized to be there. Should such trespassers be detected, then it
was the shaman's responsibility to take action against them. He
would send sickness to them, or at least bad luck. Given a deep-
seated belief in the power of the shaman, which was essential to
the operation of the system, this would have served as an effective deterrent. In the case of those individuals who may have
mustered up the nerve to actually poach on someone else's territory, the first untoward event thereafter would likely be inter-
preted as some shaman's retaliation. But, with populations as far
below carrying capacity as they appear to have been, it is unlikely
that there was much incentive to trespass in the first place.

Another crime probably handled by the shaman was misuse
of supernatural power. All individuals with great supernatural
powers were supposed to use these for the good of the group, but
at the same time they had the potential to misuse them. There
were definite controls to prevent people from using such powers
for their own gain at the expense of others. One was the belief
that supernatural powers would give out if overused. Thus, they
had to be conserved so that they could be exercised in times of
necessity. Another control was that known shamans, on account
of their potential to cause harm, were closely watched by others.
If severe misfortune hit a particular group, its members might ac-
cuse their shaman of malpractice and kill him. This probably
tended to keep shamans on their best behavior. Besides this, if a
shaman was engaged in shady practices against another group, he
ran the risk of that group's shaman finding out about it and taking
counteraction. Every shaman was thought to have the ability to
recognize another who was engaged in wrongdoing. And there
was no way to hide; for example, even though the evil shaman
could disguise himself in the form of an animal—his helper—
there were ways of finding out which animals were attached to
which shamans. One way was by watching what foods people
avoided, for the flesh of one's animal helper was taboo. By killing
the animal when the shaman was traveling about in its form, the
shaman was killed as well.

Although a number of supernatural sanctions were thought to operate without the need of any direct action on the part of humans, these were backed up by other considerations: fear of loss of social acceptance and fear of being accused of shamanistic malpractice. These sanctions involved certain taboos, as well as various "dos and don'ts" to be found in mythology. Outright taboos seem to have been few in number. Among the western Abenakis, incest was considered a crime of the worst sort. Any offender would certainly suffer supernatural punishment; they'd probably be banished from the community as well. Other taboos were probably similar to those in force among the Penobscot: suggestive joking with one's sisters, or breaking wind in their presence. Besides supernatural punishment, intense shame was involved. Most likely, too, a hunter could not eat any of his first deer or moose kill of the season, nor could a boy eat any of his first kill ever. To do so would bring very bad luck. This custom emphasized the very high value placed on sharing, a value which ensured that everyone enjoyed more or less equal access to valued resources.

One of the very important functions of western Abenaki stories was to provide people, especially children, with a moral example. This was especially true of stories relating the exploits of the trickster *Azeban*, the Raccoon. By constantly getting into trouble, he illustrated the pitfalls of not adhering to accepted practices. Unfortunately, none of the western Abenaki trickster tales have been published, but two nontrickster episodes, provided by Gordon Day for the film, *Prehistoric Life in the Champlain Valley*, serve to illustrate the role of myths in maintaining social order. The first has already been noted—the tale of the Swamp Creature. The second is the tale of the Tree Squeak, and it goes like this:

As you know, sometimes two trees stand too close together and whenever the wind blows they make a curious sound. There were once two such trees on the top of a mountain, and when the wind blew they made a strange noise, and the little animals heard it and wondered. The screech owl, who is very intelligent and always hungry, heard it and thought it was a little animal he could kill. So he flew to the tree and looked around, but he could not find any little animal and he went away. In a little while a rabbit heard it, but he is naturally timid, and thinking it could be some animal which might seize him, he ran away. Then the flying squirrel heard it and was very curious about it. He wanted to go see what made the noise, but he can only travel by throwing himself down from the top of a tree and gliding, but he cannot fly upward. So he never found out what caused the noise. An Indian who was camped nearby had some little girls, and they were very frightened of the noise. He told them it was only a tree squeak, and not to be afraid. When he returned to the village, he told his cousin about it, how the children were so frightened he had to talk almost all night to make them understand. His cousin said, "My children do not mind me. I'll use the Tree Squeak to frighten them. I'll tell them someone is hollering behind the camp, and if they don't go to sleep I'll call him back. Then they will obey me."

Generally speaking, western Abenaki myths and tales indicate the value of cooperation and unselfishness with those a person knew, which is to say all of the members of one's own major band. Conversely, one didn't interfere in their affairs. One was wary of strangers, for one never knew which of them were out to cause harm. Finally, each individual was supposed to be satisfied with existing reality. These values were consistent with a view of humans as part of a natural order, rather than superior to it. One did not attempt to alter the natural order; rather one did one's best to fit into it. On a personal level, one minded one's own business. Egalitarianism was the order of the day, and so whatever a person had was shared freely with other members of the band. Indeed, the more one had, the more one was obliged to share.

The stories which promoted these values were heard often, from earliest childhood through adulthood. Hence, the moral code was constantly reiterated and became deeply ingrained. Because of this, people generally took responsibility for their own conduct, and social control could be maintained with a minimum of intervention by others.

To summarize, Abenakis in Vermont did not operate in terms of a strict system of laws, as do most people in the world today. They did have a clear moral code which was deeply ingrained in each individual, and which was usually sufficient for day-to-day living. This, coupled with low population levels and a commonality of interests, favored reasonable social stability. When conflicts did arise, as they do in any human society, there were effective ways of handling them, usually on the family level, either through shamanism or more direct action. But for the most part, social disapproval, mediation, and the deterrents of shamanism and supernatural punishment were sufficient to ensure that conflicts did not become disruptive to society.

Roots of Abenaki Culture

On a more general note, the way of life which we have sketched in this chapter seems to have been established, at least in broad outline, in the Archaic period. Since then, a number of changes certainly took place in native culture in Vermont, but they appear to have involved differences of degree, rather than kind. Many of these—the adoption of new styles of projectile points, for example—were no more momentous than are the annual changes in automobile styling in our own culture. Others, though, represented significant improvements, as when birch bark canoes, the bow and arrow, and pottery containers largely, though not completely, replaced dugout canoes, spears, and containers of wood and bark.

The most momentous change was the adoption of horticulture, but even at that the native Vermonters never became as fully committed to growing their own food as did the native peoples of New York and New England south of Vermont. The low population levels, social organization, and world view of the western Abenakis are all more typical of hunters and gatherers than they are of horticulturalists. Moreover, the frequent and unpredictable occurrence of shorter than average growing seasons precluded too much dependence upon domestic crops for subsistence. Evidently, horticulture was adopted as a supplement (an important one nonetheless) to the existing tradition of hunting and gathering. It was carried out in such a way as to fit in with the seasonal cycle of hunting and gathering, which continued to regulate people's lives. In short, there is nothing to indicate that the overall pattern of seasonal movement within specific watersheds did not remain pretty much the same over five or six millennia.

Such cultural stability implies continuity, and this brings us back to a hypothesis stated in Chapter 3: the roots of western Abenaki culture lie in the late Archaic Vergennes culture. The case cannot yet be proven, but there are other bits of evidence which support it. There is presently widespread acceptance of the view that cultural and ethnic continuity have characterized the regions surrounding Vermont for the last 2000 years at least. In Canada north of the St. Lawrence, the Algonquian-speaking Cree-Montagnais and Naskapi are generally regarded as the ethnic, cultural, and linguistic descendants of ancient Shield Archaic peoples, who moved into the boreal forests of eastern Canada some 6000 or so years ago. Similarly, the eastern Abenakis, Passamaquoddys, Maliseets, and Micmacs are accepted by most anthropologists as the ethnic, cultural, and linguistic descendants of the people responsible for the coastal shell middens of Maine and the Maritime Provinces of Canada. South of Vermont, the seventeenth-century Algonquian-speaking peoples of Massachusetts, Rhode Island, Connecticut, and the Hudson Valley are likewise accepted by many as having ethnic, cultural, and linguistic roots extending back 2000 years in their region. Finally, it is generally accepted that the ethnic, cultural, and linguistic ancestors of the historic Iroquoian peoples have been occupying most of the rest of New York State for the last 2000 years surely, and probably since at least 1500 b.c. (1835 B.C.). Given such apparent ethnic, cultural, and linguistic stability throughout the rest of the Northeast, it would be odd if the situation in Vermont were any different.

As we have seen, the frontier between the western Abenakis of Vermont and the Iroquoian peoples of New York ca. A.D. 1600 was Lake Champlain. We have also seen that this was preceeded in late Archaic times by a frontier located a bit west of Lake Champlain, in the Adirondack Mountains. This divided Vergennes Archaic folk on the east from Brewerton Archaic folk on the west. As discussed in Chapter 3, ancestors of the Iroquoians seem to have moved in and asserted dominance over the Brewerton folk. Given the expansionist tendencies of the Iroquoians, it is not surprising that their eastern frontier should, with time, have been pushed as far as Lake Champlain. In other words, the frontier which existed in the ethnographic present between the Iroquoian Mohawks and the western Abenakis appears to have its origins in the late Archaic frontier between the Vergennes folk and their descendants on the one hand, and the Brewerton folk and the early Iroquoians who moved in on them on the other.

Another late Archaic frontier discussed in Chapter 3 which

may have persisted up to Historic times is that which ran from the Green Mountains east to the coast, just south of Vermont. In the ethnographic present, this was the frontier between western Abenakis on the one hand, and the Pocumtucks and other Algonquian-speaking peoples of southern New England on the other. On the basis of two datum points, in the Connecticut and Merrimac valleys, it looks as if the southern frontier of Vergennes or Vergennes-like culture was virtually the same. Unfortunately, these are the only two datum points we have; obviously we need more before we can be sure about this conclusion.

Again referring back to Chapter 3, we saw reason to propose the same kind of close ethnic, cultural, and linguistic relationship between the Vergennes folk and the Maritime Archaic peoples of Maine and Canada's Atlantic Provinces as existed later between eastern and western Abenakis. Moreover, the distribution of these late Archaic peoples shows a rough correspondence to that of the Wabanakis at the time of European contact. In the Atlantic Provinces and Canada, archaeological research over the past decade has shown that Maritime Archaic culture survived, in modified form, into historic times as the culture of Newfoundland's Beothuk. On the Mainland north of the St. Lawrence, Maritime Archaic culture was replaced by that of people ancestral to the modern Montagnais and Naskapi. The situation is not yet as clear in Maine and the Maritimes, but archaeologists James Tuck and Dean Snow have both presented strong arguments that the culture of the people responsible for the coastal shell mounds, which is generally regarded as ancestral to the culture of the eastern Wabanaki peoples, evolved *in situ* in Maine and the Maritimes from the Maritime Archaic. If so, then a similar relationship should exist between Vergennes and Western Abenaki culture. All of this is consistent with linguistic evidence: there is nothing in the language spoken by any of the Wabanaki peoples to suggest the presence of earlier, non-Algonquian populations in the region. While the easterners continued to exploit coastal resources, they no longer went so far offshore after sea mammals and deep sea fish. Instead, they placed more emphasis on riverine and land resources, which took them with more regularity into the interior. This being so, it is understandable that the boundary between eastern and western Abenakis would have been some-what west of that between Vergennes and Maritime Archaic peoples.

To repeat, we cannot now prove that Vermont's western Aben-akis are the descendants of the late Archaic Vergennes folk. It will take many years of work to come up with such proof, if in-deed it can be proven. On the other hand, the evidence currently at our disposal fits comfortably with the hypothesis, and there is nothing to contradict it. In our opinion, the odds are in its favor; future research is likely to increase those odds.

The apparent stability of culture in Vermont since the late Archaic period raises one last issue which must be discussed. In our modern quest for progress, we tend to place a high value on change. Consequently, it is all too easy to regard five or six mil-lennia of relative cultural stability as a sign of stagnation, or lack of progress. To do so, however, is unjustifiable. One cannot objec-tively evaluate one culture by another's values. Nor is it correct to conclude that a people like the western Abenakis and their an-cestors lacked the leisure time which would have permitted cul-tural elaboration. This is an old wives' tale that flies in the face of a large body of evidence which shows quite clearly that hunting and gathering people as a general rule have more leisure time available to them than do most non–hunting and gathering peoples.

The long term stability of aboriginal culture in Vermont is best explained in evolutionary terms. In late Archaic times, a culture emerged which was well-adapted to conditions as they existed in Vermont. By providing for patterns of behavior which allowed people to utilize the environment to their advantage, it secured their survival and saw to the reasonable satisfaction of their needs, as these were perceived. Such are the only objective crite-ria by which the success or failure of a culture may be judged. In evolution, be it biological or cultural, what works well in a given environment is usually favored over what is new and novel, un-less there is a significant change in the environment. In Vermont, the environment has remained relatively stable over the past five or six millennia. Given a successful adaptation to that environ-ment, relative cultural stability would be expected. What we are saying, then, is that the long term stability of native culture in Vermont is a clear indication of that culture's success. It was not until existing conditions were radically altered by the influx of European peoples that the adaptive advantage of the traditional culture was lost. How this came about we shall see in Chapter 6.

6. EUROPEANS COME TO VERMONT:
The Destruction of a Way of Life

ALTHOUGH it was Columbus's "discovery" which opened the lands of the western hemisphere to European settlement, it was more than 100 years before the French, British, and Dutch established settlements in northeastern North America. The French tried and failed on St. Croix Island in 1604, but were successful at Port Royal a year later, and at Quebec in 1608. The British tried and failed at the mouth of the Kennebec River in 1607; it was not until 1620 and 1628 that Plymouth and Massachusetts Bay had their beginnings. The Dutch tried and were successful at Fort Orange (Albany) in 1624. In what is now Vermont, there was no significant European settlement for still another 100 years. The French established Fort Ste. Anne on Isle La Motte in 1666, but it was not long maintained. Fort Dummer, built by the colonists of Massachusetts Bay in 1724, was the first relatively permanent European settlement in Vermont. Following its construction, a few more people from the Bay colony trickled into southeastern Vermont. The French, for their part, established Fort St. Frederic at Crown Point in 1731, made some land grants in the Champlain Valley, and established a mission at Missisquoi in 1743. But it wasn't until 1763 that Europeans in large numbers began to move into Vermont. They came largely from Connecticut, though western Massachusetts was well-represented. Fewer than 10 percent came from other places.

The Abenakis of Vermont began to feel the effects of the European discovery of America long before any European settled on their lands. We know from Peter Thomas's work at Fort Hill, the Connecticut River village established by the Sokokis in 1663, that western Abenaki culture was in the throes of substantial change by then. Although traditional work in ceramics, bone, stone, and shell was still being carried on, manufactured implements of iron, such as axes, hatchets, knives, and fishhooks, had largely replaced their traditional stone equivalents. For smoking, kaolin pipes had replaced those of native manufacture. European brass was being used extensively to make arrow points, engraving tools, needles, and punches, as well as some ornaments. Muskets were in common use, as was manufactured cloth for clothing and blankets. Traditional symbolic objects were still being made, of shell, mudstone and brass, but Jesuit rings handed out after catechism classes indicate that concepts of European world view were vying with traditional native concepts. Traditional social, political, and economic networks had been substantially altered, and traditional subsistence strategies were showing signs of strain. In short, although many elements of European culture had been absorbed and integrated into native culture, the transformation of the latter into something radically different from what it had been had actually begun by the second half of the seventeenth century and was well-advanced by the time the first British settlers arrived in 1724. This is important, for it has much to do with the rise of the myth that "Indians didn't live in Vermont." To understand both the myth, as well as the demise of traditional western Abenaki culture in Vermont, we must concern ourselves with events that happened before 1724, and in places other than Vermont.

Though seldom given much play, it is an historical fact that the first colonists of New England and New York established themselves on land which had already been cleared by natives for their own farms and villages. Indeed, they could hardly have done otherwise, for they had neither the knowledge, technology, nor organizational skills to "carve farms from the wilderness." These were to come later, gained through instruction provided by natives. For that matter, there was not any real wilderness; where not cleared, the land sustained forests which were maintained as open parkland by native peoples. This was done through periodic burning, which provided good "browse pasture" for deer and other game.

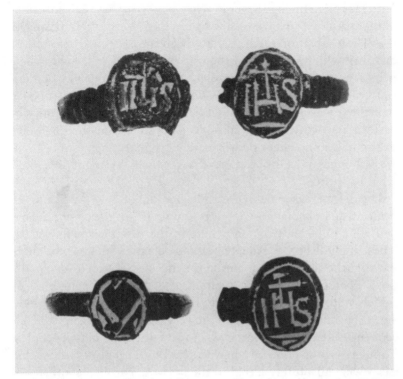

FIGURE 6-1. Jesuit rings found at Fort Hill. Such rings were handed out after catechism classes to Native Americans. Photo courtesy Peter A. Thomas.

Epidemics and Plague

Had the first colonists simply stepped ashore and helped themselves to cleared land being lived on or farmed by people at the time, they probably would have been met by serious opposition. Being few in number, they could have been disposed of by the natives then and there. But fortunately for the colonists, they found substantial tracts of cleared land not then in use. The reason for this is that a devastating epidemic in the years 1616 and 1617 had killed off natives by the thousands. Those few who survived had more than enough land for themselves, and so they were not unduly inconvenienced by the settlement of newcomers nearby. From early records, it is clear that this epidemic swept through native populations along the coast from Cape Cod at least as far north as the Kennebec River in what is now Maine. The only populations known to have escaped were those west of Narragansett Bay. Their salvation seems to have been the existence of a state of hostility which had caused them to break off contact with their neighbors before the plague. Because eastern Abenaki populations were affected, and because we have no reason to suppose that there was a lack of contact between at least some groups of eastern and western Abenakis, it is possible that the 1616 epidemic had some effect on Vermont's original inhabitants. There was, though, no European on the scene in Vermont to record what happened.

The disease responsible for the epidemic of 1616/17 has never been adequately diagnosed, but is known to have been one of several which did not exist anywhere in the Americas before 1492. These include bubonic and pneumonic plague, chicken pox, cholera, diphtheria, dysentery, influenza, measles, scarlet fever, smallpox, tuberculosis, typhus, typhoid, and whooping cough, all of which were carried unwittingly from the old world to the new by Europeans and were among the very first of the disruptive consequences of European discovery to be felt by the native peoples. Though serious enough when suffered by Europeans, these diseases were absolutely lethal to the natives. Through centuries of exposure, Europeans had developed a degree of biological resistance to these diseases. Never having had this opportunity, Native Americans had virtually no resistance to them at all. Thus, they contracted the diseases more readily than did Europeans, and of those who contracted them, fewer survived.

We can be sure that the epidemic of 1616/17 was not the first to wreak havoc among New England's natives. In Mexico, where the Spanish kept much better records than did the Dutch, French, and British further north, we know that European diseases caused a 90 percent reduction in native populations within 100 years of first contact. Since the native Mexicans were biologically the same as all the other native peoples of eastern North America, the same thing must have happened all along the eastern seaboard, including New England. The records at our disposal, imperfect though they are, support this contention.

The first European diseases probably were brought to the Northeast by the end of the first decade of the sixteenth century. As early as 1497 and 1498, the Cabots sailed the coast, to be followed by Gaspar Corte-Real in 1500. A combined party of British and Portuguese reached Labrador in 1501. By 1504, boatloads of French and Portuguese fishermen were making regular trips to the Grand Banks, coming ashore to cure their catches and trade with the inhabitants. Although Newfoundland was the scene of most of these early contacts, they soon spread to the shores of the Maritimes. Between 1504 and 1534 there was frequent contact between Basque, Breton, British, Norman, and Portuguese fishermen and Micmacs, who in turn were in regular contact with their Abenaki neighbors to the south and west. It is inconceivable that at least one fisherman, on one of these boats, wasn't sick; that is all it would have taken to start an epidemic among the Micmacs. From the Micmacs, it could have easily spread to the Abenakis, and from one group of Abenakis to another in the course of their regular social, political, and economic contacts with one another. One hundred years from 1510 brings us to the time of the first attempts at colonization in the Northeast. By then, the Micmacs are known to have suffered a major population decline. Further south and west, in Abenaki country, population reduction through disease should have been well-advanced, even if it had not yet reached 90 percent.

Just as it was not the first, the epidemic of 1616/17 was not the last to decimate the ranks of New England's native peoples. In 1633, Captain John Oldham of Massachusetts made the first recorded overland journey by an Englishman to the upper Connecticut River. Whether or not he actually caused it, Oldham was blamed by a number of natives for an outbreak of smallpox there shortly after his trip. Affecting not just the people of the Connecticut Valley, this epidemic swept through native populations at least as far east as Maine. It spread as well to the Iroquois of New York State and, within two or three years, to the people of the St. Lawrence and Ottawa valleys. Again, as they had in 1616 and 1617, thousands of natives died from the disease. By contrast, only two British families in the whole of New England suffered losses. In southeastern Vermont, the Sokokis were certainly ravaged by the disease. The same was probably true for the closely related Cowasucks to the north of them in the Connecticut Valley; nor could the Abenakis of western Vermont have escaped, surrounded as they were by afflicted populations on all sides.

But the 1633 epidemic was not the end of troubles, either. Natives, particularly those in close contact with colonists, continued to die from European diseases, even if not in epidemic proportions. Then, in 1639, there was a new outbreak of smallpox among the natives at Quebec and elsewhere along the St. Lawrence. This outbreak is known to have been caused by the arrival of natives from Abenaki country. A few years later, in 1646, there was an outbreak of a disease among Maine's Abenakis which produced a "bloody vomiting." Whether Vermont's Abenakis were affected by either of these is not known, but it is likely. By 1640 at least, the Sokokis are known to have been in close contact with Abenakis as far east as the Kennebec River, who were affected by both. The most destructive of all smallpox epidemics to strike native communities along the St. Lawrence broke out in 1669, long after close relationships were established between the French and Abenakis from Vermont. The latter could hardly have escaped involvement in this epidemic.

Whether or not Vermont's Abenakis suffered from the "bloody flux" which afflicted the natives of Massachusetts in 1652 is not known. But almost certainly, they felt the effects of the "strange diseases" which broke out among New England's natives in the winter of 1675/76, just as the Mohawks struck against "King Philip's" force in the second war of Puritan Conquest. Reports suggest that warriors of Missisquoi met with Philip and his warriors before the Mohawk attack, and later, some of the survivors of the war are known to have fled north into Vermont. Vermont's inhabitants must have suffered, too, from the smallpox epidemic which broke out among the native peoples of the St. Lawrence Valley in 1684. Once again, the disease was carried by Abenakis, who had caught it from the Iroquois. Vermont's natives were probably stricken again in 1690, when a military force raised against Canada, under Fitz-John Winthrop of Connecticut, got as far as Lake Champlain. It was there that an outbreak of smallpox forced the troops to turn back. The 1690s, too, were a time of great destruction from smallpox throughout eastern Abenaki

FIGURE 6–2. Unknown artist's impression of a smallpox epidemic among Massachusetts native peoples. By permission of Chicago Historical Society Ichi-08785.

country. Finally, French records and Ira Allen tell of an outbreak of smallpox at Missisquoi in 1730 which caused abandonment of the village. Although the survivors began to move back in 1731, resettlement was not completed until 1740.

Vermont's original inhabitants then, suffered their share of catastrophic epidemics which, along with chronic illnesses such as tuberculosis and other respiratory complaints, reduced native populations elsewhere in New England by 90 percent. Several of these epidemics preceded the founding of Fort Dummer, and even more preceded the 1763 influx of immigrants from the Puritan colonies of New England. By then, surely, there weren't many native Vermonters left. However, as we shall see, those who were left were joined by refugees from elsewhere in New England, offsetting to some degree losses by disease.

The Fur Trade

Another early consequence of European contact, less immediately disastrous to the natives, was the development of the fur
trade. Europeans—especially those of wealth and rank—developed a taste for furs long before voyagers from Europe reached the
rich fur-producing regions of North America. France, England
and, the Low countries in particular all have cold winters, and
manor houses were drafty and poorly heated. Furs, therefore, kept
the nobility warm. Because they were expensive, they served as
well to show off the wealth and high rank of those who wore
them. They were expensive because, by 1500, Europeans had long
since depleted their own stocks of fur-bearing animals. By then
they were getting their furs largely from the Russians. Although
there was still a good supply of fur-bearing animals in eastern
Russia and Siberia, it is likely that some of the "Russian" pelts
actually came from North America. Many were obtained by the
Russians through trade with the nomads of central Asia who, at
least from the time of Marco Polo, were linked to an extensive
trade network extending ultimately over the Bering Straits into
Alaska. The movement of furs from east to west across the straits
was an important part of this trade.

Two things about northeastern North America impressed the
early Dutch, British, and French explorers: the vast quantities of
codfish to be found in the offshore waters and the rich store of fur-
bearing animals on the land. The fish they could get for themselves, but lacking knowledge of the country, the habits of fur-
bearing animals, and the techniques for trapping them, they
could obtain furs only through trade with the natives. The richest
source of furs in all of North America was the St. Lawrence–
Great Lakes region, and here the French quickly established
themselves with a string of trading posts: Port Royal on the Bay of
Fundy; Tadouasac, Quebec, Trois Rivieres, and Montreal on the
St. Lawrence itself. So intent on the fur trade were the French
that for many years they allowed no settlement other than those
required to sustain their trade. Any settlement beyond this, they
felt, would complicate their dealing with the natives.

Were it not for the establishment of Fort Orange by the Dutch
in 1624, the French would have had the furs of the Great Lakes

region to themselves. The Dutch entered the fur trade in 1612, obtaining pelts from the inhabitants of the Hudson and (after 1614) Connecticut valleys. Like the French, they were more interested in this trade than they were in establishing colonial settlements. Their first settlements were all trading posts, and at Fort Orange they had access through Iroquoian middlemen to furs from the Great Lakes. Thus the Dutch, and the British who replaced them in 1664, could continue to obtain furs long after stocks in New York and New England had been depleted. But to do so they had to maintain good relations with the Iroquois, which they bent over backwards to do. Thus, the Iroquois remained strong long after 1676, by which time almost no natives were left in New England south of what are now Vermont and New Hampshire, or in the Hudson Valley south of Albany.

East of the Dutch and south of the French, the first British settlements at Plymouth and Massachusetts Bay were established as trading posts, and so they remained until 1623 and 1630 respectively. There were at the time many furs to be had in New England, but large numbers of those in the Connecticut Valley were going to the Dutch. Later, many of those of the North were to go to the French. One of the highest fur-yielding regions in all of New England was that drained by the upper Connecticut River. Here, the British squeezed out the Dutch by the simple expedient of establishing trading posts further upstream. The first of these upstream posts was established in 1633, and by 1635, William Pynchon of Springfield, Massachusetts, had secured a virtual monopoly over the Connecticut River trade. The Sokoki were involved in this trade, probably largely through other native middle men. They are first mentioned in Pynchon's day book in 1648, when a Sokoki traded two beaver pelts for two blue cloth coats. The account books of John Pynchon, who took over his father's business in 1652, show that beaver pelts were far and away the major commodity obtained from the natives. In 1654, his most successful year, he exported 3723 pounds of beaver pelts. But the pelts of otter, muskrat, mink, marten, lynx, fisher, fox, sable, raccoon, and moose were also obtained and sent off to England. In addition, some deer, wolf, and bear pelts were obtained for local consumption.

A major item sought by the natives from Europeans was manufactured cloth, including ready-made clothing. In the Connecticut Valley, this was the number one item consumed by native inhabitants. There were several reasons for this. For one thing, it took much less time and energy to transform wool or cotton cloth into clothing than it did deer or moose hides. For another, clothing of wool or cotton tends to be more comfortable than that made from animal hides, particularly where the climate is humid as it is throughout the Northeast. Finally, skin clothing is costly of raw materials. It probably took the equivalent of 4.5 deer hides per year to keep each individual Abenaki in clothing and moccasins, and of course additional hides were required for bedding and other purposes. Thus it is likely that as more time and energy were devoted to the procurement, processing, and transport of furs, including some deer and moose hides, fewer hides were available for traditional purposes. Acquisition of manufactured cloth would have made up for whatever deficit there was in the raw materials for clothing and bedding.

The other major item sought by natives in exchange for furs was wampum, the strings of ground and drilled shell beads which were used for awhile in the seventeenth century by the New England colonists as a form of currency. The center of wampum manufacture was Long Island Sound, and it was first used by coastal people for ceremonial, political, and decorative purposes long before Europeans arrived on the scene. Its use spread to the peoples of the interior, who obtained it through trade from the coastal peoples. In the seventeenth century, the exchange of wampum between groups was an important part of treaty negotiations. Small strings were exchanged where trivial matters were involved, but large broad belts were necessary for momentous matters. Figures in the belts gave them individual identities so that they could serve as mnemonic devices. These belts were carefully preserved and reviewed periodically so that their ceremonial and political meaning was remembered and passed on to succeeding generations. Wampum was also a major item in tribute payments. When one group was able to assert its dominance over another, the subjected group was required to acknowledge this relationship periodically, through payment of tribute. For much of the time between the late 1620s and 1650, the Sokokis and Mahicans, among others, were in such a tributary relationship to the New York Iroquois. In order to make the necessary tribute payments, they had to obtain sufficient wampum, which was available only from peoples to the south of them.

The political and ceremonial importance of wampum to the natives, and its prominence as an item of exchange in the fur trade, brings us to an important point which all too often is overlooked. Traditionally, peoples in the Northeast did not trade with one another solely, or even primarily, to procure consumable commodities, no matter how useful these may have been. Rather, it was the act of trade that was important, for it provided a means of maintaining contact and communication between different bands and tribes who might otherwise be hostile toward one another. Through trade, information was exchanged, conflicts resolved, and friendly relations maintained. Thus, it is understandable why these people so quickly entered into trading relationships with Europeans: trade provided the only means by which conflicts with the newcomers might be resolved.

As we have already seen in the case of the Sokokis, the native peoples obtained more than cloth and wampum from Europeans. Before the outbreak of the first Abenaki-British war in 1675, the Sokoki relied on the Pynchons and their agents at Springfield and Northampton for their kaolin pipes, iron goods, brass, and occasional glass bottles and mirrors. But trade in these commodities was nowhere near as extensive as that in cloth and wampum. There was in addition to this authorized trade a kind of trickle trade by which an occasional piece of glazed earthenware was obtained from nearby farmsteads. The Sokoki relied on the French for muskets and, presumably, lead for shot and the powder to fire it. These must have been of more than utilitarian value, for among native North Americans traditionally, weapons had great symbolic value. The exchange of real or symbolic weapons was an important means of disarming suspicion of evil design or unfriendly intent. From the French, the Sokoki also got glass beads. Ultimately, as we shall see, they began to rely on the French for more than guns and beads.

All of this trade with Europeans, as might be imagined, caused major alterations in existing trade networks. Since late Archaic times, Vermont peoples participated in long distance trade that at various times brought goods into the region from as far afield as the Great Lakes, Long Island Sound, and the Atlantic coast. The kind of alteration caused by the fur trade is vividly illustrated by the Sokoki who, at the time of contact, obtained much of the chert used to make their chipped stone implements from the peoples of western Vermont and New York. By the 1660s this was no longer the case. Instead, they were making their chipped stone "strike-a-lights," scrapers, and engraving tools of flint that was carried all the way from Europe in French and British ships as ballast.

Besides inducing a shift in native economies from subsistence to commercial activities and altering traditional trade networks, the rise of the fur trade brought about a number of other changes in native cultures. Unless they were obtained through trade with other peoples, the furs which western Abenakis traded to Europeans came from animals to be found within family hunting territories. As the rate of extraction of furs accelerated, attempts were made to more precisely allocate rights to the animals which supplied those furs. This was accomplished in part by a more precise definition of the boundaries of hunting territories. With this, the western Abenaki concept of territoriality changed from one which bore no real relation to the European concept of ownership of parcels of land, the boundaries of which are well-defined, to one which did. In addition, just who was entitled to hunt and trap within those boundaries was more precisely spelled out. An effective device for restricting access to valued resources, frequently used by tribal peoples in all parts of the world, is a specified rule of descent. Thus, an Abenaki's right to hunt or trap fur-bearing animals within a specified territory seems to have depended more and more on the fact that his father hunted and trapped there. A development of totemic ideas seems to have gone along with this increased emphasis on the patrilineal transmission of hunting and trapping rights.

Although these changes were well under way by the latter half of the seventeenth century, other events intervened to prevent their full maturation until after 1800. As we shall see, the seventeenth and eighteenth centuries saw a rise in the frequency and intensity of warfare, which not only made it increasingly difficult to control what went on in hunting territories far removed from the villages, but ultimately caused the dispersal of many peoples from their ancestral lands. Moreover, strict adherence to patrilineality was impossible in the face of the continuing high death rates which were brought about by disease and exacerbated by warfare.

As trade between Europeans and natives developed, redistribution came to play an increasingly prominent role. Redistribution is a form of exchange in which goods are accumulated by an agent of redistribution, who then sees to their ultimate distribution. On the European side, the agent of redistribution was the trader, operating out of a specific trading house under some kind of governmental supervision. In western New England, natives brought their processed furs into the "trucking houses" run by the Pynchons and their agents at places such as Springfield and Northampton. Here, in addition to wampum, the people could obtain cloth, iron objects, brass kettles, kaolin pipes, and other things which the trader kept as part of his regular stock. Trade between natives and colonists outside the trucking houses was not encouraged.

On the Abenaki side, it appears that the band chief often acted as the agent of redistribution. Originally the chief of a major band enjoyed considerable prestige, but had little authority, as we have already seen. People's needs were largely taken care of through the network of kinship relationships within family bands. But as we have also seen, the major band itself constituted a larger order kinship group, and its chief was regarded as responsible in a general sort of way for the welfare of its members. Therefore, as the need for an agent of redistribution arose, it was natural that the chief of the major band should take on the job. No doubt this was aided and abetted by the European preference for dealing with chiefs, and by shifts in intertribal relationships brought on by changing patterns of trade and new political alliances, see pages 225–227. As a consequence, the office of chief became far more important than it had been, making it possible for office holders who were adept at manipulation to increase their authority considerably. As this increased, so did their relative status. Coupled with the previously noted emphasis on the patrilineal transmission of rights, this led to the transformation of what had been an essentially egalitarian society into one in which distinctions of rank were considered important.

Although the fur trade in New England was carried out by the colonists pretty much as a straight commercial operation, such was not the case in New France. Almost from the start, French traders saw advantages to close cooperation with missionaries, and so the latter were welcome in the settlements along the St. Lawrence even when farmers and other nontraders were not. And the missionaries served the traders well; as they sought converts, they developed contacts useful to the traders. And as they proselytized, they were able to speak with eloquence of the heretical nature of the British, who had strayed from Catholicism. Heretics were evil, and good Catholics should have as little to do with them as possible. Among other things, they should trade their furs to good Catholic Frenchmen even though, as was often the case, British heretics might pay higher prices.

The French were extremely successful at converting native peoples, the Abenakis included, to Catholicism. Part of their success they undoubtedly owed to the epidemics which periodically killed so many people. Traditional cures, including those which involved shamanism, obviously offered no protection against these disasters, and this may have shaken the people's confidence in their traditional beliefs. By contrast, European medicines and rituals had the appearance of being effective against the new diseases, for the Jesuits particularly suffered far less from the various epidemics than did the natives. Of the French who cared for the natives through the epidemic of 1669/70, for example, only one became ill, but he recovered. The Abenakis particularly were firm believers in the efficacy of French religion in curing diseases of European origin.

In addition to all this, the French worked hard at their missionizing; much harder than did the British, who frequently diverted funds from missionary activities to other purposes. Unlike the British, they normally took the trouble to learn the language of the peoples among whom they worked. They also demanded less of the people for conversion than did, at least, the Puritans of New England. Moreover, they promised their converts military protection against their enemies, the Iroquois of New York, who just happened to be allies of the British and competitors of the French in the trade for furs from the Great Lakes. As early as 1651, the French promised to provide Sokoki chiefs with muskets to use against their enemies. As we have already seen, this was probably taken by the Sokoki as a specific sign that French intentions toward them were not unfriendly. The British by contrast, had a prohibition on trading or lending guns to natives.

We do not know exactly when Vermont Abenakis began trading with the French, and so were exposed to their missionizing. We do know that the first French reference to Sokokis, who lived in that part of Vermont least accessible to the French, and closest to the British, dates to 1642. By the 1660s, as we have already noticed, the Sokoki were trading with the French for muskets, lead, powder and glass beads. They were also learning their catechism, for which they were rewarded with Jesuit rings. By 1662, at least some of them were traveling all the way to Montreal for rites of the church, for that is when the names of Sokoki individuals began to appear in the register of Notre Dame de Montreal. Obviously, this implies that a significant change in western Abenaki world view had at least begun, if it was not well-advanced.

In spite of their close French connection, Vermont Abenakis continued to trade with the British from time to time when it was to their advantage to do so. For example, in 1682 the Abenakis were trading with the British at Schaghticoke, a village on the Hoosic River near its confluence with the Hudson, established by Governor Andros of New York for refugees from New England's second war of puritan conquest (King Philip's War). This trade was not to the liking of the French, even though they were not willing to pay prices as high as those the British were paying for furs. The French response was to establish a short-lived mission at Missisquoi, in an attempt to alienate the Abenakis from the English. A longer-lived mission was established at Missisquoi in 1743 in part for the same reason: to counteract trade with the British at Albany, and strengthen the attachment of the Abenakis to the French.

Although participation in the fur trade was not initially disastrous to Vermont's natives, it did ultimately work to their disadvantage. For one thing, their increasing dependence on Europeans, be they British or French, led eventually to the loss of both their traditional technology and world view. With both went the people's ability to provide for their own basic material and spiritual needs. It is ironic to note, considering that the early Euro-

FIGURE 6–3. These "Indians of Lower Canada" may have been Abenakis. By 1662, Abenakis from southern Vermont were traveling as far as Montreal for rites of the church. Lithograph by Cornelius Krieghoff, courtesy Public Archives of Canada, C-56.

pean settlers would have perished had they not been fed by natives, that John Pynchon of Springfield frequently sold even corn and beans to the natives of the Connecticut Valley. In short, they eventually could not get along without Europeans and the goods and services which they provided.

Unfortunately, for native peoples, the reverse was not true. The initial dependence of Europeans on natives vanished as soon as the natives had taught them how to deal with the North American environment. This left the fur trade; but in New England, this was destined to fail. The beaver is an animal of low fertility, and heavy trapping soon exhausts the supply of animals. One answer to this is to range further afield in search of new supplies. In New France and New Netherland (later New York), furs continued to be obtained through trade with people living further in the interior of the continent, both directly and through other native middlemen as well. New England's traders, however, were hemmed in by the French, Dutch, and the British who replaced the Dutch. Although some western furs did reach the Pynchons through a limited overland trade from the Hudson Valley, this was not sufficient to offset the decline in New England furs. The year 1654 was the high point of the Connecticut Valley fur trade, but the inevitable decline set in. By 1656, fur yields were consistently below average, and the failure was well advanced by 1665. But then, the natives had another commodity of interest to the colonists: land. By the 1650s, colonial settlements had grown to the point where land was in short supply. At the same time, the natives still desired the cloth and other items they were accustomed to obtaining through trade. Moreover, they apparently continued to view trade as the only forum for resolving their problems with the colonists. So in the 1660s, the Connecticut Valley traders began to regularly extend credit to the natives, with their prime farmland as collateral. Since it was impossible for the people to secure enough pelts to pay off their debts, they rapidly lost their lands to the British. This left them with no commodity of interest to the British, and by 1675, they were of no further use to New England's colonists.

The British Menace

Although New England's fur trade was ultimately bound to fail anyway, its failure was undoubtedly hastened by warfare which more and more interfered with trapping activities. As we have seen in earlier chapters of this book, warfare was by no means absent in northeastern North America in pre-European times. As early as 2000 b.c., there was conflict between different groups of peoples in the Finger Lakes region of New York. And in Vermont, the Abenakis were having trouble with the Iroquois as early as about 1570. But in the seventeenth century, as a consequence of European settlement, the nature, tempo, and conduct of warfare changed drastically, with disastrous results for native peoples. At first, traditional patterns of native warfare intensified, as different tribes competed to control, if not monopolize, the fur trade. This was exacerbated as natives were drawn into the power struggles of the French and British. Ultimately, the natives of New England were faced with a war of extermination unlike anything they had ever experienced before.

Almost from the moment of their arrival on the shores of

northeastern North America, the French and British unwittingly became involved in existing native enmities. The British, for their part, immediately earned a bad reputation for themselves with the Abenakis. In 1602 and 1603, Bartholomew Gosnold and Martin Pring voyaged to the coast of Maine, where they and their seamen had a good deal of contact with eastern Abenakis. And in both instances, trouble developed. The records do not tell us why, but the reasons seem clear nonetheless. The brawling, licentious conduct of sailors ashore in foreign lands has become legendary through the ages, and the British sailors of the sixteenth century were a particularly hard-bitten bunch. That they were generally rough in their dealings with native peoples is indicated by no less an authority than Sir Ferdinando Gorges, who expressed his concern that the misbehavior of British seamen and fishermen would make trouble for future colonists. To add insult to injury, the next British voyager to appear, in 1605, was George Waymouth, who kidnapped five Abenakis on Monhegan Island. Finally, in 1607, the British tried to establish a colony in eastern Abenaki country, near the mouth of the Kennebec River. Records suggest that the colonists were quarrelsome even amongst themselves, and it is not surprising that they, too, got in trouble with the natives; so badly did they treat their neighbors in the colony's second year that a Jesuit missionary was prompted to remark: "They drove the Savages away without ceremony; they beat, maltreated and misused them outrageously."

News traveled widely in aboriginal New England, and it is clear that news of any community within 200 miles was easily obtained. Not infrequently, in the Connecticut Valley, news traveled as far as 300 to 500 miles. In the 1640s, the Sokoki are known to have had strong contacts to the east as far as the Kennebec River, and there is no reason to suppose that this was anything new. We are justified in supposing, then, that word of British misconduct spread widely among Abenakis and certainly did nothing to win friends among a people who regarded all strangers with suspicion to begin with. In fact, the British seldom did anything to overcome Abenaki distrust. Their ban on trading or loaning guns to natives meant that they could not provide the natives with the traditional symbols by which suspicion of evil design or unfriendly intent were disarmed. Later, British alliance with the Iroquois, traditional enemies of the Abenaki and competitors in the fur trade, rubbed salt into existing wounds; reports of atrocities in the Puritan colonies of New England surely added to Abenaki anxieties. The situation became explosive by the latter part of the seventeenth century and erupted in open warfare in 1675.

While the behavior of Englishmen led to the development of the idea of a "British Menace," the behavior of Frenchmen, while not perfect, had quite the opposite effect. The French seem to have recognized from the start that success in the fur trade—which was at the root of their interest in North America—depended on good relations with the natives. This is why they were reluctant to allow the emigration of settlers with other interests to New France. In his eagerness to please his native companions in 1609, Champlain assisted in the slaughter of a party of their Iroquoian enemies on the west shore of Lake Champlain. This seems to have earned the French the same sort of bad reputation among the Iroquoian tribes of New York that the British had with the Abenakis. On the other hand, it had the desired effect on his Algonquian companions, and word of the deed must have gotten to the Abenakis living east of the lake. Surely this created a favorable bias toward the French, even before any face-to-face meeting between a Frenchman and a western Abenaki took place. The first record we have of such a meeting occurred in 1642, when the French rescued a Sokoki captive from his Montagnais tormentors. For this kindness, the Sokoki were grateful; they were even more grateful in 1651 when the French promised them muskets, which they could not get from the British, to use against their Iroquoian enemies. And whether the French realized it or not, the presentation of weapons was in native eyes an act which explicitly indicated that the intentions of the weapons' givers were not unfriendly.

In spite of their bad start, the British were able to come ashore peacefully at Plymouth and around Boston harbor in the 1620s, as we have already seen. Although established as trading posts, these early British outposts soon became full-fledged agricultural settlements; before long other such settlements were established elsewhere in New England. This expansion began in the late twenties as a veritable flood of Puritans poured into southern New England. By 1634, there were 10,000 British in New England south of the Merrimack River, and the number almost quadrupled over the next four years. By 1675, there were perhaps 75,000 British; in 1700 the British population of what is now Massachusetts, Connecticut, and Rhode Island was 120,000, with another 10,000 in New Hampshire. Things were entirely different in the French possessions to the north. In 1643, there were only 300 French in all of New France outside of Nova Scotia; by 1672 there were only about 7000 French along the St. Lawrence. In 1763, when the British took over, there were no more than 100,000 French in all of North America.

While the main interest of the French in North America remained from first to last the fur trade, this was not so in New England. The men and women who came in the seventeenth century to Plymouth, Massachusetts Bay, and the other colonies which were established in what is now Connecticut and Rhode Island were religious fanatics intent upon establishing a "new Zion." They considered themselves to be a "chosen people"; and, as is usually the case with people who consider themselves to be superior to all others, they saw this as giving them the right to do as they pleased, regardless of what anyone else thought about it. This attitude, coupled with the need for land to support their rapidly growing population and their preference for cleared, as opposed to forested land, inevitably led to conflict with the natives. But here, there was an obvious need for caution. They could not afford to antagonize the native peoples until they had acquired from them the skills and knowledge necessary to sustain themselves in the region, and until their numbers were sufficient to hold their own if and when it became necessary to fight.

There were other constraints on Puritan actions as well. Because they were dependent on England for supplies and credit, they could not afford to do anything that would hurt their image in the mother country. Moreover, if they persisted in activities which were at odds with the wishes of the crown and Parliament, they would run the risk of intervention in their affairs. Thus, it was risky just to move in and dispossess natives from their villages and farms, for this would violate the European concept of allodial rights. This was a property right based on effective occupation and possession "time out of mind," regardless of any formal sanction of effective sovereignty. On the face of it, this ought to have applied to native as well as to European farmers. In fact, Puritans had specific instructions from the directors of the Bay Colony to compensate natives for land taken. Unfortunately, the natives weren't always willing to sell land that the Puritans wanted. Besides, purchase of all the land they wanted would have been expensive to the settlers of colonies which were not yet self-sufficient.

In order to get what they wanted without at the same time antagonizing important people in the mother country, the Puritans from the start instituted a two-pronged policy of deliberate deception of the natives as to their real intentions, while they systematically applied as soon as it was practical the techniques of conquest which earlier had been used by England to subdue Scotland and Ireland. As described by the historian Francis Jennings, these were:

1) a deliberate policy of inciting competition between natives in order, by division, to maintain control 2) a disregard for pledges and promises to natives, no matter how solemnly made; 3) the introduction of total exterminatory war against some communities of natives in order to terrorize others; and 4) a highly developed propaganda of falsification to justify all acts and policies of the conquerors whatsoever.

A favorite concept in the acquisition of native lands was that of *vacuum domicilium*. By this concept, land not occupied and possessed by someone else was legally "waste" and could be taken by those who were capable of occupying and possessing it. The Pilgrims and other Puritans had no trouble applying the concept to the substantial tracts of cleared land which, when they arrived, were not being lived on or farmed by natives. It was not as easy to apply to those lands which were being lived on and farmed by natives, but if these people could be portrayed as wanderers, then public opinion in the mother country could be persuaded that *vacuum domicilium* applied. Even before he stepped ashore, John Winthrop, who served several terms as Governor of Massachusetts Bay, declared his intent to apply the concept to native lands.

This strategy seems to have been reasonably effective with the British government and public, but it didn't satisfy the natives. In order to handle their opposition, and also to stave off later rival claims by other colonists, Puritans did find it expedient to purchase land from the natives. In such cases, the people were often "encouraged" to sell by allowing European livestock to maraud their cornfields so that it was impossible to get a useable harvest. Sometimes an implicit, but unmistakeable, threat of force was used. And sometimes purchases of land were made from those who had no legitimate right to sell the parcel in question; nonetheless the buyer would haul the legitimate occupant into court if he did not quit the land. Needless to say, the Puritans did their best to keep word of such deals from getting back to England.

Effective though these techniques were, the Puritans sometimes resorted to conquest in order to gain land, and in order to lend credibility to the threat of force in their other dealings with natives. But in order to invoke rights of conquest without getting in trouble with the British government or public, the war of conquest had to be presented as a "just" war. Might did not make right unless there was just cause. Self-defense, of course, was accepted as just cause, and pre-emptive attack was acceptable if there appeared to be some sort of native plot to make war. Given native resentment at the treatment meted out to them by the colonists, the Puritans had little difficulty persuading people in the home country of the existence of an "Indian Menace." The first major war of Puritan conquest came in 1637, when the Pequots of Connecticut were all but exterminated in a solution as "final" as any of World War II. Rather than seek out and fight the Pequot warriors, the colonists preferred the technique of demoralization by avoiding the men and slaughtering instead as many women and children as possible. This is what they did in the Mystic Massacre, and they did it again to the Narragansetts, in the second war of Puritan conquest in 1675. Such terror tactics were new to aboriginal warfare, and had the desired effects.

Word of the "British Menace" must have reached people in Vermont, probably via the Sokokis who traded to the south, and who in the 1650s were allied with the Pocumtuck of Massachusetts against the Iroquois. Given the existing bad reputation of the British with Abenakis, we may suppose they were a source of anxiety. We may suppose, too, that Jesuit missionaries played upon these anxieties, for part of their job was to alienate natives from the British. Not only did this work to the benefit of the French fur trade, but at least as early as the 1660s, if not earlier, the French saw the Abenakis of Vermont as an important buffer between their settlements in the St. Lawrence Valley and those of their traditional enemies, the British, which were creeping inexorably northward in both New York and New England.

In spite of their misgivings about the British, or perhaps because of them, Abenaki peoples in what is now Vermont, New Hampshire, and Maine continued to trade actively with the Puritan colonists until the outbreak of warfare in 1675. This may seem paradoxical, until it is realized that trade provided the only forum through which conflicts with the colonists might be resolved short of war. But there was another reason for this trade: the British controlled access to wampum. This was particularly important to people like the Sokoki who, in 1628, found themselves in a tributary relationship to the Iroquois. As a result, they had to make annual tribute payments, and a major item in these payments was wampum.

The Abenaki–Iroquoian Wars

Although Abenaki and Iroquoian peoples had been enemies for a long time, the 1628 defeat of the Sokoki, Mahicans, and other peoples to the east of the Mohawks was directly related to the rise of the fur trade in North America. This brought about intensive competition between major powers, of which the New York Iroquois were one, for control of the trade, or at least positions of advantage. By defeating the peoples to the east of them, the Iroquois gained control over some of their competitors, as well as another outlet for their furs. Thus, they were able to divert furs from the Dutch at Fort Orange to the British at Springfield, or vice versa, as suited their needs. And their participation in the Connecticut Valley trade gave them access to the wampum manufactured by peoples living along the shores at the eastern end of Long Island Sound.

With the spread of smallpox westward into Iroquois country, following its outbreak among the peoples of the Connecticut Valley, the Iroquois withdrew into their own territory, isolating themselves from their neighbors. With this self-imposed quarantine, the Iroquoian grip on the Sokoki and other New England peoples weakened, and the latter, though still nominally tributaries, were able to act with more independence. This state of affairs lasted until 1641, when the Iroquois began a series of raids against the French to seek a vengeance for a number of past acts of violence, which had begun with Champlain's slaying of Mohawk chiefs in 1609. In 1649, the Iroquois achieved a decisive victory over France's allies in the north, the Hurons, causing their dispersal. With the Hurons defeated and the French hard pressed, Iroquois raids into New England commenced again, this time well over into Maine. The beleaguered French tried to rally the Abenakis and whatever other New England peoples, even colonists, they could to their cause; in 1651 they concluded an alliance with the Sokoki, Penacook, Mahican, and Pocumtuck.

This new alliance was not completely effective, for the natives were still wary of doing too much to annoy the Iroquois. Moreover, as nominal tributaries of the Iroquois, they were regarded as enemies by other Algonquian allies of the French. Nonetheless, in 1652, a large Sokoki raid was mounted against the Mohawks. Shortly thereafter, the Iroquois suffered a major setback at the hands of the Ottawas and fugitive Hurons, so again their attentions were diverted from the east. The Sokoki took advantage of this to continue making intermittent raids against the Iroquois. Needless to say, the Iroquois were extremely irritated by these, and by 1661, as they made known to the Dutch, they were just itching for revenge. In 1662, about 200 Iroquois warriors marched eastward, vowing to roam over the entire land seeking vengeance. This they did, terrorizing communities well eastward into Maine.

Conditions were still unsettled in 1663, when the Sokokis constructed a new fort for themselves on top of the steep promontory at Fort Hill. To the Iroquois, this was a further provocation, and a combined force of Mohawks, Senecas, and Onondagas arrived at Fort Hill in December, to lay seige to the fortress. The Sokokis, reinforced by Cowasucks and Penacooks, successfully defended themselves. Although the Iroquois were able to destroy much maize stored outside the village and burn houses within it, their losses were heavy. The Dutch saw the battered survivors limping home past Fort Orange, and were told of the loss of about 100 men. Rumor suggests that the loss was more like 200. For the Sokoki, the victory seems to have been a costly one. In the spring of 1664, they abandoned Fort Hill, and many of them sought refuge among other peoples. Some went south to the Pocumtucks. Others went north where some of them may have joined the

Cowasucks at Newberry. Others, though, went farther north, for Sokokis were beginning to appear along the St. Lawrence River at about this time. Still, a number of Sokokis did remain in their native haunts for a while longer, and were probably present in the refugee village at Vernon that sheltered "King Philip" in the winter of 1675/76.

With both sides exhausted by warfare, Dutch commissioners were able to persuade the Iroquois to consider a truce with the Abenakis. Unfortunately, someone murdered the Mohawk ambassadors who were traveling to the Pocumtuck village for discussions with the Sokokis there, and by midsummer, the Mohawks were once again bent on vengeance. By July of 1664, Sokokis and Mahicans were once again raiding the Mohawks, and the Mohawks were raiding eastward. At this point the British took over the Dutch possessions, and in their eagerness to establish good relations with the Iroquois, promised not to interfere in the troubles with the Sokoki and their allies. Late in 1664, the Iroquois mounted a massive campaign to the east. By early 1665, they had destroyed the Pocumtuck settlement on the way to which the Mohawk ambassadors had been murdered. Three years later, with great loss of lives on both sides, the Penacook village in New Hampshire was destroyed. After this battle, the ground is said to have been covered with dead bodies, which could be disposed of only by throwing them into a common grave. The final defeat of the Sokoki occurred in 1669, after which many of the survivors collected on the St. Francis River in Quebec. Although a few still lingered on in their homeland, most of the Sokoki's cleared lands along the Connecticut River had grown up in brush by the early 1670s.

The Abenaki–British Wars

This was the situation when the Sokokis were, for the first time, directly affected by Puritan policies in New England. In the middle 1600s, the trading posts in the Connecticut Valley were quickly transformed into agricultural settlements which crept closer and closer to Sokoki lands: Northampton was established in 1654, Hadley in 1659, and Deerfield in 1669. In 1671, the first block of Sokoki land in what was to become Northfield was sold to a trader from Northampton, and a year later, Massachusetts authorized the laying out of the township. In 1673, the first Massachusetts settlers arrived. By 1687, the Sokoki had sold land on both sides of the Connecticut River well up into what is now Vermont and New Hampshire, but which at the time the colonists considered a part of Massachusetts. In these land sales, the Sokoki lost their prime land for farming.

Some of the Sokoki seem to have lost their lives, as well as their lands, in a small-scale version of the Pequot and Narragansett massacres. In the spring of 1676, the men of Hadley learned of an encampment of women and old men, probably including Sokoki, at Turner's Falls, a traditional fishing spot on the Connecticut River. Since no warriors were present, the encampment was unprotected. On the morning of May 19, while the people were still asleep, over 150 men of Hadley fell upon them, killing as many of them as they could before the return of the warriors. Such terror tactics were not a part of aboriginal warfare, but after 1676 the Abenakis used them with telling effect against the frontier settlements in Massachusetts, New Hampshire, and Maine.

The years 1675 and 1676 were crucial ones for all the Abenakis of northern New England. Up until then, in spite of their deep distrust of British intentions, they had managed to avoid outright warfare with them. They were, moreover, exhausted after decades of warfare with the Iroquois, during which they suffered as well from a series of disastrous epidemics. As we have seen in the case of the Sokokis, some groups of Abenakis had already begun to disperse from their original homelands. Then, in 1675, the Second War of Puritan Conquest—King Philip's War—broke out in southern New England. Over the next year, the Abenakis watched as their southern neighbors were all but wiped out by the Puritan colonists, assisted by the Iroquois. Those natives who were not killed either fled or were reduced to reservation-like status. Some of the Abenakis were drawn into this conflict; the Turner's Falls massacre was one instance of this; an unprovoked attack on the Penacooks by Captain Samuel Mosely in 1675 was another. It must have been exquisitely clear to the Abenakis that unless they launched an all out war for survival, their turn would be next. This they did, in a series of wars which continued over the next 85 years. In them, they applied with telling effect the terror tactics which the British had previously introduced into southern New England. Through it all, they had the support of their old friends, the French, who had become engaged in a great power struggle against the British for what amounted to world domination.

The first Abenaki war with the British broke out in 1675 and did not end until 1678. On the British side, this arrested what had been the rapid northward advancement of settlements, such as those in the Connecticut Valley, and forced the evacuation of many existing frontier settlements. By the end of 1675, North-field, Massachusetts had been burned and abandoned, and every single British settlement on the Maine coast had been evacuated. On the Abenaki side, further dispersal of peoples from their original homelands took place. A number of Sokokis, along with some of their Penacook allies from New Hampshire, were among the 1000 or so refugees from King Philip's War who fled to Schaghti-coke, on the Hoosic River. Others fled to the shores of Lake Champlain, where the Iroquois later found and attacked a group of Sokokis in 1680. Still others joined those Sokoki and other Abenakis who had previously moved to communities in the St. Lawrence Valley, notably Odanak (St. Francis) and Trois Rivieres.

With the cessation of hostilities, the northward march of British settlement began anew. Northfield was reestablished in 1682, and further Sokoki sales to clear land titles in this township took place by 1687. Also in 1682, the western Abenakis redirected much of their trade from the French to the British at Schaghti-coke. The French responded to this with increased missionary activity, including the establishment of a short-lived mission at Missisquoi. In 1685, there is reference to the arrival of Chief Sadochquis at Schaghticoke with his band from Missisquoi, and two years later, Peter Schuyler's "Indians" from New York were hospitably received at Missisquoi.

The beginning of the end of this brief interlude of peace came in 1687, when trouble broke out between the French and the Iroquois. The Abenakis, as allies of the French, inevitably were drawn into this. Two years later, war between the French and British in Europe spread to North America, and Vermont became a buffer zone between these two colonial powers. Louis XIV instructed Count Frontenac to proceed by way of lakes Champlain and George to Albany, which was to be captured, and from there down the Hudson to the coast, dividing the British colonies. The British, for their part, attempted to march north via the Champlain Valley to attack the French along the St. Lawrence. Neither side was up to the job, but the Abenakis, this time with French assistance, were able to resume their raids on the frontier settlements of New England with the same devastating results (to the British) as before. Northfield was once again abandoned, in 1689, and for the second time the settlements on the coast of Maine were evacuated. Abenakis from Vermont did not confine their raiding activities to the Massachusetts settlements; they participated in the destruction of Schenectady in 1690, and in the same year, Sokokis made up the bulk of the French-led party which raided Salmon Falls in Maine.

The second Abenaki War—King William's War, as it is usually called in the history books—ended in 1697. There was then a five year period of peace, during which the British colonists licked their wounds, and a number of natives moved northward, away from British settlements and closer to those of their French allies. Among these people were a number, including some Sokokis, who had been living at Schaghticoke. Taking their departure in 1698, they declared their intention to settle on the lower Winooski River. Unfortunately for them, there were already some Sokokis and Penacooks living in the region who, for unknown reasons, did not wish these newcomers to settle among them. Assisted by their friends from Missisquoi, they ejected the interlopers from the south. Also part of the northward movement were a few people from the Missisquoi settlement itself, who moved to Odanak, on the St. Francis River, the year the French mission was moved there from Sillery (1700).

The third Abenaki war with the British, called Queen Anne's War by the historians, broke out in 1702 and lasted into 1713. This war was part of the continuing worldwide struggle between France and Britain, and once again the Abenakis, as allies of the French, were drawn into the conflict. Assisted by the French, they resumed their raids on the frontier settlements of New England. For the third time, the coastal settlements of the British in Maine were wiped out. In the south, warriors from Missisquoi raided far down the Connecticut Valley. The most famous of

FIGURE 6–4. This engraving shows the famous attack on Deerfield of 1704, in which Vermont Abenakis participated. (Drawing by William S. Fowler, from "Deerfield Archaeological Display" by Richard W. Hatch, *Bulletin of the Massachusetts Archaeological Society* 31 (3&4): 8–10, April–July 1970, by permission of the Massachusetts Archaeological Society.)

these raids occurred in 1704, when Deerfield was burned and numerous of its residents were killed or captured. In this raid, the Missisquoi warriors were assisted by the Caughnawaga Mohawks, a group of dissident Mohawks who had converted to Catholicism, established a village near Montreal, and allied themselves with the French. The main body of Mohawks, however, remained in New York and maintained their alliance with the British.

Sometime during Queen Anne's War, if not before, a native who was later to become famous arrived at Missisquoi as part of the northward drift of native peoples toward Canada. He is known to history as Grey Lock and he was apparently born into the Woronoco tribe, originally located on the Westfield River in Massachusetts. He seems to have been one of the fugitives of King Philip's War who moved to Schaghticoke; just when he moved from there to Missisquoi is not known. He was in residence at Missisquoi by 1712, though, when he led one of the last raids of the war, against Northampton.

The end of Queen Anne's War found the Cowasuck settlements of the upper Connecticut Valley temporarily deserted by their inhabitants and much of the eastern Abenaki country in the hands of the British. With the return of peace, the Cowasucks were able to reoccupy their settlements. By contrast, substantial numbers of eastern Abenakis were resettled in the west, both on the St. Francis River and at Missisquoi. There was probably further movement of Algonquian fugitives from the south to Missisquoi, as well. By 1724, substantial numbers of these "Loups," as the French called them, had taken up residence with the Abenakis of this village.

The next episode in the continuing hostilities between the Abenakis and British, unlike the preceding two, was strictly a local affair. The only British involved were the colonists of New England, while New York remained neutral. The cause, in Maine, was disagreement over the establishment of British forts and trading posts. Elsewhere, the problem was continuing pressure from expanding British settlements into western Abenaki country. In Maine, the conflict is known as Lovewell's War; in Vermont, it is called Dummer's War. It would be better called Grey Lock's War, for he was the dominant figure in its prosecution in the west.

Grey Lock led his first raid of the war in August of 1723. His targets were Northfield and Rutland in Massachusetts and although scouts and cavalry responded, they could not find the raiders who, with several captives, got clean away. Grey Lock and his men returned to raid Northfield again in October, and then returned to Missisquoi for the winter. To protect against similar raids in the future, Massachusetts voted to establish Fort Dummer, which was built in 1724. Undaunted, Grey Lock struck again in June of that year. In spite of the arrival of news of the impending raid in advance of the raiders themselves, it was wholly successful. In response, a force went looking for Grey Lock scouting as far north as Otter Creek. Grey Lock not only eluded his pursuers; he spent the entire summer raiding deep into Massachusetts: Deerfield, Northampton, and Westfield all were attacked before the raiders returned to Missisquoi in November.

Things remained quiet from November until March, and then Massachusetts went on the offensive. A party of men set out on snowshoes looking for Grey Lock. They looked for a month without success, but no sooner had they returned home than Grey Lock began his raids anew. The Connecticut Valley settlements were in turmoil when, in July, Captain Benjamin Wright, an experienced "Indian" fighter, collected fifty-nine men for an attack on Missisquoi. It took them a month to reach Lake Champlain, and they never did get further north than the Winooski River. They saw not a single "Indian" before reaching the mouth of the Wells River on the return trip. There, they got a glimpse of three natives, who got away before Wright and his men realized they were hostiles. The force returned home in something less than triumph, only to find that Grey Lock had followed them. All summer long, Grey Lock raided from Deerfield to Fort Dummer, while Wright was unable to raise another force until October.

By this time, most Abenakis had had enough of war, and in

FIGURE 6–5. Fort Dummer, Vermont's first more or less permanent British settlement, was built to protect settlements to the south from Grey Lock's raids. (From *Vermont Life* 2 (3) p. 35, by permission of Vermont Historical Society.)

Maine a peace treaty was signed in December. However, this did not bind the Abenakis at Odanak and Missisquoi. In March of 1726, word reached Massachusetts that Grey Lock was poised with a war party somewhere on Otter Creek. At this point, strenuous efforts were made through Grey Lock's brother, who was dispatched from Albany, and through Penobscot envoys at Odanak, to disuade Grey Lock from further raids. The people of Odanak were ready to call it quits and signed a treaty in July. Although they did force Grey Lock to return to Missisquoi, he himself never did sign the treaty.

Dummer's War was followed by some eighteen years of peace, if not tranquility. Once again, British settlements resumed their inexorable northward expansion in the Connecticut Valley; New Taunton (now Westminster) was founded in 1737, the refugee village at Vernon was sold in 1739, and covetous eyes were being cast on the fertile Cowas Intervales further north. Most of this settlement was in the old Sokoki country, the larger number of whom seem to have moved out a half century earlier. The Cowas Intervales were in Cowasuck country where there was still a substantial native population.

The establishment of British settlements ever closer to their own in lower Canada worried the French. They also began to worry about the loyalty of their western Abenaki allies, whose friendship the British were courting, and who persisted in trading with the British at Albany. Under the circumstances, they thought it advisable to strengthen their hold on the Champlain Valley, which they considered to be a part of New France. The British had never strenuously contested this claim, but in the absence of effective French settlement, they were likely to do so. Therefore, in the 1730s French settlements were established most notably at Chimney Point and Alburg. To protect the settlements of lower Canada, and to control Abenaki trade with the British, Fort St. Frederic was established at Crown Point in 1731. The Jesuits were instructed to do whatever was necessary to strengthen the attachment of the Abenakis to the French cause and, if they could, to lure the inhabitants of Schaghticoke away from the British to settle among the native allies of the French.

The year 1730 was a bad one for the Abenakis at Missisquoi. An outbreak of smallpox caused abandonment of the village, as those who could withdrew to other places. Most remained within the region, though, and by 1731, were moving back to the village. Meanwhile, a chaplain was assigned to Fort St. Frederic, and beginning in 1732, the records contain numerous entries of baptisms and burials of Abenakis from Missisquoi. Included among them is the baptism of Marie Charlotte, a daughter of Grey Lock, on April 21, 1737. Grey Lock's son, John Baptiste, was baptized on April 19, 1740. Since Grey Lock must have been around 80 years old in 1740, it is likely that these children were his second family.

About 1743, on the eve of the outbreak of King George's War, the French decided that Missisquoi was of such importance to them that it should have its own mission. This was to include not only a house but a chapel and sawmill. Father Etienne Lauverjat, who had previously served as a priest among the Penobscots and

FIGURE 6–6. A model of Fort St. Frederic, built by the French to protect the settlements of lower Canada against the British and to control Abenaki trade with the British. By 1732, Abenakis from Missisquoi were making use of the services of the fort's chaplain. (Model made from the original plans by A. S. Hopkins, State Conservation Department, Albany. Photo from *Proceedings of the Vermont Historical Society*, New Series, Vol. 6, 1938, between pp. 140 and 141, by permission of Vermont Historical Society.)

at the St. Francis mission at Odanak, arrived at Missisquoi in 1744, and remained there until about 1749. The sawmill was not built until about 1748, the year King George's War ended. The chapel was probably built in 1744, but at Alburg, rather than Missisquoi.

King George's War, the fifth in which the Abenakis fought the British, was part of a larger global conflict between the French and British. At Missisquoi, it was thought prudent to withdraw from the old village so as to be out of harm's way should the British succeed in raiding it, as they had tried to do during Dummer's War. But in that war, the British in New York looked the other way as New England's colonists tried to cope with Grey Lock's raids. With New York actively involved in the new war, the danger of raids on Missisquoi was increased. Although a few Missisquoi Abenakis moved as far away as the Montreal missions, it is clear that most of them merely relocated at places less well-known to the British, but still within their traditional homeland. Not only did Lauverjat's mission continue, but Missisquoi families continued to make occasional use of clerical facilities at Chambly and Fort St. Frederic. And in 1746, as many as sixty warriors were available in the Missisquoi region for a raid against Boscawen, New Hampshire. Apparently, the largest of the wartime settlements was in the present town of Alburg, which is one reason why Lauverjat's chapel was built there.

A similar relocation of settlements for strategic reasons seems to have been carried out by the Cowasucks over in the Connecticut Valley. Then, with the security of their settlements attended to, Cowasuck and Missisquoi warriors resumed their raids on the British settlements of the New England frontier. As they had been in Dummer's War, they were reinforced by a contingent of young "Loups" from Schaghticoke, who moved to Missisquoi in 1744. And as they had been in Queen Anne's War, they were encouraged and assisted by the French. Within five years of the war's official declaration, in 1744, every British settler had been driven out of what is now southeastern Vermont—then still considered to be a part of Massachusetts—save for the garrison at Fort Dummer. Though Grey Lock was still alive in 1744, he must have been too old to have participated in these raids. We do not know precisely when he died, except that it was sometime after 1744, but no later than 1753.

King George's War ended in 1748 without really settling anything in North America between the French and British. At Missisquoi, there was a return to the village by those who had sought refuge elsewhere. The "Loups" from Schaghticoke who had earlier come to Missisquoi apparently remained, at least for awhile, for they were probably visited there by the Sulpician Father Claude Mathevet between 1749 and 1754. By this latter year, only twelve families were left at Schaghticoke, but then they too departed to join their friends and relatives living among the Abenakis at Odanak.

In the Connecticut Valley, the end of the war saw the revival of British settlements abandoned but a short time before. Soon, the Cowasucks were disturbed by reports that the Cowas Intervales were to be fortified by the British. In a conference at Montreal in 1752, they reasserted their claim to the region and threatened to go to war if necessary. So by the 1750s, conditions in western Abenaki country did not differ greatly from those of the early 1740s, and the stage was set for the final major conflict between the Abenakis and British.

The so-called Seven Years War—in Canada, the War of Conquest—broke out in 1754, had its *de facto* ending in 1760, but did not officially end until 1763. At Missisquoi, events of the last war were repeated: the established village was temporarily abandoned in favor of settlements less well-known to the British, and raids were resumed on British settlements in the Connecticut Valley. But things began to go badly for the French. In 1755, they suffered a defeat on Lake George, and the war crept closer to the Champlain Valley. There, the French built Fort Carillon at Ticonderoga south of the existing Fort Saint Frederic. But the Abenakis, who had been going to Fort St. Frederic for their religious needs, stopped doing so, preferring to go north instead to Chambly and Fort St. Jean. In 1757, Montcalm, with a force that included 1800 natives of forty-one different tribes, was able to recapture Fort William Henry, but his success was a fleeting one. In 1759, General Amherst, who occupied both Forts Carillon and St. Frederic, forced the French to retreat to Isle Aux Noix at the head of the

Richelieu River. Here a number of Missisquoi families had settled for the duration of the war, not far north of their previous
wartime settlement at Alburg. In order to provide materials for
the fortifications at Isle Aux Noix, Lauverjat's old chapel at Alburg was torn down.

At this point, just after the fall of Quebec, one of the most famous events of the war took place. This was the raid on the
Abenakis living at Odanak by Major Robert Rogers and his rangers. Had they not already withdrawn to places of refuge from
their main village, it is likely that the Missisquoi Abenakis, too,
would have been attacked by Rogers or some other British force,
for all Abenakis were regarded by the British as "bloodthirsty savages" whom they despised for having kept the frontier settlements of New England in a state of terror for close to a century.
As it was, Rogers passed close by the deserted Missisquoi village
on his way to Odanak. It was some Missisquoi Abenakis, who
were keeping a close watch on their village, who discovered and
destroyed Rogers's boats.

The story of Rogers's raid has been told many times, but most
notably in Kenneth Roberts's book, *Northwest Passage*. All who
have retold the story have relied on Rogers's own account, but a
careful search for new evidence by Gordon M. Day indicates that
Rogers was significantly in error on some crucial points. Rogers
reported that he was able to achieve complete surprise in his pre-
dawn attack of October 4, killing an estimated 200 Abenakis.
This conflicts with the French report of 30 casualties. Since the
French were on the scene immediately before and after the attack, and Rogers was not able to actually count casualties, his estimate must be considered less reliable than that of the French.
Furthermore, Rogers assumed he had achieved complete surprise,
but Gordon Day has managed to locate the heirs to two detailed
family traditions which suggest otherwise. These traditions reach
back over four generations to the time of the raid. Detailed re-
membrance of momentous events over four generations is not unusual among nonliterate peoples, and in these cases, the details
allowed Day to check up on the reliability of the two traditions.
He found no reason to doubt their accuracy. Both agree that the
residents of Odanak were warned the evening before of the impending attack by a Mahican, who was a stranger at Odanak.

Rogers had with him a number of natives, including Mahicans from their reservation at Stockbridge. While these Stockbridge Mahicans were loyal to the British, the Schaghticoke Mahicans were not, and a few who were not able to get away in 1754 probably wound up at Stockbridge. Thus, one could have been with Rogers. Since a Schaghticoke Mahican would have had friends and relatives at Odanak, he would be a likely informer.

British Encroachment

With the fall of Quebec in 1759 and Montreal in 1760, the French lost their possessions in Canada and the war came to an end. With this the Cowasuck and Missisquoi Abenakis, who still had not left their respective homelands, returned to their traditional villages just as they had at the end of the preceding war. At the same time, though, white settlers, mostly from the established colonies of New England, began to pour into the nascent Republic of Vermont. South of the upper Connecticut and Missisquoi, the lands to which they came were devoid of native inhabitants. But in the north, they found the Abenakis occupying the most desirable tracts of land.

At Missisquoi, the Abenakis, who clearly had no intention of abandoning either their village or their farms, or hunting, fishing, and trapping in their traditional territories, responded to the threat of British settlement in two ways: by negotiating leases designed to ensure their long-term control, and by formal appeals to British authorities. The British authorities appealed to were those of lower Canada, even though it was New York and New Hampshire who claimed the lands between Lake Champlain and the Connecticut River. But the British in Cnada continued to take an interest in a region which, until a short time before, had been considered a part of lower Canada. And it was natural that the Abenakis, accustomed as they were to dealing with the French authorities in Canada, should deal with the British who replaced them. Furthermore, the British in Canada were inclined to be a bit more sympathetic to Abenaki concerns than were the British in New York and New Hampshire, where Abenakis had been regarded as hated enemies for almost a century. Thus the governor of lower Canada, in 1765, refused a request from Lieutenant Moses Hazen for a grant of 2000 acres of land along the lower

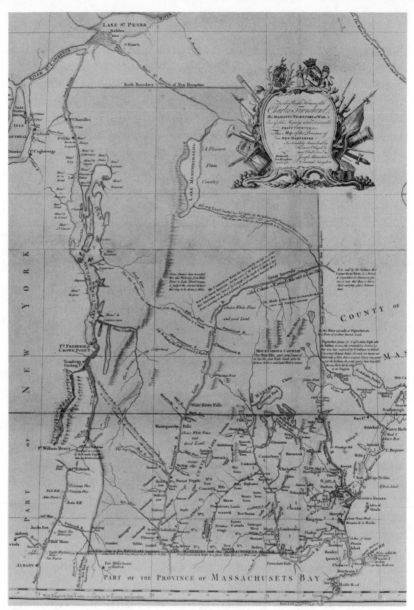

FIGURE 6–7. Vermont at the end of the Seven Years War. This is a portion of an original map by Joseph Blanchard in the special collections of the Bailey-Howe Library at the University of Vermont: "An accurate map of his majesty's province of New Hampshire in New England, taken from actual surveys of all the inhabited part, and from the best information of what is uninhabited, together with the adjacent countries, which exhibits the thetre [*sic*] of this war in that part of the world, by Col. Blanchard and the Rev. Mr. Langdon. Portsmouth, N.H. engraved by Thomas Jefferys, Geographer to His Majesty, 1761." Courtesy John Buechler, Bailey-Howe Library, University of Vermont.

Missisquoi, on the basis of Abenaki ownership. By contrast, two years earlier, the governor of New Hampshire recognized no such ownership when he granted what today are Highgate and Swanton to Samuel Hunt and Isiah Goodrich. Nor did the governor of New York when, in 1771, he granted 2000 acres that included the Abenaki village and farmlands to Simon Metcalfe.

In the same year that Hazen's request for land was denied, a lease for land along both sides of the Missisquoi was negotiated between the Abenakis and James Robertson, a merchant from St. Johns, Quebec. The agreement stipulated that the lease was to expire at the end of ninety-one years, and that an annual rent of Spanish dollars, rum, and corn was to be paid. The lease also explicitly reserved the village and twelve farms on both sides of the river below the falls for the continued use of the Abenakis. Finally, the land of those who signed the lease ws to be plowed yearly for the planting of corn sufficient for their own needs. By these terms, the lease was designed to ensure continuing Abenaki control of their ancestral lands, to assist them in their farming, and to bring in a substantial income. For his part, James Robertson was able to carry out a thriving trade and sawmill operation until 1771.

In spite of the recognition of their ownership of the Missisquoi lands acknowledged by the refusal of the Hazen grant and the negotiation of Robertson's lease, the Abenakis were still worried over threatened encroachment on their lands, probably by representatives of Hunt and Goodrich. So in August of 1766, they made a formal appeal to the authorities in Canada. The result was a meeting between the Missisquoi Abenakis and the governors of New York and Quebec on Isle La Motte. Their appeal went as follows:

Breth[n].

We are going to finish with a Remonstrance something similar but if possible more urging than the foregoing. We the Misisqui Ind[ns] of the Abinaquis or S[t]. Johns Tribe have inhabited that part of Lake Champlain time unknown to any of Us here present without being molested or any ones claiming any Right to it to our Knowledge, [nor] Except ab[t]. 18 Years ago the French Gov[t]. & Intend[t]. came there & viewed a Spot [then] convenient for a Saw mill to facilitate the building of Vessells & Batteaux [for these Lakes] at S[t]. Johns as well as for building of ships at Quebec and on the Occasion convened our People to ask their Approbation, when ac-

cordingly they consented & marked out a Spot large enough for that purpose for the cutting of Saw Timber ab^t. 1/2 League square, with the Condition to have what Boards they wanted for their own use, gratis, but on
the Commencement of last War, said Mill was deserted and the Ironwork
buried, after which [they the Ind^{ns}.] we expected that every thing of the
kind hereafter would subside, but no sooner was the peace made than
some English people came there to rebuild the Mill, and now claim 3
Leagues in breath & we dont know how many deep wch. would take in
our Village & plantations by far. We therefore request by this Belt of
Wampum that to whatever Governm^r. it may belong, the Aff^r. may be in-
quired into that we may obtain Justice it being a Matter of great Concern
to Us. We likewise beg there maynt any Traders be allowed to bring spir-
itous Liquors amongst us, the selling of which being so prejudicial & detrimental to us, if we want to purchase any we are not far from Montreal
    [illegible due to patching of manuscript]

Unfortunately for the Abenakis, they were not successful
in their appeal. At the time, the Abenakis of Missisquoi were
closely associated with those of Odanak, who in turn were members of an alliance known as the Seven Nations of Canada. The
spokesmen for this association of French mission Indians were
the Caughnawaga Mohawks, who chose this moment to assert
their own claim to hunting and fishing rights in the Champlain
Valley. Having all the farmland they needed at their own village,
they agreed in the name of the Seven Nations that native rights in
the Champlain region would be limited to hunting and fishing.
Although no one has ever been able to find a shred of justification
for the Caughnawaga claim, and the Missisquoi Abenakis did not
acquiesce, the Canadian authorities did. Thus, the Missisquoi
Abenakis lost their sole source of British support for their land
rights in the region.

    The next threat to Abenaki control of their ancestral lands
came from Simon Metcalfe, a surveyor from New York. Between
1767 and 1771, he surveyed the region, requesting grants for himself and several others. As we have already seen, New York ac-
ceded to his request, granting him 2000 acres which took in the
Abenaki's village, their farmlands, and much of Robertson's
leased lands as well. Needless to say, the Abenakis protested,
again to the authorities in Canada. The Canadians responded by
stating that the matter had been settled by the governors of New
York and Canada with the Caughnawagas in 1766. Below the 45th

parallel, the natives had free hunting and fishing rights, but the land belonged to the king and his subjects.

In spite of the setbacks they suffered, the outbreak of the Revolutionary War in 1775 found the Abenakis still living and farming on their ancestral lands at Missisquoi. With the outbreak of this new war, the Abenakis did as they had done in the two previous wars: they withdrew from their village into local retreat areas so as to be out of harm's way. There is some indication that, as before, their main place of refuge was just north of Lake Champlain. In the last war particularly, this strategy of withdrawal had served the Missisquoi Abenakis well. At its end, they were able to return to their village which had come through the war unscathed. Their friends and allies at Odanak, by contrast, had seen their village burned by Rogers and his rangers.

The Allens and Usurpation by the New United States

As the Revolutionary War drew to a close, the Abenakis reoccupied their village at Missisquoi. In 1779, there came to live among them a loyalist of Dutch descent, John Hilliker. Like Robertson before him, Hilliker respected Abenaki ownership of the land, and leased from them 100 acres at one crown per year. Five years later, Simon Metcalfe returned, and in the same year, Captain James Hunter and Charles Grajon of St. Jean purchased Robertson's lease. All three found themselves embroiled in a dispute with Ira and Levi Allen, who had been buying up the old New Hampshire grants from Goodrich, Hunt, and their associates. They took the Allens to court and promptly lost their suits. In the process, the possibility that the Abenakis might have legitimate interests was glossed over.

To appreciate what happened next, one must know something of the background and interests of the Allens. This family came to Vermont from the Puritan colony of Connecticut and brought with them the Puritan attitudes towards "Indians" that we discussed earlier in this chapter. In Vermont, Ira Allen and his brothers were intent on profiting from their various land transactions, and settled natives living on land the Allens wanted to sell to other people did not make for easy profits. So the Allens did exactly what the Puritans before them had done; they systematically set about portraying the natives as wanderers who did not effectively occupy the land, and so had no legal claim to it. And here, the Abenaki tactic of strategic withdrawal from the Missisquoi village, which had served them so well in times of war, played right into the Allens' hands. Before the intensive settlement of Vermont after 1763, the southern boundary of Canada was only vaguely defined as lying somewhere north of New England's frontier settlements, and raiders from Missisquoi were clearly Canadian Indians to the colonists of New England. Accustomed to this kind of thinking, people could be easily convinced that the people who resettled Missisquoi following the Seven Year's War, and again following the Revolution, were Canadian.

The Allens also capitalized on the close relationship the Missisquoi Abenakis had with their friends and close allies at Odanak. So close were these relations, and so much better known to the British was Odanak, site of the St. Francis Mission, that there was already a tendency to speak of Abenakis from both places— indeed, all Abenakis in the west—as St. Francis Indians. Ironically, a number of Missisquoi Abenakis had probably never in their lives been to Odanak. Nonetheless, Ira Allen and his associates consistently referred to them as "St. Francis Indians," further implying that they were from Canada and had no business being in Vermont. It also played on the fears of those who came to Vermont from elsewhere in New England, which is to say about 90 percent of the white population of Vermont. These people grew up hating and fearing Indians from St. Francis, which they regarded as the major staging area for raids on New England's frontier settlements. They were not inclined to support such people in their disputes with settlers of European descent.

The ability of the Allens to quickly seize opportunities and use them to the disadvantage of the Abenakis is illustrated by an incident that occurred in 1784. Acting, apparently, at the behest of the frustrated Captain Hunter, several "St. Francis" Abenakis are alleged to have threatened some settlers at the mouth of the Missisquoi River, appropriated a number of goods as rent, and sworn to scalp Colonel Allen if he persisted in denying their land rights. At the time, Ira Allen was using negotiations with Frederic Haldiman, the military governor of Canada, as a means of forcing the new United States to accept Vermont as the fourteenth state.

Moving quickly, he got Haldiman to reprimand Hunter and the Abenakis, and to remind everyone of the old decision that Canadian Indians, Abenakis included, had no land rights south of the 45th parallel.

Ira Allen himself seems to have engineered another incident that occurred in 1788. According to a sworn deposition, a group of Indians suddenly appeared from St. Francis, planted the British flag, and robbed two settlers, John Waggoner and William Tichout of wood. They then threatened Waggoner and Tichout, demanding as rent one-quarter of their crops. In fact, the "Indians" were not from St. Francis at all, but lived nearby at Missisquoi. Furthermore, Waggoner and Tichout were friends and comrades in arms of John Hilliker; like him, they were loyalists of Dutch descent. For eight years, Hilliker had maintained friendly and cooperative relations with his Abenaki neighbors, so it is surprising that his two friends, whom he also served as interpreter, would have had such trouble. They had settled on land expressly reserved for the Abenakis under the terms of Robertson's lease, so it is likely that they, like John Hilliker, paid rent to the Abenakis.

The peculiarities of the situation are resolved when it is realized that neither Waggoner nor Tichout could read or write. Their deposition was written by the justice of the peace who notarized it, a man named Thomas Butterfield who was in the employ of the Allens as their local land agent. The deposition which he wrote and notarized was whisked away by Ira Allen for another official reminder that the Abenakis had no rights at Missisquoi. When informed as to the contents of their deposition by a third party, Waggoner replied: "We have never mentioned anything of the sort, and it cannot possibly be so, because we can neither read nor write, unless Colonel Allen has played us this trick and without our knowledge."

On the basis of incidents such as these, it became clear to the Abenakis remaining in Vermont that they were to be dispossessed of their lands, much as the native peoples of southern New England had been dispossessed of theirs by the Puritans in the preceding century. Even so, they were reluctant to quit their lands, and remained in the majority at Missisquoi into the 1790s. In the year 1790, there were at least 70, but more likely 150 to 200 Abenakis living in fifty cabins. By contrast, the total white population a year later was 74. But more settlers were arriving, and by 1800, that figure was 858. In 1789, some Abenakis requested compensation for the loss of their lands, which they never got; a year later a number of families left to resettle at Odanak. They were joined there by a number of Cowasucks, who had just sold off much of their homeland. By 1797, conditions were so crowded at Odanak that the Abenakis there had to ask for more land to absorb the continuing influx of peoples from Vermont. Eventually, through a population explosion of sorts, descendants of the Missisquoi refugees became the dominant element at Odanak, and they remain the dominant element today: about 85 percent of the family names there over the last 150 years had their origins in the eastern part of the Champlain Valley.

But not everyone deserted northern Vermont, for the numbers of refugees coming into Odanak do not begin to equal the numbers of Cowasucks and Missisquoi Abenakis present in Vermont in the 1890s. There are also numerous references in local histories to the presence of Abenakis in the nineteenth century, particularly in the Missisquoi region. And finally, the old Abenaki names continue to appear with regularity in the records of the Catholic churches accessible to people from Missisquoi. So strong was the Abenaki sense of place, and so crowded were conditions at Odanak, that at least twenty-five to thirty Missisquoi families chose to remain within about a thirty mile radius of their ancient village.

The Abenakis who refused to leave their ancestral lands survived by adopting the tactics by which Grey Lock had eluded his pursuers in Dummer's War, and by which Missisquoi escaped destruction through three subsequent wars: they became all but invisible to the whites among whom they now lived. Outwardly, they looked and acted much more like Europeans than did their ancestors of the early seventeenth century; they wore European-style clothing, used metal rather than stone tools, fought with guns rather than bows and arrows, emphasized the patrilineal transmission of important property, recognized distinctions of rank, were generally fluent in speaking a European language (French), and had even adopted Christianity (Catholicism). Such native practices as they did retain—hunting, fishing, the cultivation of corn, beans, and squash, use of canoes and snowshoes, and the smoking of tobacco—had long since been adopted by the British and were no longer distinctively native.

In spite of this convergence between Abenakis on the one hand and Europeans and their descendants on the other, important (even if less immediately visible) differences remained. For the Abenakis of Missisquoi, loss of their farmlands forced them to break up into smaller, more transient groups heavily dependent on hunting, fishing, and gathering for subsistence, supplemented by the sale of baskets and other craft items. This lifestyle they maintained until they were able to regroup into small, but sedentary communities at places like Swanton's Back Bay section. More significantly, they retained (and still do) a core of values and traditions that are distinctively their own. As Francis Hsu, a past president of the American Anthropological Association put it:

Cultures borrow much from each other in role matters such as foods, artifacts, etiquette, theories of nature, and tools for control of human beings and things. But there is little evidence that people change in any fundamental way, and, as a whole, their feeling about themselves, about each other, and about the rest of the world.

In short, no matter how "European" Abenakis appear on the outside, they remain their own people.

7. NATIVE AMERICANS IN VERMONT TODAY

ACCORDING to the U.S. census, there were in 1970 all of 229 Native Americans living in Vermont. A mere five years later, the Boston Indian Council's Manpower census reported 1700 Native Americans as living in Vermont, 80 percent of whom were Abenakis. Yet, there was no great influx of Native Americans from other places into Vermont, nor is there any more reason to doubt the veracity of the Boston Indian Council's figures than there is those of the Census Bureau. What happened simply was that, between 1970 and 1975, there was a resurgence of pride in their ethnic identity on the part of Vermont's Abenakis. Following the loss of their lands at Missisquoi at the end of the eighteenth century, they found that the way to survive was to look and act in ways that did not identify them as Indians in the eyes of the whites among whom they had to live. But they knew who they were and remained in close communication with one another, even regrouping in the middle of the nineteenth century into Swanton's Back Bay community. But it was not until after the rise of Native American activism throughout North America that these people were ready to declare publicly that they were what they had known themselves to be all along: Abenakis, descended from Vermont's pre-European population.

The history of Abenakis in Vermont through the nineteenth and the first three quarters of the twentieth century has been all but unknown until recently, at least to those who are not Abenakis. It was not until the late 1970s that John Moody, a graduate of Dartmouth College, began a systematic search of church records and other documentary sources overlooked until then in order to reconstruct that history. Although his research is not yet finished, Moody has found that, as a general rule, the documentary evidence confirms the oral traditions of the Abenakis themselves.

FIGURE 7–1. Symbolic of the Abenaki renaissance in Vermont is this picture of Vicki Wells, an Abenaki from Missisquoi, at work on the 1700-year-old Winooski site. Photo by Sherry Russell-Armitage, courtesy Public Relations, University of Vermont.

In fact, Moody, in common with most others who have worked with people who until recently relied on memory rather than written records to maintain their traditions, has been continually impressed by the detailed memory Abenakis have today of events that happened long in the past.

Moody's best written data for the first half of the nineteenth century come from church records. From the early 1800s until 1830, there was neither mission nor priest available to Catholic Abenakis in the Champlain Valley. For such sacraments as marriage and baptism, the services of priests had to be sought elsewhere. Records at St. Luc in Quebec indicate that by 1810, Abenaki families were traveling north from their homes in Vermont to seek the ministrations of the clergy there, as their ancestors had once traveled south to Fort St. Frederic for the same reasons. Abenaki names listed in the records at St. Johns, Iberville, St. Valentin, St. George, and St. Bernard suggest that this practice continued well into the 1830s. The eventual appearance in Burlington of a missionary, Father Jeremiah O'Callaghan, served to fulfill some of the religious needs of the Abenakis. During his travels in the Champlain Valley beginning in 1830, Father O'Callaghan visited Abenaki communities on a periodic basis and maintained such records as the Baptismal Register of 1830–57. (The extant marriage register from this period was destroyed in a recent fire in Burlington; death records have disappeared, probably as a result of the fire as well.)

By the time of the 1850 census, a small Abenaki enclave, consisting of several old Missisquoi families, had gathered in the Back Bay area of Swanton. Other families were located outside of Back Bay, on the old lands along the Missisquoi River and in the delta. One of the first Abenakis to purchase land in Swanton during this period was Michel Saint Francois, who was by occupation a teamster. He also participated in the more traditional subsistence activities: hunting, fishing, trapping, gardening, and herb collecting.

After 1860, numerous references to Abenakis and other natives appear in both town and church records, including those at St. Albans and at Swanton. In the 1870 census of South Hero, a group of natives were listed as "basketmakers." Elderly informants interviewed by Moody recall that until the 1930s, two and possibly three interconnected bands composed of perhaps 100 to 150 Abenakis lived at Grand Isle, St. Albans Bay, and Missisquoi. Those at St. Albans and Grand Isle, along with others at Milton and (later) Charlotte, unlike those at Swanton, continued to maintain close contact with Odanak, and were more apt to share with them their more nomadic lifestyle. But by 1940, these communities had disappeared, as their members dispersed, were assimilated into white culture, or adopted the ways of the more sedentary Swanton Abenaki community. The latter community, by contrast, not only survived, but expanded considerably over the years following 1850. It became the physical and social expression of Abenaki continuity in the Missisquoi region.

What seems to have happened, after being forced off their lands along the river, is that the Missisquoi Abenakis adopted a more transient lifestyle, similar to that of their friends and allies at Odanak. Indeed, some people from Missisquoi actually went to live at Odanak. Moving about from one campsite to another, they hunted and fished mostly in the region bounded on the south by the Missisquoi River, and on the east and west by the St. Francis and Richelieu rivers. People from Odanak, too, hunted and fished here, and there was continued interaction between Abenakis from both places. But while the Odanak community continued to emphasize hunting and fishing, along with the making of baskets and other goods for sale, the tendency among the Missisquoi Abenakis was to return as soon as possible to a more sedentary and less visibly "Indian" way of life. Thus, many were soon to be found farming and working as laborers in several communities on or near Missisquoi Bay, often intermarrying with neighboring French or loyalist families. So they became essentially "invisible" to the white population, while the people of Odanak, some of whom ultimately returned to Vermont, remained more highly visible as they traveled about, gathering herbs for the market, making and selling baskets, and working the fairs and carnivals. When not identified as "Indians," such peoples were often inter-preted to be "gypsies."

Tribal spokesmen estimate that, as of 1980, there are between 1500 and 2000 Abenakis living in Vermont. The largest commu-nity is still located in the Swanton-Highgate area; other Abenakis live in St. Johnsbury, Orleans, Waterville, Hyde Park–Eden, or are scattered elsewhere around the state. In Swanton, the Abenaki community is tightly knit. The old family band organization per-sists in the recognition of large extended family groups, with a male—not necessarily the oldest—the recognized leader. Politi-cally, the band concept is expressed in the names of the organized Abenaki units, the largest and most viable being the St. Fran-cis–Sokoki band.

The St. Francis–Sokoki band is organized with a chief, cur-rently Homer St. Francis, and a governing body, the seven-mem-ber Tribal Council. All are elected to two-year staggered terms by card-carrying Abenakis. The band's tribal headquarters is located in the old railroad depot building in Swanton (Figure 7–2), which is shared with the service agency for all Native Americans in Ver-mont, the Abenaki Self Help Association, Inc. (ASHAI). In addi-tion to Abenakis, ASHAI serves people from other tribes who have come into Vermont over the past 200 years, such as Micmac, Passamaquoddy, Penobscot, and Mohawk. A seven-person board

FIGURE 7-2. Swanton's old railroad depot, now headquarters for the Abenaki St. Francis-Sokoki Band.

of directors, elected for two-year terms by the membership, is the decision-making body; it is presently composed wholly of members of the St. Francis–Sokoki band. Both ASHAI and the Tribal Council share the same goals and objectives. Of highest priority are (1) self-sufficiency; (2) acquisition of a land base for a reserve which would contain a community center, administration offices, school, museum, and day care facilities; (3) fishing and hunting rights; (4) Federal recognition, and (5) symbolic recognition.

Compared to previous decades and even centuries, the visibility of the Abenakis in Vermont during the past few years has been striking. In a report to Governor Thomas P. Salmon in 1976, Jane Baker offered three reasons why the Abenakis chose to restructure their native organization in a formal and public way. All three relate to the 1980 high priority goals, stated above. The first is the Swanton–St. Albans area's depressed socioeconomic conditions, with high unemployment rates and low incomes: "It is clear that perhaps over 95 percent of their active members are living below, to well below, the recently declared national poverty level." The second has to do with the state's enforcement of fish and game regulations during the last quarter century, a process that, in the 1960s, began to seriously interfere with their traditional subsistence hunting, fishing, and trapping. The third reason involves Abenakis' difficulties in getting along with the dominant white communities, and it also "involves the developing profile of Indians with an accompanying sense of dignity and pride replacing the invisible, unmentionable sense of the last two hundred years." Undoubtedly, other factors were involved as well, but for whatever reasons, the "reemergence" was accomplished in short order.

A chronological listing of events or activities that the Abenakis consider to be of crucial importance in their most recent history, prepared by ASHAI personnel, includes the following:

1972: Abenaki Tribal Council reformed

1975: Vermont Native American Indian Census (carried out by the Boston Indian Council)

1975: Vermont Abenaki Tribal Council recognized by Odonak and Becancour Band Councils

1976: Vermont Abenakis recognized by the State of Vermont by Executive Order Number 36, November 24.

1977: Executive Order Number 36 revoked by Executive Order Number 3, January 28.

To this list might be added other events of some significance that occurred during the 1970s:

1974: Indian Manpower Office established in Vermont by the Boston Indian Council

1976: Petition for Abenaki hunting and fishing rights submitted to the State of Vermont

1976: *Report to Governor Thomas P. Salmon of the State of Vermont Regarding the Claims Presented by the Abenaki Nation* submitted by Jane Stapleton Baker, October 15

1977: Abenaki Public Forum held at the University of Vermont, February 26

1979: Completion of *Missisquoi: Abenaki Survival in Their Ancient Homeland*, a manuscript by John Moody

In the years 1972–75, efforts were directed primarily toward internal and organizational concerns, a period of regrouping that produced a formal entity—the Tribal Council of the Abenaki Nation—and a Native American census, funded through the Boston Indian Council. 1976 proved to be a critical year for the Abenaki

sense of self-awareness; the traditional low profile was irrevoca-
bly turned full face. In the early summer of that year, a petition
was circulated throughout the state, requesting exemption from
established fish and game regulations for the Abenaki:

We the undersigned residents of the state of Vermont hereby petition
the governor, state legislature and all other appropriate authorities of the
state of Vermont to immediatly [sic] recognize the rights of the people of
the Abenaki Nation to fish and hunt on all lands and waterways throughout the state (except, for safety reasons, within a minimum distance of at
least 500 feet from any occupied dwelling, barn, or farm animal).
We recognize that hunting and fishing is not sport for Native Americans
but is their traditional means of economic and cultural survival. As such,
we demand that the state of Vermont and all its appropriate authorities
recognize the rights of Abenaki people to fish and hunt without restriction as to season, size of catch, or state licensing.

The controversy generated by this petition and the resultant pub-
licity was considerable. Between 1300 and 1400 signatures—
many those of whites—were presented to the Vermont Fish and
Game Commissioner. The controversy stemmed from several
sources. For one thing, the petition represented the first concentrated Abenaki effort to publicize their existence, which was in
itself a revelation, if not a shock, to many white Vermonters. Of
concern also was the effect that apparently unlimited hunting
and fishing would have on fish and game populations, particularly deer. Further, concern was expressed regarding the impact
such policy would have on sportsmen and tourism. A final concern involved the implications inherent in any specific group
claiming special rights of access to the state's resources.

A public forum addressing these and other issues was held at
the University of Vermont the following spring. Panel participants consisted of Homer St. Francis, Ronnie Canns, and Kent
Ouimette, representing the Abenaki of Vermont; Chief Walter
Watso of Odanak, and Bill Williams, an Iroquois active in New
England Native American affairs. During the discussion, Canns
clarified what had been meant by "unlimited": Abenaki hunting
and fishing would be limited and restricted by the Abenakis
themselves. Restrictions included needless destruction of wildlife, hunting ducks or deer in the spring, and commercial sale of
specific game or fish to others.

FIGURE 7–3. Homer St. Francis (center), chief of Vermont's St. Francis-Sokoki Band, confers with Chief Walter Watso of Odanak (left) and Bill Williams, an Iroquois who lives in New Hampshire, at the 1977 forum on Abenaki hunting and fishing rights. Photo by Carolyn Bates, *Burlington Free Press*.

Even more controversial than the circulation of the petition was Governor Salmon's Executive Order Number 36, issued on Thanksgiving Day, 1976, which conferred state recognition status to the Abenaki Nation and established a Governor's Commission on Indian Affairs (see Appendix A). Recognition was granted on the basis of research conducted by Jane Baker and her summary report submitted to the governor on October 15. Baker made use of Abenaki informants, ethnographic and historic literature, government documents, and interviews with government officials. In addition to formal recognition and the establishment of a commission, other recommendations from her report were included in the executive order, but in the form of a charge to the commission:

In addition, the Commission shall prepare a report and recommendation for the Governor and the Legislature on the request by the Abenakis for unrestricted hunting and fishing rights within the State of Vermont; the inclusion of Abenaki Tribal members in the guardianship and management of the Missisquoi [sic] Wildlife Refuge; and the request that legal title to the Monument of St. Francis, located north of Swanton, be transferred to the Abenaki people.

On February 28, 1977, Executive Order 36 was revoked by Governor Richard A. Snelling in his Executive Order Number 3 (see Appendix B). The new executive order referred to "persons of American Indian heritage who are residents of Vermont," rather than to Abenakis specifically. Thus, no distinction was made between those to whom allodial rights might apply, and those to whom they would not. Among the duties of the members of the newly created Vermont Commission for Indian Affairs were ". . . advising the appropriate authorities of any pattern or instance of unlawful discrimination against persons of American Indian heritage," as well as ". . . communicating, as widely as possible, to all citizens of Vermont and to persons of American Indian heritage, information of use and interest relating to Indian affairs," and

. . . investigating problems common to persons of American Indian heritage who are residents of this State, both urban and rural. The Commission shall provide appropriate assistance to Indian organizations and individuals in their dealings with agencies of federal, state, and local government and gaining access to social services, education, employment opportunities, health, housing, civil rights, and other services and programs and their funding.

Although the Abenakis no longer have official state recognition status, cooperation of some state agencies has been good. Currently the state recognition issue is not as critical to their welfare as federal recognition would be. Relationships between the Abenaki and the federal government, represented by the Bureau of Indian Affairs, United States Department of the Interior, are not formal, in that the Abenaki are not currently recognized as a "tribe," but fall under the Department's definition of an Indian "group." This is an important distinction, since "Such acknowledgment of tribal existence by the Department is a prerequisite to the protection, services and benefits from the Federal Government available to Indian tribes."

The reason eastern Native Americans in general have not had federal recognition is that it was their misfortune to be subdued prior to the creation of an independent United States. Although a few treaty relationships with eastern tribes were established, for the most part the newly formed United States government tended to leave the "Indian" affairs of the original thirteen states in the hands of those states and concentrated instead on native groups living on the western frontier, a policy which was maintained in later years by the BIA.

In practical terms, the nonreservation Native Americans of the eastern United States, including the Abenakis, have been the recipients of federal funding such as CETA for some projects, but only tribal status will provide access to the BIA's services and benefits that would be most useful to them. The criteria employed by the BIA for tribal recognition, published in the *Federal Register* of September 5, 1978, are included below in abbreviated form:

a. A statement of facts establishing that the petitioner has been identified from historical times until the present on a substantially continuous basis, as an "American Indian," or "aboriginal."

b. Evidence that a substantial portion of the petitioning group inhabits a specific area or lives in a community viewed as American Indian and distinct from other populations in the area and that its members are descendents of an Indian tribe which historically inhabited a specific area.

c. A statement of facts which establishes that the petitioner has maintained tribal political influence or other authority over its members as an autonomous entity throughout history until the present.

d. A copy of the group's present governing document, or in the absence of a written document, a statement describing in full the membership criteria and the procedures through which the group currently governs its affairs and its members.

e. A list of all known current members of the group and a copy of each available former list of members based on the tribe's own defined criteria.

f. The membership of the petitioning group is composed principally of persons who are not members of any other North American Indian tribe.

g. The petitioner is not, nor are its members, the subject of congressional legislation which has expressly terminated or forbidden the Federal relationship.

According to spokesmen, the Abenakis are currently working to satisfy the criteria and plan to petition for tribal status.

Despite the lack of federal recognition, most of the Abenakis' economic successes thus far have occurred through the assistance of Indian service agencies. One of these is the Boston Indian Council, which was discussed previously. The BIC is a service agency for the New England region, but works most closely with the Native American community in Boston, composed of eight to nine thousand Micmac, Passamaquoddy, Penobscot, Wampanoag, Maliseet, Mohawk, and others. In addition to publishing a monthly newspaper, the *Circle,* they offer such programs and activities as a health clinic, halfway house, day care center, seniors and adult education programs. BIC's interaction with the Abenakis in Vermont has been primarily in the area of funding; currently the agency funds ASHAI's position of job developer. The Administration for Native Americans, also located in Boston, publicizes grant availabilities to qualified groups, serves as supervisory administrators of grants, and offers advice on federal matters. ANA is responsible for the development of ASHAI's food and nutrition program. Communication among various Native American groups is facilitated through association with the Federal Regional Council/Indian Task Force, a Community Services Administration agency. Abenaki representatives attend monthly meetings to participate in discussions and resolution of issues and problems of common interest to all Native Americans. It was the CSA that funded an initial grant in 1976 to establish food cooperatives, community gardens, and crisis relief programs in the Abenaki community. That the Abenaki identify with common problems shared by Native Americans outside of New England was documented by the presence of ASHAI personnel and tribal members at the Longest Walk in Washington, D.C., a protest that culminated in a week-long demonstration in July, 1978. The purpose of the protest was to lobby against proposed legislation that had been placed before Congress, including the North American Equal Opportunity Act, a bill that would terminate all government treaties with American "Indians." Ties with the Canadian Abenaki government are strong, as well. Chief Watso of Odanak was a panel discussant at the Abenaki Forum, and the Tribal Councils of Becancour and Odanak formally recognized the existence and aboriginal rights of the Vermont Abenakis in a resolution dated August 20, 1976 (see Appendix C). This was reaffirmed in a second resolution, following Governor Salmon's recognition, on January 8, 1977 (see Appendix D).

While maintaining good relationships with other aboriginal groups is good policy and promotes group solidarity, Vermont's Abenakis are still faced with such problems as low incomes and unemployment. Baker's statistics for the St. Albans–Swanton area, previously cited, are essentially correct for 1980, according to Miles Jensen, director of ASHAI. Exacerbating the chronic unemployment and low income is the educational level of the Abenakis, many of whom are high school dropouts. Several approaches have been involved in ASHAI's attempts to provide educational opportunities for persons at all levels. In the summer of 1979, ASHAI secured an Adult Basic Education grant; a few months later, fifty-eight adults were enrolled in three basic areas: life-coping skills, basic literacy, and the General Equivalency Diploma program. The GED program, which prepares individuals who have not completed high school to earn their diplomas by means of tutoring, has been particularly effective. By March of 1980, ten persons of various ages had passed the GED tests. Another program, funded through an Indian Education grant, will serve as an adjunct to academic services provided by schools within the Franklin County Northwest school district. This program consists of providing qualified counselors, tutors, and school policy interpreters who are available to students, parents, and teachers. It is geared to fit the special needs of Abenaki students who are seeking alternatives to more traditional school services. A new office has been established to administer these and other educational activities and programs: the Abenaki Tribal Learning Center was officially opened on February 14, 1980 in Swanton.

Long-range educational goals include the establishment of an accredited Abenaki school, which is viewed as an important com-

ponent of the proposed reserve, the development of a cross-cul-
tural educational program for young people from Vermont and
Odanak and the development of courses to teach the Abenaki
language. Chief St. Francis has expressed his hope that a crafts
program involving Vermont and Odanak, Abenaki youths can be
established. Although the ash splint–sweet-grass basketry is no
longer an important industry at Odanak, some artifacts are still
produced for the tourist trade. One example of the reintroduction
of a traditional item of material culture has been noted by Gordon
Day: a carved wooden "medicine" pole, which in former times
was kept by the river's edge on the reserve. Borrowing perhaps
from elements of the Northwest Coast ceremonial totem poles,
the modern equivalent was first manufactured for the 1960 annual celebration at Odanak, with carved turtle and bear representing symbols of Abenaki moieties (these moieties are based on
the tribal origins of those who contributed to the mixed village at
Odanak). Chief St. Francis envisions that a crafts program would
serve a dual purpose: the manufacture of basketry and perhaps
the production of miniature medicine poles, among other items,
would not only promote an interest in traditional Abenaki crafts,
but would provide supplemental income for the participants.
With the aid of a VISTA volunteer, the first phase of this cultural
education program has already begun. Plans to develop a language
program may prove to be more difficult. Gordon Day reports that
in 1974, only twenty-one fully competent speakers of the language—all elderly—were at Odanak; an undetermined number of
other younger or middle-aged Abenaki exhibited varying levels of
proficiency, mostly "passive." Although not part of the organized
educational efforts, at least one Abenaki has introduced herbal
medicine to the larger Swanton community, an interesting fact in
light of Day's description of the achievements of Abenaki "plant
doctors," who were as effective during the colonial period as they
are at Odanak today.

As should be clear from the above discussion, many of the goals
that the Abenakis have set for themselves have not yet been
fulfilled. While some of the economic and educational programs
are expanding, the Abenaki community in Franklin County is far
from self-sufficient. Aboriginal rights were again an issue on
April 22, 1978, when a Fish-In was held on the west bank of the

Missisquoi in Swanton (Figure 7–4). The purpose of the demonstration was to publicize their request for free licenses and unlimited access to fishing spots (except for posted spawning grounds) for purposes of obtaining food. Thirty-four persons were cited for fishing without licenses by Fish and Game wardens. As of this writing, legal action is still pending at St. Albans District Court. The preparation of Federal recognition forms continues, and Vermont state officials have recently expressed interest in revitalizing the Vermont Commission for Indian Affairs, which has been inactive since 1978. Symbolic recognition, in the form of obtaining title to the Swanton Monument, has not yet been granted. This stone monument was erected in 1901 to commemorate the location of the first church in Vermont, built for the "St. Francis Indians" (Missisquoi) by the Jesuits in the eighteenth century. It is located not far from the Boucher site, the Early Woodland cemetery discussed in Chapter 4, on a terrace above the Missisquoi River, an area that the Abenakis consider to be sacred ground. Individual Abenakis have on their own initiative performed groundskeeping tasks at the monument in the past as they still do today.

FIGURE 7–4. The 1979 Missisquoi Fish-In. Photo courtesy Miles Jensen.

FIGURE 7–5. The Monument of St. Francis, located on a terrace above the Missisquoi River. Photo courtesy Peter A. Thomas.

Their wish is to become spiritual caretakers of this small plot of land as well. Dialogues continue with the owners of the monument, the Roman Catholic Diocese of Burlington.

After all that Vermont's Abenakis have been through since Champlain's visit of 1609, one is struck by their remarkable will to survive as a people in the face of incredible odds. Their experience has been, in many ways, similar to those of small tribal groups the world over:

Frequently they find that they must forfeit their indigenous identity and be pressed into a mold that allows them no latitude or motivation to rise above the lowest rung of the social ladder. From an autonomous people with pride and a strong sense of their own identity as a people, they all too often are transformed into a deprived underclass with neither pride nor a sense of identity.

The Abenakis have chosen another way. Like many indigenous peoples in almost all parts of the globe, they have decided that they have a right to their own identity and should be allowed to work out their own way of being different. When a whole people give up and disappear as a people, just because their continued presence is inconvenient or upsetting to some, all of humanity is in trouble. The Abenakis have not given up and disappeared, and we can all take encouragement from that fact.

BIBLIOGRAPHICAL NOTES

IN THIS BOOK, we have spared the reader from footnotes or other specific references to the relevant literature in the body of the text. We have done this deliberately so as not to interrupt the flow of the text, or impose potential barriers between the reader and what we are trying to say. On the other hand, it is essential that proper credit be given to the work and ideas of others, that specific references be given so that the critical reader can check on our use of sources, and that leads be provided for those who wish to pursue their own avenues of research.

To take care of these essentials, and to provide us with an opportunity to expand upon some points made in the text, bibliographical notes for each chapter follow. A complete bibliography is on page 283.

Chapter 1

The statement which opens this chapter is from Hancock et al. (1978: 28); it serves as one example of a current and widely available work which repeats the myth of an "empty Vermont"; it is by no means the only example which might have been selected.

The most reliable references to French and English knowledge of Vermont Indians are the works of Gordon Day (1965a, 1965b, 1971, 1973b, 1975, 1978) and Thomas (1973, 1979b). Another important source, once it is published, will be Day's *Canadian Abenakis*, which will be part of the National Museum of Man's Popular Series. Also useful, so long as one is aware that it contains errors, is Pierce (1977). A translation of Champlain's 1609 observations on Vermont will be found in Bassett (1976: 3–7). On the cleared lands found by the English settlers, see Crockett (1921: 59–60), Sanders (1812: 170; see also p. 173) and Thomas (1973).

The specific articles cited in *Vermont History* are Day (1965b) and Laurent (1955). Day is a happy exception to the general rule that anthropologists write mostly for each other's benefit. Their writings are to be found mostly in journals which are little known to the non-anthropologist, hard to find when they are known, and written in such a way as to be difficult for the non-anthropologist to understand. Another exception is Haviland (1969), but this is now outdated.

Further examples of Native American articles in *Vermont History* are the numerous articles by Huden (1955a,b; 1956a,b; 1957a,b,c; 1958). Huden was a pioneer in the study of aboriginal occupations of Vermont; unfortunately, it is the fate of pioneers to be subsequently proven wrong about many things. Huden's importance for the study of Vermont's native peoples, therefore, lies more in what he started than in what he said. Much of the latter has been modified, and in many cases invalidated, by a subsequent research.

The Vermont Historical Society (VHS) sponsored excavation was that of Brooks (1971:24–32) at the Rivers site. In 1941, Henry Slocum chaired an archaeology committee of the VHS, the goal of which was to survey the state to find a site worth excavating (see Loring 1972).

Reliable sources on who lived in Vermont in the seventeenth century are Day (1965a,b; 1971; 1973b; 1978) and Thomas (1973; 1979b). Huden's (1958) listing of "Recent Algonkians" is more a catalogue of peoples in Vermont who were driven out of homelands in other parts of New York and New England by the British, than it is of peoples indigenous to Vermont. Day gives Otter Creek as the boundary of Abenaki territory, which it may have been, except that comparable watercourses throughout New England normally lay at the core, rather than edges of band territories (Snow 1968). Those which did occasionally serve as boundaries, such as the Richelieu River, were generally quite long and/or complex (Morrison 1977b:241). It is, therefore, unlikely that Otter Creek itself was at the edge of anyone's territory. Its use in the seventeenth century as part of a travel route to and from Sokoki (Abenaki) territory on the Connecticut (Bostock 1955:237; Broehl 1959:27; Hall 1858:33), its inclusion as part of the Champlain, rather than Hudson watershed, and the similarity of its archaeological materials to those further north in the Champlain Valley all lead us to the conclusion that the Otter Creek watershed probably was Abenaki rather than Mahican country. Its Abenaki name was *Onegikwizibó*, which means "Otter River" (Day 1977:30).

The discussion of languages is drawn largely from Goddard (1978a,b), Haas (1960), Snow 1976b, 1977a), and Tuck (1975b), and has benefited greatly from Gordon M. Day's comments on a first draft. Snow's (1977a) paper raises so many important problems which are usually overlooked by archaeologists that every archaeologist in the Northeast who has not yet done so should read it immediately. On the principles of linguistic classification, with a classification of Native American languages, see Driver (1969: Chapter 3). On language chains, see Goddard (1978b:70), Swadesh (in Hymes 1964:581), and Tuck (1975b). On the lack of evidence for borrowing from any ancient, non-Algonquian language, see Goddard (1978b:77).

Material on Vermont's environmental setting is drawn largely from *Vermont Land Capability*, put out by the Vermont State Planning Office in 1974 (and which, on page 15, has the inevitable ". . . Vermont was a no-man's-land lying between warring peoples . . ." statement). This has been supplemented by material from Funk (1976:5–6), Thomas (1973; 1979b), and Willey (1966:10).

For a short, easy to read introduction to what archaeology is all about, and how archaeologists operate, see Haviland (1979: Chapters 1 and 2). For a more thoroughgoing introduction, the standard work is Hole and Heizer (1977). For a good example of ethnohistoric research, and the problems involved, see Jennings (1976). For problems in radiocarbon dating, see Stuckenrath (1977). The correction for carbon 14 dates used in this book is from Clark (1975).

The beginning date for the ethnographic present is straightforward enough, but its ending date is not. Although native cultures must have begun to adjust to the European presence early in the seventeenth century, meaningful direct contact with Europeans did not begin until the 1640s, when there was some contact with English surveyors and traders in southern Vermont and New Hampshire. French dealings with the Sokoki, from the same region, began in 1642. Probably, native culture had not changed too much by then, although there had been displacement of Mahicans by the 1630s, and the Connecticut Valley peoples were hit by a devastating epidemic in the same decade.

Thomas's (1979b) work at the Fort Hill site at Hinsdale, New Hampshire, indicates that although native culture was still quite vigorous as late as 1663–64, the European presence was having a noticeable impact. By then, European trade items were replacing and supplementing native technology, traditional subsistence strategies were undergoing modification and showing signs of strain, and elements of Roman Catholic world view were gaining acceptance.

Chapter 2
Discussion of American Indian origins will be found in any recent text dealing with North American Indians, of which there are several. One of the best up-to-date, as well as readable, discussions is in the Time-Life book, *The First Americans* (Claiborne et al. 1973). A more detailed discussion of the availability of the Bering land bridge and ice-free McKenzie corridor relative to early archaeological remains in North America is Bryan (1969; but see also Fladmark 1979).

Good discussions of the Laurentide ice and its recession relative to New England and the Northeast are Funk (1972 and 1976:207–212) and especially Borns (1973). The classic work on Lake Vermont and the Champlain Sea is Chapman (1937), which has been updated and related to radiocarbon dates by Wagner (1972). For glacial Lake Hitchcock, see Curran and Dincauze (1977) and Hartshorn (1969).

The primary source on the Reagen site is Ritchie (1953), and what he refers to as "the total series" of artifacts are illustrated in Ritchie (1957: Plates 12–18). However, the illustrated artifacts add up to a few less than those mentioned in the 1953 article, and there are some other minor discrepancies. Further useful thoughts on the Reagen material will be found in Funk (1976:229), but what we urgently need is a thorough restudy of the artifacts, including the 25 percent which have not been studied by Ritchie or anyone else. Methods of lithic analysis have become much more sophisticated than they were in the early 1950s. Applied to the totality of the Reagen collection, they can probably tell us much more about it than we now know. The proposed dating for the Reagen site is our own reconsideration of the old, as well as some new, evidence. For the Labrador material referred to, see Renouf (1977); the Lake Winnipesaukee date is from a feature associated with a Plano living floor (Klein 1977:645).

Our summaries of Debert and Bull Brook owe much to the summaries of Dragoo (1976), Funk (1972, 1976), Ritchie and Funk (1973), and Salwen (1975). The major publications on these sites are Byers (1954, 1955, 1959) and MacDonald (1968).

The only reasonably complete inventory of Paleoindian material from Vermont consists of an article by Stephen Loring (1980), at the time a graduate student in anthropology at the University of Massachusetts in Amherst. We have relied heavily on his work, supplemented by that of Squire (1977b), Vogelmann (1972), and informant data gathered by James B. Petersen (a senior anthropology student at the University of Vermont). Our assessment of the relationship between Paleoindian finds and shorelines of the Champlain Sea is based on an accurate plotting of these shorelines on 15 minute series USGS topographic maps, by Tom Vogelmann, done when he was a senior at the University of Vermont. These maps are on file in the University's department of anthropology. For complete descriptive data on the fluted points which we have listed in Table 1, see Loring (1980).

The Davis site is described, and its relation to the Champlain Sea is discussed, by Ritchie (1969:19–22). Our information on Sawyer's Crossing No. 1 comes from Curran (1977; also summarized in Klein 1977:645).

Ideas about postglacial vegetation have changed considerably in the past few years. It used to be thought that as glaciers grew and climates became colder, tundra and northern forest belts like those of today shifted southward in response. Conversely, as glaciers melted and climates warmed, these vegetation belts shifted northward once again. We now know that this is much too simple a picture, and that recolonization of glaciated areas by vegetation was significantly affected by soil conditions, moisture, temperature, and the speed with which different kinds of seeds could spread northward. As a result, postglacial vegetation was in a more or less constant state of evolution, and was not precisely like any present-day vegetative assemblage. One must, therefore, be cautious in using the literature on postglacial changes in vegetation. In our discussion here, we have relied heavily on Carr, Worley, and Davis (1977) *Post-Lake Vermont History of a Pond and Wetland in the Champlain Basin*, Bradstreet and Davis (1975) *Mid-Postglacial Environments in New England with Emphasis on Maine*, and Curran and Dincauze (1977) *Paleoindians and Paleolakes: New Data from the Connecticut Drainage* (see also Fagan 1978).

The animal resources available in postglacial forests are discussed in Fagan (1978), Funk (1972, 1976:209–210, 1977), and Salwen (1975). The marine mammals of the Champlain Sea have been summarized by Harrington (1977); the suggestion that they were exploited by Paleoindians comes from Vogelmann (1972) and, more recently, Loring (1980).

The concept of the North American Big Game Hunting Tradition is defined and discussed in Willey (1966:37–51). Its emergence in eastern North America is summarized by Dragoo (1976b). The suggested analogy between northeastern Paleoindians and the caribou hunting Inuit of interior Alaska comes from Funk (1976:226). On material which predates the emergence of the Big Game Tradition, see Adovasio et al. (1978).

The model of movement of Paleoindians into Vermont is our own, but its roots lie in arguments about the spread of human populations in arctic regions made by J. L. Giddings (1954:28). For a general summary of the characteristics of hunting and gathering societies, see Haviland (1978:154–165). For a discussion of the relationship between population density and dispersal among mammals, see Christian (1970). The 1200 years, more or less, which is suggested as the time available for movement of Paleoindians into Vermont, is based on radiocarbon dates from Dutchess Quarry Cave (Funk 1976:206) and our dating of Vermont Paleoindian remains, both dealt with earlier in Chapter 2.

· The summary of what we know about the first inhabitants of Vermont, besides drawing upon material already presented in Chapter 2, relies upon our general anthropological understanding of hunting and gathering peoples, as summarized by Haviland (1968: see especially pp. 154–165, 288–290, 338 and 340–342). Although many reconstructions of Paleoindian society utilize Service's (1971:48–50) patrilocal band model (see for example Fitting 1977:370), we find Funk's (1976:226) analogy with the ambilocal, bilateral, caribou hunting Inuit of interior Alaska more apt. In fact, the patrilocal band model never has had much basis in reality. Not only are most hunting and gathering societies not patrilocal, but some which have been described as patrilocal either are not, or seem to have become so quite recently. Moreover, rigid adherence to patrilocality would militate against the adaptive flexibility normally required by the hunting and gathering way of life.

The suggestion of a Paleoindian withdrawal from the Champlain Valley up the St. Lawrence comes, once again, from Stephen Loring (1980). The probability that the salt waters of the Champlain Sea were flushed out within ten years of its ending, to be followed by a lake of low productivity, was pointed out by Ian Worley in personal communication with Haviland. For a discussion of the relevant material from southern Labrador and its possible relation to late Paleoindian remains from Vermont, see Renouf (1977).

Chapter 3

Our discussion of past environments throughout this chapter relies on the same sources noted for Chapter 2, with the addition of two others. One of these is a paper by Dincauze and Mulholland (1977) which is invaluable for understanding how environmental factors may have affected early Archaic occupations in New England. The other, a personal communication between Ian Worley of the University of Vermont's botany department and Haviland, deals with the origin of Lake Champlain's wetlands.

Recent general discussions of the beginnings of the Archaic in the East are Dragoo (1976b) and Griffin (1978). For southern Labrador, see Renouf (1977); our information on the sequence at Lake Winnipesaukee is Bolian (n.d.; see also Klein 1977:645). The success in recognizing early Archaic sequences throughout so much of the East has had a certain "band wagon" effect with respect to the northeastern lake-forest region. Where once no early Archaic materials were recognized, there is now some tendency to assume they are common everywhere. To make such an assumption is to ignore the continued lack of firm evidence against the proposition that human populations underwent a significant decline in many parts of the region, even though it may not have been totally deserted as once thought. For discussion of the early Archaic in the lake-forest region, see Funk (1977), Salwen (1975), Snow (1977b), and Tuck (1975b:144–146). On the early Archaic of southern New England, see

Dincauze (1971:19) and Dincauze and Mulholland (1977). Our information on the distribution of early Archaic material in Vermont is drawn from Squire (1977b) and Peter A. Thomas (personal communication with Haviland).

The possible persistence of early and middle Archaic materials into later times is raised by Loring (1972), Ritchie (1979:5), Ritchie and Funk (1973:38, 337), and Squire (1977b:5). As an important theoretical point to keep in mind, although older ideas of the far Northeast as little more than a kind of "receiving area" for things invented earlier elsewhere are no longer acceptable, it is still a fact that some things were dropped by peoples outside the region a lot earlier than within it. A general case in point is continued reliance on hunting and gathering for subsistence. Possible cases of a more specific nature are the presence of Brewerton points in early and even middle Woodland sites in Vermont (Squire 1977b:9, 61). Although the possibility of digging errors immediately comes to mind, none of these sites included identifiable Archaic components. Even more certain cases are discussed in Chapter 4. Clearly, we should not assume that just because a particular tool or custom was abandoned in southern New England or New York at a particular time that this was necessarily the case further north and east. More work needs to be done on this.

Vermont archaeology is plagued by the lack of acceptable site reports which present with precision and in detail the basic data from excavation. The situation is not much better elsewhere in the Northeast. With respect to Vermont sites discussed in this chapter, the only adequate report is Sargent's (1960) for Sumner's Falls (see also Sargent 1969:30 and Dincauze 1975:30 on this site). Our information on the other Vermont sites comes from the following sources: *KI*, Daniels (1963:26, 28–31), Ritchie (1968:1–3; 1969:85–89), Snow (1976c:37 for the idea about ironwood atlatls), and Wright (1974:77 for the most reliable inventory of artifacts); *Donovan*, Bailey (1939b:7–23); *Rivers*, Bailey (1939a:3–6), Brooks (1971:24–32); *Otter Creek No. 2*, Funk (1976:235, 238), Ritchie (1979), Ritchie and Funk (1973:340), and Tuck (1977:38); *East Creek*, Loring (1972:152–170); *Auclair and Ewing*, Anonymous (1970), Bacon (1975), Basa (1971), Petersen (1977; 1978c), and Squire (1977b); *Isle La Motte*, Ritchie (1969:132–134).

Our discussion of Vergennes and related materials outside of Vermont is based on the following sources: *Allumette Island*, Funk (1976:235) and Ritchie (1969:xix; 1971:4; 1979:15–16, 19); *Bridge site*, Ritchie (1968:3; 1969:xviii); *Lake George–Hudson Valley region*, Funk (1976: especially 197, 235–236, 237, 241, 244, Figure 21 and Table 28); *Hirundo*, Sanger (1975) and Sanger, Davis, MacKay and Borns (1977); elsewhere in *Maine and the Maritimes*, Bourque (1975:40) and Sanger (1975:62, 72); *Neville*, Dincauze (1976: especially 110–111, 124–126, 135); *Southern New England*, Dincauze (1975:26 and 1976:125). See also Ritchie and Funk (1973:48) for general Northeastern distribution.

Our conclusions about the dating of the Vergennes Archaic are our own, but the facts on which the discussion rests are from the following sources: Dincauze (1975:26; 1976:110–113), Funk (1976:235, 237, 243,

271, 272, 307); Ritchie (1968:2; 1971:4–5; 1979:19), Ritchie and Funk (1973:45, 46), Sanger (1975:62), Sanger, Davis, MacKay and Borns (1977:465) and Snow (1975:51). The concept of a "Laurentian Archaic" was formulated by Ritchie (1969:79), who, although he clearly recognizes an element of regionalism, consistently refers to Vergennes, Vosburg, and Brewerton as "phases." The Vergennes he regards as the classic expression out of which Vosburg and Brewerton developed (Ritchie 1969:84), even though he sees the origins of the Laurentian as lying to the south of the Great Lakes (Ritchie 1969:82), while the Vergennes does not extend west or south of the Champlain Valley. Here, we have a second compelling reason to abandon the Laurentian concept. The lumping together of Vergennes, Vosburg, and Brewerton has blinded us all to the likelihood that the origins of the Vergennes on the one hand and Vosburg and Brewerton on the other may lie in different directions. Those things which they have in common may be the result of convergence and borrowing, rather than a carry over from a common ancestry.

The way archaeologists have been conditioned to think by the Laurentian concept is apparent in recent papers by Sanger, Snow, and Tuck. Sanger (1975) simply accepts the notion that Vergennes, as part of the Laurentian which is supposed to have developed in the south and west, is intrusive into Maine. This leads him to believe that the Vergennes folk spoke a Proto-Iroquoian language. Tuck (1975b, 1977) is not quite so passive in his acceptance of this notion, aware as he is of the strong connections between Vergennes and the Maritime Archaic. Nonetheless, accept it he does, complete with the idea that the Vergennes folk spoke Proto-Iroquoian. Snow (1976c:34), however, will have none of the Proto-Iroquoian hypothesis; he regards the Laurentians (i.e. the Vergennes, Vosburg, and Brewerton folk) as speakers of Proto-Algonquian. Not even in passing do any of these three raise the possibility that the origins and language of the Vergennes folk may have been quite different from those of the other "Laurentians." Perhaps Bourque (1975:40) comes close: he sees great appeal to positing a relationship between Vergennes material in Maine with that in the "red paint" burials of the Maritime Archaic. Turnbaugh (1977:92) is clearly close: he has independently suggested that maritime peoples turned inland sometime after 4000 b.c.

On the Inuit ("Eskimo") theories of Vergennes origins see Ritchie (1969:80) or Turnbaugh (1977:87). As examples, see Bailey (1939b:7–8, 20–21) and Daniels (1963:27–31). On "intrusion from the south and west" theories, see Sanger (1975) and Tuck (1975b). On the Maritime Archaic, see Tuck (1971, 1975a) and Snow (1975).

Our understanding of the nature and origins of the foreign elements which went into the making of the Vergennes Archaic owes much to discussions by Funk (1976:237) and Tuck (1977). An understanding of the means by which these elements were introduced requires an assessment of the probability of diffusion having occurred. Our judgment that the probability of diffusion of ground slate technology from the Maritime Archaic to the Vergennes is practically nil is based on Fitzhugh's (1975) important comparative study of this technology among peoples of the northern hemisphere. Our observations on the relative importance of indigenous and foreign elements in the growth of Vergennes are based on our anthropological knowledge of the roles played by internal and external forces in the shaping of human cultures generally (see, for example, Haviland 1978: Chapters 1 and 15).

On the characteristics of Native American culture areas which persist over extended periods of time, see Willey (1966: 5). The relationship between language and culture is always difficult to deal with archaeologically, but cannot be ignored. For an excellent summary of problems and potentials, see Willey (1966:16). Our discussion draws on the same sources listed for Chapter 1, but relies most heavily on Snow (1976b and 1977a). For *in situ* theories of Iroquoian origins, see Lounsbury (1978:336), Ritchie (1969:301), and Ritchie and Funk (1973:359–368). For similar theories of Algonquian origins, see Goddard (1978b:70, 77), Snow (1975; 1976b; 1977a; 1978:60, 67, 69) and Tuck (1975b).

Recognition of the "hybrid nature" of all cultures is important for an understanding of the significance of those elements which came into Vermont following the establishment of the Vergennes Archaic. All too often, archaeologists tend to think in terms of cultures as somehow "pure," a concept that vaguely implies that archaeological remains which include artifacts not known in "pure" deposits have been contaminated by mixing. If, then, a style of projectile diagnostic of one culture becomes prominent in another area, this all too often is taken to indicate some kind of cultural replacement. The fact is, not only styles of projectile, but whole complexes of hunting equipment may diffuse with impunity, and one style of projectile—or even a whole technological complex, for that matter—does not equal a whole culture. Furthermore, the notion implied by the "pure culture" concept, that cultures remain unchanging for prolonged periods of time, is unwarranted (see, for example, Colson 1976). Rates of change certainly vary enormously over time, but cultures never stand still; to some degree they are always in a state of flux as they respond to influences both from within and without. In short, it would be very surprising if foreign elements were not added to the Vergennes Archaic from time to time, and a Vergennes assemblage which includes, for example, Brewerton projectiles, is no less "pure" than are those in which such projectiles are absent.

The various styles of projectile which were introduced into Vermont over the last three millennia b.c. are discussed by Squire (1977b). Additional information relating to specific archaeological sites comes from the sources already cited. As things stand, in spite of our lack of well-controlled data on the Auclair and Ewing sites, we regard them as particularly important for an understanding of the late Archaic. Every technological element which came into Vermont from 3000 to 500 b.c. appears to be mixed together at these sites. This is exactly what we would expect if the sites were continuously utilized by indigenous "Vermonters" without significant interruption over this period, but were disturbed by plowing in historic times. Of course, there is an alternative hypothesis, that there was a series of discrete occupations at these sites by different peoples. But this is not as economical an interpretation and, in science, the most economical interpretation is always accepted until an alternative has been demonstrated to be more likely. What we really need, obviously, is careful excavation of sites like Auclair and Ewing which have escaped disturbance.

For discussion of small-stemmed and notched points, Normanskill points, and broad points south of Vermont, see Funk (1976:268–276) and Ritchie (1971:5–9). If Snow (1977a) is right about the location of the Proto-Iroquoian homeland, it seems to us highly likely that the small-stemmed and notched points and associated implements which seem to originate in the same region were introduced into the Northeast by Proto-Iroquoian peoples. According to Floyd Lounsbury (1978:336), Northern Iroquoian languages have probably been spoken in central New York and Pennsylvania for as many as four millennia. This being so, we should look for the arrival of Proto-Iroquoians in New York sometime before 2000 B.C. and not after, as Snow suggests. Linguists estimate the separation of Proto-Muskogean from Proto-Algonquian to have taken place between 3000 and 4000 B.C. This could have been caused by a general expansion of Proto-Iroquoian peoples out of their Appalachian homeland. It is likely that such an expansion would have carried some Proto-Iroquoians as far north as southwestern New York State by the end of fourth millennium B.C. And indeed we find that by 3245 B.C. (2500 b.c.), the Lamoka folk, who so closely resemble in physical type the Archaic peoples of the Southeast (Ritchie 1969:46), were in place. We find that, in tentatively identifying the Lamoka folk as Proto-Iroquoian, we have independently come up with the same idea which occurred to Byers (1961) almost twenty years ago.

Evidence for conflict in central New York around 2000 b.c. (2520 B.C.) between Lamoka people, who we think were Proto-Iroquoian, and Brewerton people, who were probably Proto-Algonquian, comes from the Frontenac Island site (Ritchie 1971:6). The failure of Lamoka culture to replace Brewerton in northern New York need not imply that the Lamoka folk were the losers. What we may have here is a situation analogous to the Aztec rise to dominance in Mesoamerica. The Aztecs were a nomadic people who lived to the north of Mesoamerica, and whose culture originally was quite different from that of the Mesoamericans. Through conquest, the Aztecs were able to impose their dominance over the Mesoamericans, but they did not impose their culture upon them. Instead, they themselves adopted the culture of the people they conquered.

In northern New York, the conflict between Lamoka and Brewerton peoples was followed by a new culture, the archaeological remains of which are overlain on Frontenac Island by those of the Frost Island phase. Snow (1977a:110) is inclined to identify Frost Island, which dates to around 1500 b.c. (1835 B.C.) as Proto-Iroquoian. What we may have here, though much work needs to be done to verify it, is a record of Proto-Iroquoian intrusion, conflict, and ultimate domination in the old Brewerton homeland.

On long distance trade in the late Archaic, see Ritchie (1968:4; 1969:80, 101). On late Archaic burial cults, see Ritchie (1955), Robbins (1968) and Tuck (1970; 1971). For the anthropological approach to religion, see Wallace (1966). On Ritchie's analogy between the late Archaic and the Historic Abenaki, see Ritchie and Funk (1973:343). Given the probability that late Archaic peoples in Vermont spoke a Proto-Algonquian dialect, then it follows from evidence discussed in the notes to Chapter 5 that their social organization is unlikely to have differed in any significant way from that of the western Abenakis of the ethnographic present.

Chapter 4

The Woodland is perhaps the most complex and poorly understood period in the Northeast. For purposes of placing this time period within the context of a generalized eastern North American prehistoric sequence, see Willey (1966, Chapter 5), Dragoo (1976b), and Stoltman (1978). An overview of the Northeast is provided by Trigger (1978) and Ritchie (1969; see especially Chapter 4, the Woodland Stage). For transitional late Archaic—early Woodland manifestations in the Northeast, see Tuck (1978a), and for middle and late Woodland, Fitting (1978). The Hudson Valley sequence is discussed in Salwen (1975), Funk (1976), and Snow (1977a). On the earliest domestic plants, see Chomko and Crawford (1978).

A heavy reliance has been placed on ceramic analysis in this chapter, for the most part drawn from studies conducted by James B. Petersen (1977; 1978a; 1978b; 1978c; 1979; 1980; Power, Cowan, and Petersen 1980; and personal communication with Power). Squire (1977b) was used throughout the chapter for projectile point distribution; the discussion of skeletal remains recovered at the Boucher and Rivers sites was based on analysis conducted by Haviland.

Our discussion of the Intervale's resources utilized Anderson (1975), Seymour (1979), Siccama (1971), and Spear (1970). Sources for aboriginal plant use include Vogel (1970), Vogelmann (1977), and Yarnell (1964). Available studies of the Winooski site are Catania (1978), Cowan (1979), Petersen (1979; 1980), Power (1978, 1979a; 1979b), and Power, Cowan, and Petersen (1980). For the comparative discussion of middle Woodland manifestations outside the state, see Fitting (1978), Ritchie and Funk (1973), and Wright (1967) for the early period; and after A.D. 500, discussions by Brumbach (1977), Funk (1976), Funk, Weinman, and Weinman (1966), and Tuck (1978a).

In addition to the Winooski site, other sites and sources include the McNeil Generating Plant site (Thomas and Bourassa 1978) and the Chace Mill sites (Thomas and Bayreuther 1979). Also related to the Intervale Woodland occupation but not mentioned in the chapter by site name are reports by Haviland (1969a; 1973). The passage on Seneca villages is quoted from Wallace (1969:22).

As previously noted, few middle Woodland sites outside the Intervale have been reported in a comprehensive or even adequate fashion. Exceptions are the Missisquoi Wildlife Refuge sites (Thomas and Robinson 1979) and Sutherland Falls (Squire 1977a). Data for the remainder are at times confused, due in part to the sporadic nature of the investigations, but also because of the presence of unrecognized multiple Woodland occupations. For the Ewing site, see Anonymous (1970); Bacon (1975); Basa (1971); Cowan (1977); Catania (1978); Petersen (1977; 1978c; 1979); Stvan (1978), and Varney (n.d.). Bailey (1939b), the major reference for the Donovan site, also discussed Rivers in his report. Other references for the

Rivers site are Brooks (1971), Barber's (1972) study of pit remains, and Basa, in an interview conducted by Grossinger (1975).

Information pertaining to both middle and late Woodland materials and sites in the southwestern portion of the state were drawn from Thomas and Campoli (1979), and Thomas (1979c); see also Snow (1978) for related data and Brasser's (1978b) discussion of the Mahican. See Funk (1976) on the rarity of evidence for middle Woodland settlements in the Hudson Valley. Other sites included in the middle Woodland portion of the chapter are Skitchewaug (Petersen 1978a); Sumner Falls (Sargent 1960); and Isle La Motte (Moorehead 1922).

The absence of early Woodland habitation sites and the nature of the Adena relationships perceived in cemetery sites are problems common to all northeastern prehistorians. In Vermont, these problems are compounded by the uneven quality of the cemetery investigations. The most useful source of information for the Swanton site is Perkins (1873); see also Perry (1868), and Moorehead (1922). Brief descriptions of both Swanton and the East Creek sites are found in Willoughby (1935:85–86; 94–95) and some of the objects from both are illustrated in Huden (1971). Information for the Boucher site is derived from Louise Basa (personal communication with Power; Basa 1974; 1975) and from Grossinger's (1975) interview with Basa. Since there are no extant field notes from the East Creek site, Loring's (1972) study of the materials provided the basis for the discussion; some use was also made of Gifford (1948). The Bennett site is also a problem; however, a summary of site contents occurs in Ritchie (1944:199–200). The references to early Woodland cemetery materials from Burlington and Woodstock are from Loring (1972).

Our discussion of the Meadowood and Middlesex phases is drawn from Ritchie (1969:180–200) and more recent interpretations by Snow (1977a). The situation in which Meadowood materials such as side-notched projectile points and cache blades have been located outside of Iroquois territory appears to be analogous to a phenomenon observed in late Woodland times. The small, well-made Madison projectile points, at home in Iroquois territory, are also present, but far less commonly, in areas east of the heartland, including Vermont (see, for example, Funk 1976:301).

For an understanding of the Middlesex phase, studies by Webb and Snow (1945), and Webb and Baby (1957) are of value, since they have formed the basis for the models of proposed transmission of traits from the Ohio Valley. Members attending an Adena Conference (Swartz 1971) have more recently articulated some of the problems inherent in the Adena concept. Ritchie's (1969:201–245) discussion of the Middlesex culture as "Adena of the North" also includes the historical development of his ideas regarding Adenoid population migration into the Northeast and further summarizes the hypothesis that he formulated with Don Dragoo (Ritchie and Dragoo 1960). For a review of the "migrationist school of explanation" and alternative models that have contributed to the fall from grace of migration as the most plausible explanation for culture change, see Adams, Van Gerven, and Levy (1978). Grayson's (1970) criticism of the Ritchie-Dragoo theory and more recent comments on Adena in the Northeast by Dragoo (1976a), Snow (1977a) and Tuck (1978b) present convincing arguments for alternative interpretations. It is of significance, too, that Dragoo (1976a; 1976b) stresses *in situ* development in his summary of prehistory.

In our own discussion of early Woodland *in situ* development from late Archaic cultures, specific instances were cited in which Archaic artifacts were found in cemetery contexts. There are several possible explanations for their presence. First, these items may have been kept by early Woodland peoples as "heirlooms" in the same sense that heirlooms are treasured today; second, using another modern analogy, artifacts may have been surface collected by early Woodland peoples, thus they were collectors of prehistoric artifacts during prehistoric times. Finally, the likelihood exists that such items, while diagnostic of Archaic peoples, had not entirely gone out of use. This interpretation would conform to the evidence for cultural lag, particularly as it relates to pottery motifs and methods of manufacture that we describe during the late Woodland discussion. Thus, we think it the most likely interpretation.

Detailed information on Owasco and post-Owasco ceramics in New York state is from Ritchie (1969: 300–324) and Tuck (1978a). A discussion of Iroquoian ceramics and their presence in non-Iroquois territory can be found in Brumbach (1975). Late Woodland manifestations in New England are also described by Snow (1978). Tuck (1978a) presents a lucid summary of the introduction of horticulture and its ramifications. The lone horticultural site known so far in Vermont—Donohue—is reported in Thomas and Bumstead (1979). Our discussion of the relative merits of adopting horticulture from the point of view of a generalized hunter-gatherer was drawn from Haviland (1979, Chapter 12). On the appearance of maize and storage pits in eastern New York, see Funk (1976: 295, 296).

Many of the late Woodland sites with multiple Woodland occupations represented have been previously discussed, and sources listed. These include Ewing, Donovan, Rivers, Sumner Falls, Skitchewaug, and data known from southwestern Vermont. Sites and references not previously cited here are Chipman's Point (Bailey 1940), the Warrel Farm site (Bacon 1976; Petersen 1979), Fort Hill (Thomas 1979b), and other Connecticut Valley sites: Vt-Wd-14, Ft. Dummer, and Great Bend (Petersen 1978a).

Archaeological evidence for Woodland manifestations pertaining to the St. Lawrence Iroquois was drawn from Barré and Girouard (1978), Clermont (1978), and Marois (1978); Trigger and Pendergast (1978) explore the history and disappearance of these groups from the St. Lawrence Valley.

From the standpoint of cultural reconstruction, the problems involved in a good understanding of the Woodland period in Vermont are obvious and need not be reiterated here. On the positive side, more usable information has been amassed in the past decade than in all previous years combined. In just the last few months, fourteen new sites have been located during the course of survey work in the Middlebury area, fifteen were found in the vicinity of Wells, and seven in Pownal-Bennington (Thomas and Robinson 1980; Thomas and Bayreuther 1980; Thomas, Bayreuther, Bourassa, Campoli, and Doherty 1980). Of the thirty-six sites, eight have produced Levanna points and related materials, and many others may represent Woodland occupations. The data base is thus rapidly expanding and will permit more detailed interpretations of the cultural complexity that is present during the last of Vermont's prehistoric periods.

Chapter 5
This chapter could not have been written had it not been for the archival, ethnographic, and historic research on western Abenakis carried out by Gordon M. Day over the past two decades. All of his works listed in the bibliography have been drawn on to write the bulk of our own ethnographic account. Although we have generalized, we recognize that there was some variability in western Abenaki culture, depending on where particular bands lived. Since the majority of the people at St. Francis, among whom Day has worked, came from Missisquoi, his data tend to be weighted in favor of western Abenakis in the north, where moose hunting was probably more prominent than among the southernmost western Abenakis. Fortunately, Peter Thomas (1979b) has provided us with excellent supplementary material on the Sokokis, and we have drawn heavily from his work as well as Day's. Thomas's work is especially useful for its detailed listing and evaluation of subsistence resources. On the other hand, Thomas's data on subsistence resources at Fort Hill cannot be taken literally to reconstruct subsistence activities as they were carried out at the start of the seventeenth century. Fort Hill was a community under siege, and this certainly must have altered normal subsistence activities, especially those customarily carried out at some distance from villages. Not only that, but something like twenty years of trade with the British and the demographic devastation wrought by diseases of European origin (see Chapter 6) must have affected traditional subsistence practices as well.

For "fleshing out" our account, we have relied heavily on the works of Frank G. Speck (1918, 1920, 1935, 1940). But a number of other works have been especially useful in providing ideas or information on specific points. A useful source which pulls together the observations of the British chroniclers on the eastern Abenakis is Wasserman (1954). The information on which our introductory paragraph is based comes from Jennings (1976) and Morison (1965:58). The rest of our introductory remarks are based on our earlier discussion of the Abenaki homeland (Chapter 1), as well as the articles by Day, Goddard, and Snow in Trigger, ed. (1978). The Thoreau reference is the Lunt edition (Thoreau 1950:107, 111–112).

Our discussion of aboriginal population sizes and densities relies heavily on Chapter 2 of Jennings (1976), the most reliable treatment of the subject available for New England. Our estimate of western Abenaki population density in Vermont is consistent with a recent estimate of aboriginal population density among the Micmacs (Miller 1976), which in turn is consistent with the 90 percent reduction within 100 years of contact which Jennings argues was the rule in southern New England. On family hunting territories, see Snow (1968) and Hallowell (1949). See also our remarks in Chapter 2 on territories among hunters and gatherers in general. On subsistence differences between the native peoples of northern and southern New England, see Thomas (1976:7–9, 1979b: Chapter 3) and Day (1953; 1975: n 583; 1978:153).

Our material on maple syrup production comes from Butler and Hadlock (1957). On medicinal plants and herbs used by natives, see Vogel (1970). Extensive descriptions of eastern Abenaki canoe making are to be found in Speck (1940) and Thoreau (1950).

Numerous articles have been written on the social organization of Wabanaki peoples; we have found those of Frisch (1977), Hallowell (1928), McGee (1975), and Murdock (1965) especially useful. Our treatment of western Abenaki kinship requires some discussion. The earliest record we have of kinship terms from a western Abenaki community is that contained within the French-Abenaki dictionary compiled by the Jesuit Father Joseph Aubery, who resided at Odanak between 1709 and 1755. His list of terms is quite complete, and the explanations of usage are given in precise detail (Hallowell 1928). We are extremely fortunate to have this information, but we must recognize that there are important problems to be faced in making use of it. The first problem is that the terms recorded are in an eastern dialect, and eastern Abenakis are known to have been present at Odanak, even if they were outnumbered by westerners. Since the kinship systems of the other Wabanaki peoples are known to have been similar to one another, we are probably safe in assuming that eastern and western Abenaki systems were not significantly different from one another. Furthermore, it is reasonable to suppose that easterners moving into a western community would have conformed to existing practices in that community. Thus Aubery's terms, though in eastern dialect, probably are a reasonable guide to western Abenaki kinship in the early eighteenth century.

The second problem is that the terms recorded by Aubery are those which were in use after seventy-five or more years involvement in the European fur trade. This is important, for it is generally accepted that the fur trade brought about significant changes in Native American societies. Those which probably occurred in western Abenaki society are described in Chapter 6 and are of a sort which sooner or later would cause changes in kinship nomenclature (see Haviland 1978:224). Since kinship nomenclature can undergo significant change within a single generation (see Hallowell 1928:117) we must ask: can we be sure that the terms recorded by Father Aubery sometime in the first half of the eighteenth century were in use near the start of the seventeenth?

Father Aubery's dictionary leaves no doubt but what bifurcate collateral terminology was in use early in the eighteenth century for relatives on the first ascending and descending generations. Although the terms for the son and daughter of one's sibling of the same sex are derivatives of the terms for one's own son and daughter, they are not the same, and this kind of nomenclature behaves as bifurcate collateral (Aberle 1961:712, 715). Bifurcate collateral is the most frequent terminology for North America as a whole, and Driver (1969:259) suggests that it is probably the oldest type on the continent. In the Northeast, it is the dominant terminology for aunts and uncles and is characteristic of most Algonquian-speaking peoples (Driver 1969:259, 261). According to Driver (1969:

261), all Algonquian-speaking peoples probably possessed bifurcate collateral terminology. We are probably on safe ground, then, in projecting bifurcate collateral backwards to the western Abenakis of precontact times.

In North America, bifurcate collateral terminology is positively correlated with nonunilineal, or cognatic, organization ("bilateral descent," Driver 1969:259), but it may occur with matrilineal or patrilineal organization. When it does, bifurcate-merging terms often occur as alternatives and ultimately replace bifurcate collateral terms (Driver 1969:259). This is one indication that patrilineal organization probably was not a feature of western Abenaki society in precontact times; this is in accord with the practice of ambilocal residence and a lack of matrilineal or patrilineal extension of incest taboos.

The problem arises when we consider how siblings and cousins were classified. Once again, Aubery's dictionary leaves no room for doubt; Iroquois cousin terms were characteristic of Abenaki kinship at Odanak in the early eighteenth century. In North America, Iroquois cousin terms are positively correlated with unilineal (matrilineal or patrilineal) descent (Frisch 1977:19). By contrast, Hawaiian terminology is strongly correlated with cognatic organization in North America (Driver and Massey 1957:420, and compare Maps 156, 161). What, then, are we to make of this seeming inconsistency in what we presume to be western Abenaki kinship terminology? The answer, we think, is that the Iroquois terminology of the early eighteenth century represents a recent change from an older terminology. Given an existing tendency to favor patrilocal over matrilocal residence, even though the latter was perfectly acceptable, the increased emphasis on the patrilineal transmission of hunting and trapping rights inspired by the fur trade (discussed in Chapter 6) is precisely the sort of development which would favor the emergence of Iroquois cousin terminology (see for example Murdock 1949:231). This is even more likely when we realize that the Sokokis, who were prominent in the founding of Odanak, were in a tributary relationship to the Iroquois through much of the same period when they became involved in the fur trade (see Chapter 6).

Hawaiian cousin terminology is characteristic of about 50 percent of North American aboriginal societies and is more widely distributed than any other type (Driver and Massey 1957:420). Like bifurcate collateral terminology, it is positively correlated with cognatic organization. In the Northeast, it is characteristic of the eastern Wabanaki peoples, as well as the Algonquian-speaking peoples to the north (Frisch 1977:46, 54; see also McGee 1977, who corrects Frisch's attribution of Eskimo terminology for the Micmac).

This suggests that such terminology is quite old in the region. Independently, and on other grounds, Murdock (1949:347) once suggested that Hawaiian terminology may at one time have been characteristic of all Algonquian-speaking peoples. Ambilocal residence, as practiced by the western Abenakis and their neighbors to the north and east (Frisch 1977:38), inevitably produces a local kin group, some members of which are related in the male, and some in the female, line of descent. Although not a descent group, its membership resembles that of genuine am-bilineal descent groups as these are known in other parts of the world, and so would favor Hawaiian cousin terms (see Murdock 1960:14).

All things considered, then, we regard the terminology recorded by Fa-ther Aubery in the early eighteenth century as just what we might expect in the case of a formerly cognatic society with bifurcate collateral–Hawaiian nomenclature which came under strong Iroquoian influence at the same time that the fur trade favored an increased emphasis on pa-trilineality. On the first ascending generation, the use of a term for mother's sister derived from that for mother, and on the first descending generation use of terms for parallel nephew and niece derived from those for son and daughter may represent the bare beginnings of a shift to bifur-cate-merging terms more in keeping with the new Iroquois cousin terms. This is in accord with the observation of Driver and Massey (1957:421) that, in a number of Native American societies, cousin terminology seems to have changed more rapidly than that for aunts and uncles.

If all Algonquian-speaking peoples at one time had bifurcate collat-eral–Hawaiian terminology, as seems indicated by the above, then our hypothesis argued in Chapter 3 that the Vergennes folk spoke a dialect of Proto-Algonquian takes on added significance. It would mean that the Vergennnes folk, too, possessed such terminology, with its sociological correlates. This, in turn, helps support our argument, stated near the end of this chapter, that the roots of western Abenaki culture lie in the Ver-gennes Archaic.

In addition to our discussion of the adaptive advantages of cognatic so-cial organization in this chapter, see our earlier discussion in Chapter 2. On Abenaki chiefs, one should see the papers by Alvin Morrison (1976) and Nicolas N. Smith (1977). On the conduct and motives for warfare in northeastern North America, see Jennings (1976: Chapter 9). The rela-tionship between resource depletion and Iroquoian warfare is noted by Salwen (1975:58 and 63). On warfare among slash and burn agricultural-ists generally, see Vayda (1961).

In our discussion of the individual life cycle, the reference to the rat-tlesnake belief is Klauber (1956:1166–1167) (our thanks to Gordon Niel-sen for calling this to our attention). Klauber notes two other Abenaki practices involving rattlesnakes: use of the powdered flesh to cure fevers, and use of smoke-dried rattlesnake gore to cure toothache. The tale of the swamp creature is retold in the film, *Prehistoric Life in the Cham-plain Valley* (Vogelmann et al. 1972), the text having been supplied by Gordon M. Day. The Krogman and Hrdlička observations on Native American life expectancy and old age will be found in Vogel (1970:142).

For background on the concept of world view, the reader should con-sult the classic papers on the self and behavioral environment by A. Ir-ving Hallowell (in Hallowell 1955). In our discussion, we have drawn on material from Hallowell's (1946; 1955: Chapter 6) paper on the psycho-logical characteristics of northeastern native peoples, as well as Chapter 4 of Jennings (1976; the quote is from p. 51). Jennings's comparison of the religious beliefs and practices of Native Americans with those of Euro-peans in the seventeenth century ought to be required reading. The tie between shamanism and petroglyphs is discussed by Snow (1976d,

1977c). The Bellows Falls and Brattleboro petroglyphs are described by Hall (1958:582–592). On the contrast between the world views of hunter-gatherers and food producers, see Haviland (1978:300).

Quoted material in our discussion of world view is from the following sources: Passamaquoddy drumming, Speck (1920:241); corn legend, Thompson (1966:51–52); *Odzihózo*, Day (1971:11); great serpent legend, script provided by Gordon M. Day for Vogelmann et al. (1972); story of the Tree Squeak, script provided by Gordon M. Day for Vogelmann et al. (1972).

Chapter 6

Much of our introductory material for this chapter is drawn from Day (1973), Morison (1965), and Van DeWater (1974). The source for our information on Fort Hill is Thomas (1979b); on the open lands available to the first English settlers, Jennings (1976, especially pp. 15, 33, 34, 40, 66, 80, 172, 173, 178) and Salwen (1975:62–63). On "Indian" maintenance of open woodlands, see Day (1953 and 1975: n. 583).

The best discussion of the role of European diseases in reducing New England's aboriginal populations is in Jennings (1976, especially, but not limited to, Chapter 2). We have supplemented this with material from A. G. Bailey (1937:Chapter 7, see also p. 19), Cook (1973), Day (1973), Thomas (1979b), Vaughan (1965), and Vogel (1970). Thomas's study is particularly valuable for its focus on the native peoples of the middle Connecticut Valley, including the Sokokis, and for its unearthing of a statement by Roger Williams which suggests that there may have been as many as four epidemics prior to that of 1616. On the earliest contacts between natives and Europeans in the Northeast, see Morison (1971).

There is a voluminous literature on the fur trade in North America; we have relied heavily on Thomas's (1979b) masterful study of the Connecticut Valley fur trade. This supplies us not only with the details of the trade, but also the motivations for it and some of the changes it wrought in native societies. Supplementary material, however, has been drawn from A. G. Bailey (1937), Brasser (1978a), Day (1973, 1975, 1978), Gramley (1977), Hall (1977), Morrison (1976), Snow (1968), Thomas (1973), and our own analysis of Abenaki kinship at Odanak (see notes to Chapter 5). For broader regional perspective, we have relied on Jennings (1976: Chapter 6), supplemented by information from Vaughan (1965) and Morison (1965).

Our idea of the "British Menace" was developed by putting together existing information on the psychological characteristics of northeastern Algonquians (Hallowell 1946), British-Abenaki relations before 1620 (Vaughan 1965: Chapter 1; the Jesuit quote is from p. 14), the behavior of the Puritans in New England up to the second war of conquest (Jennings 1976: Part II; the quoted material is from pp. 212–213), the effectiveness of information exchange among New England's natives before their conquest (Thomas 1979b), and the significance of weapons exchange among North American native peoples (Hall 1977). Attitudes towards the French can be gleaned from A. G. Bailey (1937), Day (1973, 1975), Morison (1965), Morrison (1977b), and Thomas (1979b). Our population figures for comparing the growth of French and English settlements are drawn from Morison (1965) and Vaughan (1965). On the expansion of British settlement in the Connecticut Valley, see Thomas (1976 and 1979b) and Van DeWater (1974).

The best source on the warfare between the Iroquois and Sokoki is Thomas (1979b); supplementary information on the other western Abenakis will be found in the various works of Gordon M. Day. For the later Abenaki-British wars, and the native peoples' withdrawal from Vermont, we have relied primarily on Day (1962a; 1962b; 1965b; 1971; 1973a; 1973b; 1975; 1978) and Moody (1979). On early French settlement of Vermont, see Coolidge (1938), and on early British settlement, see Van DeWater (1974: Chapters 1–3).

For events following 1763, we have relied almost exclusively on Moody (1979). In a brilliant piece of scholarly detective work, Moody has come up with ironclad evidence that Vermont's native peoples did not just conveniently disappear when settlers from New York, New England, and Canada wanted their land. For anyone—historian, anthropologist, or whatever—Moody's work is indispensable for an understanding of what was happening in Vermont in the latter part of the eighteenth century.

The Abenaki appeal of 1766 we have quoted from the *Papers of Sir William Johnson* (Vol. 12, p. 173), who became Canada's Superintendent of Indian Affairs following the fall of New France (our thanks to John Moody for providing this). Waggoner's comment of 1788 regarding Colonel Allen's "trick" is quoted here from Moody (1979:13–14, 30); the document of which it is a part is in the special collections at the University of Vermont's Bailey Library, where Moody found it. Francis Hsu's comment is quoted from Hsu (1977:807).

Chapter 7

Much of the information in this chapter was provided by Miles Jensen, Director of ASHAI, and Jean Sbardellati, ASHAI Job Developer (personal communication to Power); the chronological list of Abenaki events was also provided by her. Our summary of post-1800 Abenaki history is drawn from Moody (1979:62–80). For more detailed information on the report to Governor Thomas P. Salmon, see Baker (1976). Census figures were drawn from Baker (1976:I:C–1) and Pierce (1977:51–52); income and unemployment statistics are from Baker (1976:IA–5; IB:1) and Jensen (personal communication to Power). Quotes regarding Abenaki tribal reorganization are from Baker (1976:IB–1–4). Discussion of Bureau of Indian Affairs procedures is from the *Federal Register* (Vol. 43, No. 172, Tuesday, September 5, 1978:39561–39563). Chief Homer St. Francis's comments on the crafts program were made during a visit to a "Vermont Indians" class at the University of Vermont in November, 1978. For all references to Odanak (except recognition of the Abenaki), see Day (1978). The end quote is from the third edition, in preparation, of Haviland (1978).

BIBLIOGRAPHY

Aberle, D. F.
   1961   Matrilineal Descent in Cross Cultural Perspective. In D. M. Schneider and K. Gough, eds., *Matrilineal Kinship*, pp. 655–727. Berkeley: University of California Press.

Adams, W. Y., D. P. Van Gerven, and R. S. Levy
   1978   The Retreat from Migrationism. In J. Siegel, A. R. Beals, and S. A. Tyler, eds., *Annual Review of Anthropology, Vol. 7*, pp. 483–532. Palo Alto: Annual Reviews Inc.

Adovasio, J. M., J. D. Gunn, J. Donahue, and R. Stuckenrath
   1978   Meadowcroft Rockshelter, 1977: An Overview. *American Antiquity* 43(4):632–651.

Anderson, J. K.
   1975   Fisheries. In *Winooski River Basin Water Quality Management Plan*, pp. 5-1, 5-2. Agency of Environmental Conservation. Manuscript on file, Special Collections, Bailey Library, University of Vermont, Burlington.

Anonymous
   1970   Vt-Ch-3, Progress Report. *VAS Newsletter* 3:1–2.

Bacon, Edgar
   1975   Vt-Ch-5, The Ewing Site, Shelburne, Vermont. *VAS Newsletter* 2(1):4–5.
   1976   The Warrel Farm Site, Vt-Ca-13. *VAS Newsletter* 3(2):3.

Bailey, A. G.
   1937   The Conflict of European and Eastern Algonquian Cultures 1504–1700. *Publications of the New Brunswick Museum, Monograph Series* No. 2.

Bailey, J. H.
   1939a   Archaeology in Vermont 1938. In J. C. Huden, ed., *Archaeology in Vermont*, pp. 3–6.

   ———.
   1939b   A Ground Slate Producing Site Near Vergennes, Vermont. *Bulletin of the Champlain Valley Archaeological Society*, 1(2):1–29.

   ———.
   1940   A Stratified Rock Shelter in Vermont. *Proceedings of the Vermont Historical Society* 8(1):3–30.

Baker, J. S.
   1976   *Report to Governor Thomas P. Salmon of the State of Vermont Regarding the Claims Presented by the Abenaki Nation.* Montpelier, Vt.: Office of the Governor.

Barber, Russell
    1972   Analysis of Manufacture and Use Reconstruction for Lithic Artifacts. Typescript on file, Department of Anthropology, University of Vermont, Burlington.

Barré, Georges et Laurent Girouard
    1978   Les Iroquoiens: premiers agriculteurs. In Claude Chapdelaine, ed., *Images de la Préhistoire du Quebéc*, pp. 43–54. Recherches Amérindiennes au Québec. Montreal.

Basa, Louise
    1971   Vt-Ch-3; Progress Report, Summer 1971. *VAS Newsletter* 5:4–5.
    ———.
    1974   Report on the Boucher Site (Vt-Fr-26), Highgate, Vermont. *VAS Newsletter* Special Number: 5–6.
    ———.
    1975   The Boucher Site: A Progress Report. *VAS Newsletter* 1:6.

Bassett, T. D. S. (ed.)
    1976   *Outsiders inside Vermont: Three Centuries of Visitors' Viewpoints on the Green Mountain State.* 2nd ed. Canaan, N.H.: Phoenix Publishing.

Bolian, Charles E.
    n.d.   An Archaeological Survey of the Lakes Region of New Hampshire. Mimeograph, Department of Anthropology, University of New Hampshire, Durham.

Bolton, R. P.
    1930   Indian Remains in Northern Vermont. *Indian Notes*, Vol. 7, (1):57–69. Museum of the American Indian, Heye Foundation. New York.

Borns, H. W., Jr.
    1973   Possible Paleoindian Migration Routes in the Northeast. *Bulletin of the Massachusetts Archaeological Society* 34 (1–2): 13–15.

Bostock, A. K.
    1955   Searching for Indian Relics in Vermont. *Vermont History* 23(3):233–240 and (4)327–332.

Bourque, Bruce
    1975   Comments on the Late Archaic Populations of Greater Maine: The View from the Turner Farm. *Arctic Anthropology* 12(2): 35–45.

Bradstreet, T. E. and R. B. Davis
    1975   Mid-Postglacial Environments in New England with Emphasis on Maine. *Arctic Anthropology* 12(2):7–22.

Brasser, T. J.
    1978a   Early Indian-European Contacts. In Bruce G. Trigger, ed., *Handbook of North American Indians*, Vol. 15, Northeast, pp. 78–88.
    ———.
    1978b   Mahican. In Bruce G. Trigger, ed., *Handbook of North American Indians*, Vol. 15, Northeast, pp. 198–212.

Broehl, Wayne G.
1959   *Precision Valley*. Englewood Cliffs, N.J.: Prentice-Hall.
Brooks, Edward
1971   A Laurentian Site in Addison County, Vermont. In J. C. Huden (ed.) *Archaeology in Vermont*, pp. 24–32.
Brumbach, Hetty Jo
1975   "Iroquoian" Ceramics in "Algonkian" Territory. *Man in the Northeast* 10:17–28.

————.
1977   Report of Excavations at the Archaeological Site in the Village of Schuylerville, New York. Manuscript on file, Department of Anthropology, SUNY, Albany, N.Y.
Bryan, A.L.
1969   Early Man in America and the Late Pleistocene Chronology of Western Canada and Alaska. *Current Anthropology* 10(4): 339–365.
Butler, E. L. and W. S. Hadlock
1957   Use of Birch-Bark in the Northeast. *The Robert Abbe Museum, Bar Harbor, Maine Bulletin 7*.
Byers, D. S.
1954   Bull Brook—A Fluted Point Site in Ipswich, Massachusetts. *American Antiquity* 19:343–351.

————.
1955   Additional Information on the Bull Brook Site, Massachusetts. *American Antiquity* 20:274–276.

————.
1959   Radiocarbon Dates for the Bull Brook Site, Massachusetts. *American Antiquity* 24:427–429.

————.
1961   Second Comment on William A. Ritchie's "Iroquois Archaeology and Settlement Patterns." In W. N. Fenton and John Gulick, eds., *Symposium on Cherokee and Iroquois Culture*, pp. 47–50.
Carr, P. G., I. A. Worley, and M. W. Davis
1977   Post-Lake Vermont History of a Pond and Wetland in the Champlain Basin. In *Proceedings of the 4th Annual Lake Champlain Basin Environmental Conference*, pp. 71–112. Institute for Man and Environment, SUNY, Plattsburgh, N.Y.
Catania, V. A.
1978   Flotation and Analysis of Ewing (Vt-Ch-5) and Winooski (Vt-Ch-46) Soils. Typescript on file, Department of Anthropology, University of Vermont, Burlington.
Chapman, D. H.
1937   Late Glacial and Postglacial History of the Champlain Valley. *American Journal of Science* 34:89–124.
Charland, T. M.
1961   Un Village d'Abenaquis sur la Rivière Missisquoi. *Revue d'Histoire de l'Amérique Français* 15(3):319–332.

———.
1964   *Les Abenakis d'Odanak: histoire des Abenakis d'Odonak, 1675–1937.* Montreal: Les Editions du Levrier.

Chomko, S. A. and G. W. Crawford
1978   Plant Husbandry in Prehistoric Eastern North America: New Evidence for Its Development. *American Antiquity* 43:405–408.

Christian, J. J.
1970   Social Subordination, Population Density and Mammalian Evolution. *Science* 168:84–90.

Claiborne, Robert and the editors of Time-Life Books
1973   *The First Americans.* New York: Time-Life.

Clark, R. M.
1975   A Calibration Curve for Radiocarbon Dates. *Antiquity* 49:251–266.

Clermont, Norman
1978   Le Sylvicole Initial, in C. Chapdelaine, ed., *Images de la Préhistoire du Québec,* pp. 31–42. Recherches Amérindiennes au Québec. Montreal.

Colson, Elizabeth
1976   Culture and Progress. *American Anthropologist* 78:261–271.

Coolidge, G. O.
1938   The French Occupation of the Champlain Valley from 1609 to 1759. *Vermont History* 6(3):143–311.

Cook, Sherburne
1973   The Significance of Disease in the Extinction of the New England Indian. *Human Biology* 45(3):485–508.

Cowan, F. L.
1977   History and Present Status of the Ewing Site Investigations. *VAS Newsletter* 5(3):3–7.

———.
1979   Winooski Site Summer Work Turns to the Lab and Reflection. *VAS Newsletter* 26:3–6.

Crockett, W. H.
1921   *Vermont—The Green Mountain State.* New York: The Century History Co.

Cunningham, W. M.
1948   A Study of the Glacial Kame Culture in Michigan, Ohio, and Indiana. *Occasional Contributions from the Museum of Anthropology of the University of Michigan No. 12,* Ann Arbor.

Curran, M. L.
1977   Early Man in the Connecticut River Drainage: An Archaeological Testcase in Southern New Hampshire. Manuscript, Department of Anthropology, University of Massachusetts, Amherst, Mass.

Curran, M. L. and D. F. Dincauze
1977   Paleoindians and Paleo-lakes: New Data from the Connecticut Drainage. *Annals of the New York Academy of Sciences* 288:333–348.

Daniels, T. E.
1963   *Vermont Indians.* Poultney, Vt.: Journal Press.
Day, G. M.
1953   The Indian as an Ecological Factor in the Northeastern Forest. *Ecology* 34(2): 329–346.

_____.
1962a   English-Indian Contacts in New England. *Ethnohistory* 9(1): 24–40.

_____.
1962b   Rogers' Raid in Indian Tradition. *Historical New Hampshire* 17:3–17.

_____.
1965a   The Identity of the Sokokis. *Ethnohistory* 12:237–249.

_____.
1965b   The Indian Occupation of Vermont. *Vermont History* 33:365–374.

_____.
1971   The Eastern Boundary of Iroquoia: Abenaki Evidence? *Man in the Northeast* 1:7–13.

_____.
1973a   Greylock and the Missisquoi Settlement. Paper Presented at the Spring 1973 meeting of the Vermont Archaeological Society, Burlington, Vt.

_____.
1973b   Missisquoi: A New Look at an Old Village. *Man in the Northeast* 6:51–57.

_____.
1975   The Mots Loups of Father Mathevet. *National Museum of Man, Ottawa, Publications in Ethnology* No. 8.

_____.
1976   The Western Abenaki Transformer. *Journal of the Folklore Institute* Vol. 13(1):75–89.

_____.
1977a   Indian Place Names as Ethnohistoric Data. In William Cowan, ed., *Actes du Huitième Congrès des Algonquianistes*, pp. 26–31. Carleton University, Ottawa.

_____.
1977b   The Western Abenaki of Quebec and Vermont. Paper presented at the Spring 1977 meeting of the Vermont Archaeological Society, Waterbury, Vt.

_____.
1978   Western Abenaki. In Bruce G. Trigger, ed., *Handbook of North American Indians, Vol. 15, Northeast*, pp. 148–159.

_____.
1979   Arosagunticook and Androscoggin. In William Cowan, ed., *Papers of the Tenth Algonquian Conference*, pp. 10–15, Carleton University, Ottawa.
Diamond, Stanley (ed.)
1960   *Culture in History, Essays in Honor of Paul Radin.* New York: Columbia University Press.

Dincauze, D. F.
1971 An Archaic Sequence for Southern New England. *American Antiquity* 36:194–198.

——.
1972 The Atlantic Phase: A Late Archaic Culture in Massachusetts. *Man in the Northeast* 4:40–61.

——.
1975 The Late Archaic Period in Southern New England. *Arctic Anthropology* 12(2):23–34.

——.
1976 The Neville Site: 8000 Years at Amoskeag, Manchester, New Hampshire. *Peabody Museum Monographs*, No. 4.

Dincauze, D. F. and M. T. Mulholland.
1977 Early and Middle Archaic Site Distributions and Habitats in Southern New England. *Annals of the New York Academy of Sciences* 288:439–456.

Dobyns, H. F.
1966 Estimating Aboriginal American Population: An Appraisal of Techniques with a New Hemispheric Estimate. *Current Anthropology* 7(4):359–416.

Dragoo, D. W.
1976a Adena and the Eastern Burial Cult. *Archaeology of Eastern North America* 4:1–9.

——.
1976b Some Aspects of Eastern North American Prehistory: A Review 1975. *American Antiquity* 41(1):3–27.

Driver, Harold E.
1969 *Indians of North America*, 2nd ed. Chicago: University of Chicago Press.

Driver, H. E. and W. C. Massey
1957 Comparative Studies of North American Indians. *Transactions of the American Philosophical Society* 47:165–465.

Fagan, L. A.
1978 A Vegetational and Cultural Sequence for Southern New England 15,000 BP to 7000 BP. *Man in the Northeast* 15–16:70–92.

Fenton, W. N. and John Gulick (eds.)
1961 Symposium on Cherokee and Iroquois Culture. *Smithsonian Institution, Bureau of American Ethnology, Bulletin* 180, Washington, D.C.

Fitting, J. E.
1970 *The Archaeology of Michigan*. Garden City, N.Y.: Natural History Press.

——.
1977 Social Dimensions of the Paleoindian Adaptation in the Northeast. *Annals of the New York Academy of Sciences* 288:369–374.

——.
1978 Regional Cultural Development, 300 B.C. to A.D. 1000. In B. G. Trigger, ed., *Handbook of North American Indians*, Vol. 15, *The Northeast*, pp. 44–57.

Fitzhugh, William
  1975   A Comparative Approach to Northern Maritime Adaptations.
         In William Fitzhugh, ed., *Prehistoric Maritime Adaptations of
         the Circumpolar Zone*, pp. 339–386.
Fitzhugh, William, (ed.)
  1975   *Prehistoric Maritime Adaptations of the Circumpolar Zone.*
         The Hague: Mouton.
Fladmark, K. R.
  1979   Routes: Alternate Migration Corridors for Early Man in North
         America. *American Antiquity* 44 : 55–69.
Frisch, Jack A.
  1977   Cognatic Kinship Organization Among the Northeast Algon-
         kians. *Saint Mary's University, Department of Anthropology
         Occasional Papers in Anthropology* No. 2.
Funk, R. E.
  1972   Early Man in the Northeast and the Late Glacial Environment.
         Man in the Northeast 4 : 7–39.
  _____.
  1976   Recent Contributions to Hudson Valley Prehistory. *New York
         State Museum, Memoir 22*, Albany.
  _____.
  1977   Early to Middle Archaic Occupations in Upstate New York. In
         R. E. Funk and C. F. Hayes, eds., *Current Perspectives in
         Northeastern Archaeology—Essays in Honor of William A.
         Ritchie*, pp. 21–29.
  _____.
  1978   Post-Pleistocene Adaptations. In B. G. Trigger, ed., *Handbook
         of North American Indians, Vol. 15, Northeast*, pp. 16–27.
Funk, R. E. and C. F. Hayes, III (eds.)
  1977   *Current Perspectives in Northeastern Archaeology—Essays in
         Honor of William A. Ritchie.* Researches and transactions of
         the New York State Archaeological Association 17(1). Albany.
Funk, R. E., Paul Weinman, and Thomas Weinman
  1966   The Burnt Hill Phase: Regional Middle Woodland at Lake
         George. *Bulletin of the New York State Archaeological Asso-
         ciation*, 37 : 1–20.
Giddings, J. L.
  1954   Early Man in the Arctic. In R. S. MacNeish, ed., *Early Man in
         America*. San Francisco: W. H. Freeman.
Gifford, S. M.
  1948   A Brief Summary of Three Years' Digging on the Orwell Site.
         The Bulletin of the Fort Ticonderoga Museum 8(1):26–28.
         Fort Ticonderoga, N.Y.
Goddard, Ives
  1978a Central Algonquian Languages. In B. G. Trigger, ed., *Hand-
         book of North American Indians, Vol. 15, Northeast*, pp.
         583–587.
  _____.
  1978b Eastern Algonquian Languages. In B. G. Trigger, ed., *Hand-
         book of North American Indians, Vol. 15, Northeast*, pp.
         70–77.

Gramly, R. M.
1977   Deerskins and Hunting Territories: Competition for a Scarce Resource of the Northeastern Woodlands. *American Antiquity* 42:601–605.

Gramly, R. M. and S. L. Cox
1976   A Prehistoric Quarry—Workshop at Mt. Jasper, Berlin, New Hampshire. *Man in the Northeast* 11:71–74.

Grayson, D. K.
1970   Statistical Inference and Northeastern Adena. *American Antiquity* 35(1):102–104.

Griffin, J. B.
1978   Late Prehistory of the Ohio Valley. In B. G. Trigger, ed., *Handbook of North American Indians, Vol. 15, Northeast,* pp. 547–559.

Grossinger, Richard
1975   Interview with Louise Basa in Burlington, Vermont, in *Vermont Io #21:211–18.* Berkeley: Book People.

Haas, M. R.
1960   Some Genetic Affiliations of Algonkian. In Stanley Diamond, ed., *Culture in History, Essays in Honor of Paul Radin,* pp. 977–992.

Hadlock, W. S.
1945   War Among the Northeast Woodland Indians. Master's thesis, University of Pennsylvania, Philadelphia.

Hall, B. H.
1858   *History of Eastern Vermont.* New York: Appleton and Co.

Hall, R. L.
1977   An Anthropocentric Perspective for Eastern United States Prehistory. *American Antiquity* 42:499–518.

Hallowell, A. I.
1928   Recent Historical Changes in the Kinship Terminology of the St. Francis Abenaki. *Proceedings of the Twenty-Second International Congress of Americanists* (New York), pp. 519–544.

———.
1946   Some Psychological Characteristics of the Northeastern Indians. In Frederick Johnson, ed., *Man in Northeastern North America,* Papers of the R. S. Peabody Foundation for Archaeology 3:195–225.

———.
1949   The Size of Algonkian Hunting Territories, A Function of Ecological Adjustment. *American Anthropologist* 51:35–45.

———.
1955   *Culture and Experience.* Philadelphia: University of Pennsylvania Press.

Hancock, William, Paula Lane, Lindsay Huntington, and J. E. Kelley
1978   *The Vermont Atlas and Gazeteer.* Yarmouth, Maine: David De Lorme and Co.

Harrington, C. R.
1977   Marine Mammals in the Champlain Sea and the Great Lakes. *Annals of the New York Academy of Sciences* 288:508–537.

Hartshorn, J. H.
1969   Geography and Geology of Glacial Lake Hitchcock. In W. R. Young, ed., *An Introduction to the Archaeology and History of the Connecticut Valley Indian*, pp. 19–27.

Haviland, W. A.
1969a   Excavations at Pine Island, *VAS Newsletter* 2:3–4.

_____.
1969b   Men Hunted in Vermont in 7000 B.C. *Vermont Life* 24(2):53–55.

_____.
1970   Archaeological Sites of the Champlain Valley. *Lake Champlain Basin Studies No. 8.* University of Vermont, Department of Resource Economics.

_____.
1973   Mounds in Vermont: Prehistoric or Historic? *VAS Monograph #2.*

_____.
1975   *Vermont Indians and Prehistory for Schools: A Selected Annotated List of Sources for Teachers.* Montpelier: Vermont Historical Society.

_____.
1978   *Cultural Anthropology,* 2nd ed. New York: Holt, Rinehart and Winston.

_____.
1979   *Human Evolution and Prehistory.* New York: Holt, Rinehart and Winston.

Hoijer, Harry (ed.)
1946   Linguistic Structures of Native America. *Viking Fund Publications in Anthropology, No. 6.* New York: Wenner Gren Foundation for Anthropological Research.

Hole, Frank and Robert Heizer
1977   *Archaeology, A Brief Introduction.* New York: Holt, Rinehart and Winston.

Hsu, F. L. K.
1977   Role, Affect and Anthropology. *American Anthropologist* 79:805–808.

Huden, J. C.
1955a   Indian Place-Names in Vermont. *Vermont History* 23(3):191–203.

_____.
1955b   Indians in Vermont—Present and Past. *Vermont History* 23(1):25–28.

_____.
1956a   The Abenaki, the Iroquois, and Vermont. *Vermont History* 24(1):21–25.

_____.
1956b   The Problem: Indians and Whitemen in Vermont, When and Where (1550–)? *Vermont History* 24(2):110–120.

_____.
1957a   Adventures in Abenakiland. *Vermont History* 25(3):185–193.

———.
1957b   Indian Troubles in Early Vermont. *Vermont History* 25(3):
288–291, 26(1):38–41, (3):206–207.

———.
1957c   Iroquois Place-Names in Vermont. *Vermont History* 25(1):
66–80.

———.
1958   Indian Groups in Vermont. *Vermont History* 26(2):112–115.

———.
1971   *Archaeology in Vermont* (revised edition). Rutland, Vt.:
Charles Tuttle Co.

Hymes, Dell (ed.)
1964   *Language in Culture and Society.* New York: Harper and Row.

Innis, H. A.
1930   *The Fur Trade in Canada.* New Haven: Yale University Press.

Jennings, Francis
1976   *The Invasion of America.* New York: W. W. Norton.

Johnson, Frederick (ed.)
1946   *Man in Northeastern North America.* Papers of the R. S. Peabody Foundation for Archaeology 3, Andover, Mass.

Johnson, Sir William
1921–
1965   *The Papers of Sir William Johnson.* James Sullivan *et al.*, eds.
15 vols. Albany: University of the State of New York.

Klauber, L. M.
1956   *Rattlesnakes: Their Habits, Life Histories, and Influence on
Mankind.* Berkeley: University of California Press.

Klein, J. L.
1977   Current Research: Northeast. *American Antiquity* 42(4):643–
647.

Laurent, Stephen
1955, 6 The Abenakis: Aborigines of Vermont. *Vermont History*
23:286–295, 24:3–11.

Loring, Stephen
1972   An Appraisal of Vermont Archaeology. Manuscript on file, Office of the State Archaeologist, Division for Historic Preservation, Montpelier, Vt.

———.
1973   *A Bibliography of Vermont Archaeology.* Burlington, Vt.: Vermont Archaeological Society.

———.
1980   Paleoindian Hunters and the Champlain Sea: A Presumed Association. *Man in the Northeast* 19:15–41.

Lounsbury, F. G.
1978   Iroquoian Languages. In B. G. Trigger, ed., *Handbook of North
American Indians, Vol. 15, Northeast,* pp. 334–343.

MacDonald, G. F.
1968   Debert: A Paleo-Indian site in central Nova Scotia. *National
Museum of Canada Anthropology Papers No. 16.*

Marois, R. J. M.
1978   Le Gisement Beaumier: essai sur l'evolution des décors de la céramique. *Collection Mercure.* Dossier No. 75, Commission Archéologique du Canada, Musée National de l'Homme. Ottawa.

Martin, C. S.
1974   The European Impact on the Culture of a Northeastern Algonquian Tribe: An Ecological Interpretation. *William and Mary Quarterly,* 3rd series, 31:3–26.

Mason, R. J.
1962   The Paleo-Indian Tradition in Eastern North America. *Current Anthropology* 3:227–278.

Masta, H. L.
1932   *Abenaki Indian Legends, Grammar and Place Names.* Victoriaville, Quebec: La Voix des Bois-Francs.

Maurault, J. A.
1866   *Histoire des Abenakis depuis 1605 Jusqu'à nos Jours.* Quebec: Imprimé à l'atelier typographique de la "Gazette de Sorel."

McGee, H. F., Jr.
1975   A Note on Wabanaki Kinship. *Man in the Northeast* 10:78–80.

_____.
1977   *The Case for Micmac Demes.* In William Cowan, ed., *Actes du Huitième Congrès des Algonquianistes,* pp. 107–114.

Meeks, H. A.
1975   The Geographic Regions of Vermont, A Study in Maps. *Geography Publications at Dartmouth,* No. 10, Hanover, N.H.

Miller, V. P.
1976   Aboriginal Micmac Population: A Review of the Evidence. *Ethnohistory* 23(2):117–127.

Moody, John
1979   Missisquoi: Abenaki Survival in their Ancient Homeland. Manuscript on file with the author, Sharon, Vt.

Moorehead, W. K.
1922   *A Report on the Archaeology of Maine.* Andover, Mass.: Andover Press.

Morison, S. E.
1965   *The Oxford History of the American People.* New York: Oxford University Press.

_____.
1971   *The European Discovery of America: The Northern Voyages A.D. 500–1600.* New York: Oxford University Press.

Morrison, A. H.
1976   Dawnland Directors: Status and Role of 17th Century Wabanaki Sagamores. In William Cowan, ed., *Papers of the Seventh Algonquian Conference,* pp. 495–514.

_____.
1977a   Tricentennial, Too: King Philip's War Northern Front (Maine, 1675–1678). In William Cowan, ed., *Actes du Huitième Congrès des Algonquianistes,* pp. 208–212.

1977b   Western Wabanaki Studies: Some Comments. In William
         Cowan, ed., *Actes du Huitième Congrès des Algonquianistes*,
         pp. 230–243.
Murdock, G. P.
1949   *Social Structure.* New York: Macmillan.

———.
1960   Cognatic Forms of Social Organization In G. P. Murdock, ed.,
         Social Structure in Southeast Asia. Chicago: Quadrangle
         Books.

———.
1965   Algonkian Social Organization. In M. E. Spiro, ed., *Context
         and Meaning in Cultural Anthropology*, pp. 24–35. New York:
         The Free Press.
Newman, W. S. and Bert Salwen (eds.)
1977   Amerinds and their Paleoenvironments in Northeastern North
         America. *Annals of the New York Academy of Sciences*, Vol.
         288. New York: The New York Academy of Sciences.
Perkins, G. H.
1873   On an Ancient Burial Ground in Swanton, Vermont. *Proceed-
         ings of the American Association for the Advancement of Sci-
         ence*, 22:76–100.

Perry, J. B.
1868   On the Swanton Site. *Proceedings of the Boston Society of
         Natural History*, 23(3):247–254.
Petersen, J. B.
1977   A Study of the Prehistoric Ceramics of Vt-Ch-5, the Ewing
         Site. Typescript on file, Department of Anthropology, Univer-
         sity of Vermont, Burlington.

———.
1978a   Aboriginal Ceramics in the Connecticut River Valley. Type-
         script on file, Department of Anthropology, University of Ver-
         mont, Burlington.

———.
1978b   A History of Archaeological Research in Vermont. Unpub-
         lished manuscript, Division for Historic Preservation, Mont-
         pelier.

———.
1978c   Prehistoric Ceramics from the Ewing Site. *VAS Newsletter*
         May: 6.

———.
1979   Prehistoric Pottery in Vermont. *VAS Newsletter* 27:1–4.

———.
1980   *The Middle Woodland Ceramics of the Winooski Site A.D.
         1–1000.* Vermont Archaeological Society New Series, Mono-
         graph No. 1.
Pierce, Ken
1977   *A History of the Abenaki People.* Burlington, Vt.: University
         of Vermont Instructional Development Center.

Porter, F. J.
  1970   Wildlife. *Lake Champlain Basin Studies* #7-A. Burlington, Vt.: Department of Resource Economics, University of Vermont.
Power, M. W.
  1975   *Archaeology in Vermont: A Summary of Information and Resources for Teachers.* Montpelier, Vt.: Vermont Historical Society.

——.
  1978   *Archaeological Mitigation at the Winooski Site, Northwestern Vermont.* Proposal submitted to the U.S. Department of the Interior, Interagency Archaeological Services–Atlanta, Heritage Conservation and Recreation Service. On file, Department of Anthropology, University of Vermont, Burlington.

——.
  1979a Middle Woodland Subsistence and Settlement: A Preliminary Model. *VAS Newsletter,* 28:1, 10–11.

——.
  1979b *The Winooski Site: A Test Case for a Middle Woodland Settlement Subsistence Model.* Paper presented at the annual meeting of the Society for American Archaeology, Vancouver.
Power, M. W., F. L. Cowan, and J. B. Petersen
  1980   Artifact Variability at the Multi-component Winooski Site. *Man in the Northeast* 19:43–55.
Renouf, Priscilla
  1977   A late Paleo-Indian and Early Archaic Sequence in Southern Labrador. *Man in the Northeast* 13:35–44.
Rippeteau, Bruce
  1973   Late Archaic, Transitional and Early Woodland Tree Ring Corrected Dates in Northern United States. *Man in the Northeast* 6:61–67.
Ritchie, W. A.
  1944   The Pre-Iroquoian Occupations of New York State. *Rochester Museum of Arts and Sciences, Memoir No. 1.* Rochester, N.Y.

——.
  1953   A Probable Paleoindian Site in Vermont. *American Antiquity* 18(3):249–258.

——.
  1955   Recent discoveries suggesting an Early Woodland burial cult in the northeast. *New York State Museum and Science Service,* Circular 40, Albany.

——.
  1957   Traces of Early Man in the Northeast. *New York State Museum and Science Service Bulletin 358,* Albany.

——.
  1968   The KI Site, the Vergennes Phase and the Laurentian Tradition. *New York State Archaeological Association Bulletin* 42:1–5.

——.
  1969   *The Archaeology of New York State.* Rev. ed. Garden City, N.Y.: Natural History Press.

———.
1971   The Archaic in New York. *New York State Archaeological Association Bulletin* 52:2–12.

———.
1979   The Otter Creek No. 2 Site in Rutland County, Vermont. *The Bulletin and Journal of the Archaeology of New York State* 76:1–21.

Ritchie, W. A. and D. W. Dragoo
1960   The Eastern Dispersal of Adena. *New York State Museum and Science Service, Bulletin* 379. Albany.

Ritchie, W. A. and R. E. Funk
1973   Aboriginal Settlement Patterns in the Northeast. Memoir 20, *New York State Museum and Science Service*, Albany.

Robbins, Maurice
1968   *An Archaic Ceremonial Complex at Assawompsett.* Attleboro, Mass.: Massachusetts Archaeological Society.

Ross, I. B.
1935   Remains of an Ancient People Found in Vermont. *The Vermonter* 40(12). White River Junction, Vermont.

Russell, H. S.
1980   *Indian New England Before the Mayflower.* Hanover, N.H.: University Press of New England.

Salwen, Bert
1975   Post-Glacial Environments and Cultural Change in the Hudson River Basin. *Man in the Northeast* 10:43–70.

Sanders, D. C.
1812   *A History of the Indian Wars with the First Settlers of the United States, Particularly in New England.* Montpelier, Vt.: Wright & Sibley.

Sanger, David
1975   Culture Change as an Adaptive Process in the Maine-Maritimes Region. *Arctic Anthropology* 12(2):60–75.

———.
1979   The Ceramic Period in Maine. In D. Sanger, ed., *Discovering Maine's Archaeological Heritage*, pp. 99–115. Augusta: Maine Historic Preservation Commission.

Sanger, David, R. B. Davis, R. G. MacKay, and H. W. Borns, Jr.
1977   The Hirundo Archaeological Project—An Interdisciplinary Approach to Central Maine Prehistory. *Annals of the New York Academy of Sciences* 288:457–471.

Sargent, H. R.
1960   The Sumner Falls Site. *New Hampshire Archaeologist* 10:7–12.

———.
1969   Prehistory in the Upper Connecticut Valley. In W. R. Young, ed., *An Introduction to the Archaeology and History of the Connecticut Valley Indian*, pp. 28–32.

Schlesier, K. H.
1976   Epidemics and Indian Middlemen: Rethinking the Wars of the Iroquois, 1609–1653. *Ethnohistory* 23(2):129–145.

Service, E. R.
   1971   *Primitive Social Organization*, 2nd ed. New York: Random House.
Seymour, F. C.
   1969   Flora of Vermont. *Agricultural Experimental Station Bulletin* 660, University of Vermont, Burlington.
Siccama, T. G.
   1971   Presettlement and Present Forest Vegetation in Northern Vermont with Special Reference to Chittenden County. *The American Midland Naturalist*, 85(1):153–172.
Smith, N. N.
   1977   The Changing Role of the Wabanaki Chief and Shaman. In William Cowan, ed., *Actes du Huitième Congrès des Algonquianistes*, pp. 213–22.

——.
   1979   The Adoption of Medicinal Plants by the Wabanaki. In William Cowan, ed., *Papers of the Tenth Algonquian Conference*, pp. 167–172. Carleton University, Ottawa.
Snow, D. R.
   1968   Wabanaki Family Hunting Territories. *American Anthropologist* 70:1143–51.

——.
   1975   The Passadumkaeg Sequence. *Arctic Anthropology* 12(2):46–59.

——.
   1976a   Abenaki Fur Trade in the Sixteenth Century. *The Western Canadian Journal of Anthropology* 6(1):3–11.

——.
   1976b   The Archaeological Implications of the Proto-Algonquian Urheimat. In William Cowan, ed., *Papers of the Seventh Algonquian Conference*, pp. 339–346.

——.
   1976c   *The Archaeology of North America.* New York: Viking Press.

——.
   1976d   The Solon Petroglyphs and Eastern Abnaki Shamanism. In William Cowan, ed., *Papers of the Seventh Algonquian Conference*, pp. 281–288.

——.
   1977a   Archaeology and Ethnohistory in Eastern New York. In Funk and Hayes, eds., *Current Perspectives in Northeastern Archaeology—Essays in Honor of William A. Ritchie*, pp. 107–112.

——.
   1977b   The Archaic of the Lake George Region. *Annals of the New York Academy of Sciences*, 288:431–438.

——.
   1977c   Rock Art and the Power of Shamans. *Natural History*, 86(2): 42–49.

——.
   1978   Late Prehistory of the East Coast. In B. G. Trigger, ed., *Handbook of North American Indians*, Vol. 15, *Northeast*, pp. 58–69.

Spear, R. N., Jr.
  1970   Wildlife—Part II: Birds. *Lake Champlain Basin Studies*, No.
          7-B. Department of Resource Economics, University of Ver-
          mont, Burlington, Vt.
Speck, F. G.
  1918   Penobscot Transformer Tales. *International Journal of Ameri-
          can Linguistics* 1(3): 187–244.

  _____.

  1920   Penobscot Shamanism. *Memoirs of the American Anthropo-
          logical Association*, 6(3): 239–288.

  _____.

  1935   Penobscot Tales and Religious Beliefs. *Journal of American
          Folklore* 48(187): 1–107.

  _____.

  1940   *Penobscot Man*. Philadelphia: University of Pennsylvania
          Press.
Squire, Mariella
  1977a   An Archaeological Survey of the Proposed Water Pollution
          Control Project for Proctor, Vermont. Report on file, Division
          for Historic Preservation, Montpelier, Vt.

  _____.

  1977b   Classification of Projectile Points from the Champlain Valley
          in Vermont. Masters thesis, Department of Anthropology,
          State University of New York, Buffalo.
Stoltman, J. B.
  1978   Temporal Models in Prehistory: An Example from Eastern
          North America. *Current Anthropology* 19(4): 703–746.
Stuckenrath, Robert
  1977   Radiocarbon: Some Notes from Merlin's Diary. *Annals of the
          New York Academy of Sciences* 288: 181–188.
Stvan, E. R.
  1978   Analysis of the Ewing Site Ceramics. Typescript on file, De-
          partment of Anthropology, University of Vermont, Burlington.
Swadesh, Morris
  1964   Linguistics as an Instrument of Prehistory. In Dell Hymes, ed.,
          Language in Culture and Society, pp. 575–584.
Swartz, B. K., Jr., (ed.)
  1971   *Adena: The Seeking of an Identity*. Muncie, Indiana: Ball
          State University.
Thomas, P. A.
  1973   Squakhaeg Ethnohistory: A Preliminary Study of Culture
          Conflict on the Seventeenth Century Frontier. *Man in the
          Northeast* 5: 27–36.

  _____.

  1976   Contrastive Subsistence Strategies and Land Use as Factors for
          Understanding Indian-White Relations in New England. *Eth-
          nohistory* 23(1): 1–18.

  _____.

  1979a   Initial Management Summary, Cultural Resources as They Re-
          late to the LaPlatte River Watershed Plan. *Department of An-
          thropology University of Vermont Report No. 8*, Burlington.

————.
1979b   In the Maelstrom of Change: The Indian Trade and Cultural
         Process in the Middle Connecticut River Valley: 1635–1665.
         Ph.D. dissertation, University of Massachusetts, Amherst.

————.
1979c   Pownal RS BRS 0107(4) Bridge Relocation in Pownal, Vermont
         Phase I: Archaeological Reconnaissance. *Department of An-
         thropology University of Vermont Report #12, Burlington.*

Thomas, P. A. and W. A. Bayreuther
1979   Chace Mill Hydroelectric Project: Phase I and II Archaeologi-
         cal Assessment. *Department of Anthropology University of
         Vermont Report #13,* Burlington.

————.
1980   Wells RS 0145(7) Phase I Archaeological Assessment. *Depart-
         ment of Anthropology University of Vermont Report # 25,*
         Burlington.

Thomas, P. A., W. A. Bayreuther, M. L. Bourassa, Gina Campoli, and P. J.
Doherty
1980   The Pownal-Bennington Highway Project: Fo19-1(4), (5), (6),
         Fo12-1 Phase I: Field Reconnaissance for Prehistoric and His-
         toric Sites. *Department of Anthropology University of Ver-
         mont Report #24,* Burlington.

Thomas, P. A. and M. L. Bourassa
1978   McNeil Generating Plant Phase II Intensive Archaeological
         Survey. *Department of Anthropology University of Vermont
         Report #2,* Burlington.

Thomas, P. A. and M. P. Bumstead
1979   Burlington-Colchester M5000(3) Connector: Phase II Intensive
         Archaeological Survey. *Department of Anthropology Univer-
         sity of Vermont Report #6,* Burlington

Thomas, P. A. and Gina Campoli
1979   An Initial Study of the Prehistory and Historic Archaeological
         Sensitivity of the Bennington Area. *Department of Anthropol-
         ogy University of Vermont Report #22,* Burlington.

Thomas, P. A. and B. S. Robinson
1979   Missisquoi National Wildlife Refuge: A Cultural Resource
         Survey. *Department of Anthropology University of Vermont
         Report #10,* Burlington.

————.
1980   Phase I Archaeological Assessment Middlebury F219-3(20).
         *Department of Anthropology University of Vermont Report
         #23,* Burlington.

Thompson, Stith
1966   *Tales of the North American Indians.* Bloomington: Indiana
         University Press.

Thompson, Zadock
1842   *History of Vermont, Natural, Civil and Statistical in Three
         Parts with a Map of the State and 200 Engravings.* Burlington,
         Vt.: C. Goodrich.

Thoreau, H. D.
  1950   *The Maine Woods Arranged with Notes by Dudley C. Lunt.*
          New York: Bramhall House.
Trager, G. L.
  1965   Languages of the World. *Colliers Encyclopedia* 14:300–310.
Trigger, B. G.
  1971   The Mohawk-Mahican War (1624–28): The Establishment of a
          Pattern. *Canadian Historical Review* 52:276–286.

  _____.

  1978   Cultural Unity and Diversity. In B. G. Trigger, ed., *Handbook
          of North American Indians, Vol. 15, Northeast,* pp. 798–804.
Trigger, B. G. (ed.)
  1978   *Handbook of North American Indians, Vol. 15, Northeast.*
          Washington: Smithsonian Institution Press.
Trigger, B. G. and J. F. Pendergast
  1978   Saint Lawrence Iroquoians. In B. G. Trigger, ed., *Handbook of
          North American Indians, Vol. 15, Northeast,* pp. 357–61.
Tuck, J. A.
  1970   An Archaic Indian Cemetery in Newfoundland. *Scientific
          American* 222(6):112–121.

  _____.

  1971   An Archaic Cemetery at Port Au Choix, Newfoundland.
          American Antiquity 36:343–358.

  _____.

  1975a   Maritime Adaptation on the Northeastern Atlantic Coast. In:
          William Fitzhugh, ed., *Prehistoric Maritime Adaptations of
          the Circumpolar Zone,* pp. 255–267.

  _____.

  1975b   The Northeastern Maritime Continuum: 8000 Years of Cul-
          tural Development in the Far Northeast. *Arctic Anthropology*
          12(2):139–147.

  _____.

  1977   A Look at Laurentian. In Funk and Hayes, eds., *Current Per-
          spectives in Northeastern Archaeology—Essays in Honor of
          William A. Ritchie,* pp. 31–40.

  _____.

  1978a   Northern Iroquoian Prehistory. In B. G. Trigger, ed., *Hand-
          book of North American Indians, Vol. 15, Northeast,* pp.
          322–333.

  _____.

  1978b   Regional Cultural Development 3000 to 300 B.C. In B. G. Trig-
          ger, ed., *Handbook of North American Indians, Vol. 15,
          Northeast,* pp. 28–43.
Turnbaugh, William
  1977   An Archaeological Prospect of the Ulu or Semi-Lunar Knife in
          Northeastern North America. *Archaeology of Eastern North
          America* 5:86–94.
United States Government
  1978   *Federal Register,* Vol. 43, No. 172.

Van DeWater, F. F.
  1974   *The Reluctant Republic Vermont 1724–1791.* Taftsville, Vt.:
           Countryman Press.
Varney, Ken
  n.d.   Vermont Archaeology Notes. Unpublished notes on file, De-
            partment of Anthropology, University of Vermont, Burlington.
Vaughan, A. T.
  1965   *New England Frontier: Puritans and Indians 1620–1675.*
           Boston: Little Brown.
Vayda, A. P.
  1961   Expansion and Warfare Among Swidden Agriculturalists.
            American Anthropologist 63 : 346–358.
Vermont State Planning Office
  1974   *Vermont Land Use Capability.* Montpelier: Vermont Planning
           Office.
Vogel, V. J.
  1970   *American Indian Medicine.* Norman, Okla.: University of
           Oklahoma Press.
Vogelmann, James
  1977   Medicinal Plants of Vermont Indians. Typescript on file, De-
            partment of Anthropology, University of Vermont, Burlington.
Vogelmann, T. C.
  1972   Post Glacial Lake History and Paleolithic Man in the Cham-
            plain Valley. Typescript on file, Department of Anthropology,
            University of Vermont, Burlington.
Vogelmann, T. C. and others.
  1972   *Prehistoric Life in the Champlain Valley.* Film available from
           the University of Vermont Media Services, the Vermont De-
           partment of Libraries Audio-Visual Unit, and the Vermont
           Historical Society.
Wagner, W. P.
  1972   The Ice Margins and Water Levels in Northwestern Vermont.
            *New England Intercollegiate Geological Guidebook, 64th An-
            nual Meeting,* pp. 317–342.
Wallace, A. F. C.
  1966   *Religion: An Anthropological View.* New York: Random
           House.
  ———.
  1969   *The Death and Rebirth of the Seneca.* New York: Alfred A.
           Knopf.
Wasserman, Maurice
  1954   The American Indians as seen by the Early Chroniclers. Ph.D.
            dissertation, University of Pennsylvania, Philadelphia.
Webb, W. S. and R. S. Baby
  1957   *The Adena People No. 2.* Columbus: Ohio Historical Society.
Webb, W. S. and C. E. Snow
  1945   The Adena People. *University of Kentucky Reports in An-
            thropology and Archaeology, No. 6.* Lexington, Ky.

Westveld, Marinus and others.
   1956   Natural Forest Zones of New England. *Journal of American Forestry* 54:332–38.
Wherry, J. D.
   1979   Abnaki, Etchemin, and Malecite. In William Cowan, ed., *Papers of the Tenth Algonquian Conference*, pp. 181–190. Carleton University, Ottawa.
Willey, G. R.
   1966   *An Introduction to American Archaeology, Volume I: North and Middle America*. Englewood Cliffs, N.J.: Prentice Hall.
Willoughby, C. C.
   1935   *Antiquities of the New England Indians*. Peabody Museum of American Archeology and Ethnology, Harvard University, Cambridge, Mass.
Wright, J. V.
   1967   The Laurel Tradition and the Middle Woodland Period. *National Museum of Canada*, Bulletin 217.
   ———.
   1972   The Shield Archaic. *National Museum of Man, Publications in Archaeology No. 3*. National Museum of Canada, Ottawa.
Yarnell, R. A.
   1964   Aboriginal Relationships Between Culture and Plant Life in the Upper Great Lakes Region. *Anthropological Papers, Museum of Anthropology, University of Michigan No. 23*. Ann Arbor: University of Michigan.
Young, W. R. (ed.)
   1969   *An Introduction to the Archaeology and History of the Connecticut Valley Indian*. Springfield, Mass.: Museum of Science, New Series 1(1).

APPENDIXES

APPENDIX A

WHEREAS,   Vermont has a unique history of recognizing the requests of minority groups, in that the State of Vermont was the first state to abolish slavery; and

WHEREAS,   in 1974, certain native American people living within the State of Vermont as members of the Abenaki Tribe, reconstituted as their governing body the Abenaki Tribal Council; and

WHEREAS,   the Abenaki Tribal Council as the governing body of the Abenaki Indian Tribe exercises internal governmental functions; and

WHEREAS,   people of the Vermont Abenaki Tribe can trace their lineage in Vermont well into the 19th century; and

WHEREAS,   Vermont Abenakis have resided primarily in the northern counties of the State of Vermont; and

WHEREAS,   the Canadian Government has recognized the Abenaki people of the Odanek and Becancourt Reservation in the Province of Quebec; and

WHEREAS,   the Quebec Abenakis endorse and recognize the tribal status of Vermont Abenakis; and

WHEREAS,   there may be as many as 1,700 people living in Vermont claiming to be direct descendents of the original Abenaki Indian Tribe, and research indicates that many of these people are descendents; and

WHEREAS,   many of these people suffer from low education attainment, severe poverty, inadequate housing and high unemployment; and

WHEREAS,   Congress has appropriated several millions of dollars of federal funds to provide benefits and services to Native Americans; and

WHEREAS,   without State recognition, Native Americans residing in Vermont cannot qualify for these programs; and

WHEREAS,   the definition of Native American is varied, according to federal interpretation, and initial research indicates the existence of Native Americans residing in Vermont;

NOW, THEREFORE, I, Thomas P. Salmon, by virtue of the authority vested in me as Governor of the State of Vermont, do hereby recognize these Native Americans by federal definition as members of the Abenaki Indian Tribe; and

THEREFORE,   in furtherance of the above recognition, I hereby establish the Governor's Commission on Indian Affairs.

GOVERNOR'S COMMISSION ON INDIAN AFFAIRS

1. The Governor's Commission on Indian Affairs shall investigate problems common to Indian residents of the State, as well as the special concerns of the Abenaki Tribe, and shall assist the Abenaki Tribal Council in its dealings with agencies of State and Local government.

2. The Commission shall further develop the initial research to provide historical data to define the Native American population in Vermont, and shall prepare a report to the Governor and Legislature. All State Agencies shall cooperate with the Commission in the performance of this function.

3. Each State Agency shall be responsible for evaluating its own services which are received by the Native American population, and shall propose means to provide adequate services. The head of each State Agency providing, or capable of providing, services to Native Americans is hereby directed to determine within three months whether or not federal, state or other funds are available to improve such services. Where it is determined that funds may be available for services and benefits to Native Americans, the Agency and the Abenaki Tribal Council shall work together to prepare applications for such funds. The Commission's advice on such matters may be sought and the Commission shall be informed of all funding proposals submitted by State Agencies.

4. The Commission shall meet at least four times a year, and shall be comprised of five members, of whom two shall be appointed by the Abenaki Tribal Council, two shall be appointed by the Governor, and the fifth shall be chosen by the previous appointed four members.

5. The Commission shall address itself to the
    problems of poverty, lack of education and
    high unemployment which exists within the
    Native American and Abenaki population.

6. In addition, the Commission shall prepare
    a report and recommendation for the
    Governor and the Legislature on the request
    by the Abenakis for unrestricted hunting and
    fishing rights within the State of Vermont;
    the inclusion of Abenaki Tribal members in
    the guardianship and management of the
    Mississquoi National Wildlife Refuge; and
    the request that legal title to the Monument
    of St. Francis, located north of Swanton, be
    transferred to the Abenaki Tribe.

IN WITNESS MY NAME HEREUNTO

Subscribed and the Great Seal

of the State of Vermont here-

unto affixed, at Montpelier,

this 24th day of November, A.D.,

1976.

GOVERNOR

By the Governor:

Secretary of Civil and Military Affairs

EXECUTIVE ORDER NUMBER 36

APPENDIX B

EXECUTIVE DEPARTMENT

E X E C U T I V E   O R D E R

WHEREAS,   the State is aware of problems common to
persons of American Indian heritage who are
residents of Vermont; and

WHEREAS,   it is necessary to investigate such problems
and aid in their resolution in order to promote
the public safety, health, and welfare of the
inhabitants of Vermont:

NOW, THEREFORE,   I, Richard A. Snelling, declare it to be the
public policy of this State to take an active
interest in the problems common to persons of
American Indian heritage who are residents of
Vermont and do hereby order that a commission
to be known as the:

VERMONT COMMISSION FOR INDIAN AFFAIRS

be created.

1. The Vermont Commission for Indian Affairs
shall consist of five (5) members to be
appointed by the Governor.

2. The members of the Commission shall be
appointed for terms to coincide with the term
of the Governor making such appointment.
Members of the Commission may be removed by the
Governor. The Governor shall appoint a Commission
chairperson, in consultation with the Commission
members.

3. The powers and duties of the Commission shall
include the following:

        a. meeting and functioning at any
place within the State, and advising the appropriate authorities of any pattern or instance of
unlawful discrimination against persons of American
Indian heritage;

b.   investigating problems common to persons of American Indian heritage who are residents of this State, both urban and rural. The Commission shall provide appropriate assistance to Indian organizations and individuals in their dealings with agencies of federal, state, and local government and gaining access to social services, education, employment opportunities, health, housing, civil rights, and other services and programs and their funding;

c.   accepting contributions from any source to assist in the operation of the Commission. The Commission shall seek to enlist the cooperation of public, private, charitable, religious, labor, civic, and benevolent organizations. Funds obtained from such sources may be used by the Commission for operational expenses. The Commission may not be a repository or dispensary agency for program funds from any source;

d.   communicating, as widely as possible, to all citizens of Vermont and to persons of American Indian heritage, information of use and interest relating to Indian affairs;

e.   from time to time, but not less than once a year, reporting to the Governor, advising on programs affecting Indian affairs and describing the efforts and work performed by the Commission, its programs and policies, and results thereof.

5. Executive Order number 36, dated November 24, 1976 is hereby revoked.

IN WITNESS MY NAME HEREUNTO

Subscribed and the Great Seal

of the State of Vermont here-

unto affixed, at Montpelier,

this 28 day of January ,

A.D., 1977.

_____
GOVERNOR

By the Governor:

_____
Secretary of Civil and Military Affairs

EXECUTIVE ORDER NUMBER 3

APPENDIX C

1976-77
File reference – Nº de réf. du dossier

BAND COUNCIL RESOLUTION

RÉSOLUTION DE CONSEIL DE BANDE

NOTE: The words "From our Band Funds" "Capital" or "Revenue", which ever is the case, must appear in all resolutions requesting expenditures from Band Funds.

NOTA: Les mots "des fonds de notre bande" "Capital" ou revenu" selon le cas doivent paraître dans toutes les résolutions portant sur des dépenses à même les fonds des bandes.

THE COUNCIL OF THE LE CONSEIL DE LA BANDE INDIENNE	ABENAKIS OF ODANAK AND BECANCOUR	Current Capital Balance Solde de capital	$
AGENCY DISTRICT	MONTREAL	Committed – Engagé	$
PROVINCE	QUEBEC	Current Revenue balance Solde de revenu	$
PLACE NOM DE L'ENDROIT	ODANAK-BECANCOUR	Committed – Engagé	$
DATE Friday 20 DAY – JOUR	August MONTH – MOIS AD 19 76 YEAR – ANNÉE		

DO HEREBY RESOLVE:
DÉCIDE, PAR LES PRÉSENTES:

That we, the **Abenakis of Odanak** and Becancour, recognize the Abenakis of the State of Vermont as our BROTHERS and request that:

1. The State of Vermont recognize the Indians of that State as Aboriginals of the North American Continent.

2. To be treated and provided for by the State Government and the U.S Federal Government (B.I.A).

3. That their land claims be recognized.

4. That their hunting and fishing rights be recognized.

C.C: Indians of Quebec Association.

[handwritten] ... on This Date aug 27 1976 from Chief Watso by Homer St Francis —

ODANAK BAND COUNCIL

.... (Chief – Chef)

.... (Councillor – conseiller)

.... (Councillor – conseiller)

.... (Councillor – conseiller)

.... (Councillor – conseiller)

BECANCOUR BAND COUNCIL

.... (Chief)

.... (Councillor – conseiller)

.... (Councillor – conseiller)

.... (Councillor – conseiller)

.... (Councillor – conseiller)

A quorum for this Band
Pour cette bande le quorum est
consists of
fixé à
Council Members
Membres du Conseil

FOR DEPARTMENTAL USE ONLY – RÉSERVÉ AU MINISTERE

1. Band Fund Code Code du compte de bande	2. COMPUTER BALANCES – SOLDES D'ORDINATEUR		3. Expenditure Dépenses	4. Authority – Autorité Indian Act. Sec Art. de la Loi sur les Indiens	5. Source of Funds Source des Fonds
	A. Capital	B. Revenue – Revenu			[ ] Capital [ ] Revenue – Revenu
	$	$	$		

6. Recommended – Recommandable

Approved – Approuvable

.... Recommending Officer – Recommandé par

Date

Approving Officer – Approuvé par

SWANTON, VERMONT, FRANKLIN COUNTY:
At Swanton this 30th day of August, 1976, HOMER ST. FRANCIS personally appeared, and acknowledged this instrument by him sealed and subscribed to be his free act and deed. Before me.

APPENDIX D

57/76-77

File Reference - Nº de réf. du dossier

BAND COUNCIL RESOLUTION
RÉSOLUTION DE CONSEIL DE BANDE

NOTE: The words "From our Band Funds" "Capital" or "Revenue", which appear in the case, must appear in all resolutions requesting expenditures from Band Funds

NOTA: Les mots "des fonds de notre bande" "Capital" ou "revenu", selon le cas doivent paraître dans toutes les résolutions portant sur des dépenses à même les fonds des bandes

THE COUNCIL OF THE LE CONSEIL DE LA BANDE INDIENNE	ODANAK AND BECANCOUR	Current Capital Balance Solde de capital	$
AGENCY DISTRICT	MONTREAL	Committed – Engagé	$
PROVINCE	QUEBEC	Current Revenue balance Solde de revenu	$
PLACE NOM DE L'ENDROIT	ODANAK AND BECANCOUR	Committed – Engagé	$
DATE 5 DAY – JOUR	January MONTH – MOIS AD 19 77 YEAR – ANNÉE		

DO HEREBY RESOLVE:
DÉCIDE, PAR LES PRÉSENTES:

That we, the Abenakis of Odanak and Becancour, recognize the Band Council of the St-Francis and Sokoki Bands of Abenakis in the State of Vermont and their duly elected successors as the legal government of the Abenaki Nation of Vermont, and we recognize the Tribal Chairman or his designate and his duly elected successor as the representative and spokesman for the Abenakis of the State of Vermont.

Received on this date Jan. 8, 1977 from Chief Walter Watso by hand at Swanton, Vermont by:

A quorum for this Band
Pour cette bande le quorum est

consists of
fixé à

Council Members
Membres du Conseil

ODANAK BAND COUNCIL

BECANCOUR BAND COUNCIL

(Councillor – conseiller)

(Councillor – conseiller)

(Councillor – conseiller)

(Councillor – conseiller)

(Chief – Chef)

Chief

(Councillor – conseiller)

(Councillor – conseiller)

(Councillor – conseiller)

(Councillor – conseiller)

(Councillor – conseiller)

(Councillor – conseiller)

FOR DEPARTMENTAL USE ONLY – RÉSERVÉ AU MINISTÈRE

1. Band Fund Code Code du compte de bande	2. COMPUTER BALANCES – SOLDES D'ORDINATEUR		3. Expenditure Dépenses	4. Authority – Autorité In Ilan Act Sec Art. de la Loi sur les Indiens	5. Source of Funds Source des fonds
	A. Capital	B. Revenue – Revenu			☐ Capital ☐ Revenu Revenue
	$	$			
6. Recommended – Recommandable			Approved – Approuvable		
Date	Recommending Officer – Recommandé par		Date	Approving Officer – Approuvé par	

On this, the 10th day of January, A.D. 1977, personally appeared Homer St. Francis and acknowledged the foregoing instrument to be his free act and deed.

R. "Knot" Ouimette, Notary Public

INDEX

Abenaki Appeal of 1766, 241–42
Abenaki Petition of 1976, 253, 254, 282
Abenakis, 89, 207, 221, 273. *See also* War: between British and Abenakis
  Eastern, 148–49, **151**, 199, 200, 201
    and the British, 220, 232, 277
    and disease, 206, 208–9
    traditional culture, 164, 166, 179, 186, 192, 278. *See also* Penobscots
  Western, **2**, 3, 148–50, 266, 277, 278
    and the British, 213, 217–19
    chiefs, 175–76, 181, 182, 194, 215, 280
    as descendants of earlier prehistoric peoples, 79, 89, 150, 198–201
    and disease, 206, 208
    and the Iroquois, 142, 144
    settlements, **2**, 152–53, 159, 160
    technology, 164–67
    traditional culture, 151–98, 279–81. *See also* British menace; Cowasucks; Culture, Indian; Diet, Indian; Sokokis; War: between British and Abenakis and between Iroquois and Abenakis
Abenaki Self Help Association, Inc., 251–52, 253, 258, 259, 282
Abenaki Tribal Learning Center, 259
Aberle, David F., 278
Adams, Richard, xix
Adams, W. Y., 275
Adaptation, concept of, 7, 37, 88, 172, 201–2
Addison, Vt., 29, 30
Addison County, Vt., 108, 113, 140
Adena, 13, 91–92, 118, 120, 121, **122**, 126, 127, 128, 130, 275
Adirondack Mountains, 57, 199

Administration for Native Americans, 258
Albany, N.Y., 203, 211, 217, 229, 234
Alburg, Vt., 234, 236, 238
Algonquians, 144, 177, 184, 189, 192, 221, 226, 232, 272, 278–79, 281. *See also* Languages: Algonquian
Algonquin, 3
Allen, Ira, 209, 243–45, 282
Allen, Levi, 243
Allodial rights, 222–23, 256
Allumette Island site, Ontario, 57, **58**, 70, 270
Amarascoggins, 149, **151**
Amherst, Baron Jeffrey, 237
Anderson, J. K., 274
Andros, Sir Edmund, 217
Animals, rights of, 187–88
Archaeological methods, 15–17
Archaeological proof, nature of, 16
Archaeology, defined, 16
Archaic
  culture, 13, 44–45, 53–54, 85–89, 90, 110, 128–29, 198
  origins, 45–46, 69–72, 269
  period, 12–13, 15, 45–46, 115
  sites, 45, 46, 48, 54–57, 59, 105, 107, 109, 111, 113, 270–71, 272. *See also* Artifacts
Artifacts. *See also* Pottery; Projectile points; Abenakis: Western: technology
  Archaic, **47**, 49–52, 54–57, **78**, 85, 127, 129, 270, 272, 276. *See also* Ground slate tools
  early Woodland, 116–17, 118, 119, 120, 121–22, 124–27, 128–29, 131
  late Woodland, 140
  middle Woodland, 97, 100, 101, **102**, 103, 104, 105, 107–9, 111
  Paleoindian, 22–25, 26, 27, 30, 31, **34**, 267

LIBRARY OF CONGRESS CATALOGING IN PUBLICATION DATA

Haviland, William A.
    The original Vermonters.

    Bibliography: p.
    Includes index.
        1. Indians of North America—Vermont.   2. Abnaki
Indians.   I. Power, Marjory W.   II. Title.
    E78.V5H37   974.3'00497   80-55465
    ISBN 0-87451-196-8   AACR2